Interrupt-Driven PC System Design

Interrupt-Driven PC System Design

Joseph McGivern

Annabooks

San Diego

Interrupt-Driven PC System Design

by

Joseph McGivern

PUBLISHED BY

Annabooks
11838 Bernardo Plaza Court
San Diego, CA 92128-2414
USA

619-673-0870
http://www.annabooks.com

Printed in the United States of America

ISBN 0-929392-50-7

First Printing March 1998

About the Author

Joseph F. McGivern

Joe McGivern received his BS degree in Electrical Engineering, specializing in Computer Engineering, from Michigan Technological University in the fall of 1989. For several years following he was active in the development of PC based real-time data acquisition and control systems. Consistently challenged by the PC's general lack of interrupt resources, he broke from his established career path and developed an ISA passive backplane technology which provided each expansion slot on the backplane with its own unique hardware interrupt. The technology, known as the *Interrupt Expansion Facility* or *IEF* was featured on the cover of ECN magazine in May 1995. Joe has published articles and continues to speak on the subject of interrupt processing to engineers from around the world.

Through these experiences, Joe has gained a comprehensive understanding of the behavior of interrupts within a PC, and of their practical use in the design of real-time systems. This information has formed the basis for "Interrupt-Driven PC System Design".

Dedication

This book is dedicated to my loving parents

Beatrice Sara McGivern &

Joseph F McGivern Jr.

Without whom, Lord knows, I hadn't a snowballs chance.

Acknowledgements

- To Billy Cole - Software Engineer extraordinare and great friend, whose exceptional talents were employed to breathe life into the many software examples offered throughout this book.

- To John Choisser for the opportunity, Tim Bohan for his day to day support and encouragement and to the entire Annabooks family, whose continued support and hard work made this project a reality. Thank you all!

- I'd like to especially thank Mr. Peter White, that one, pivitol high school teacher who gave me free run of my High School's new computer lab complete with 16 TRS80 Model III computers (16K of RAM) and one console unit with 64K of RAM. See what ya' started Mr. White.

- To all my family, friends and colleagues who saw fit to support and encourage me throughout the writing of this book.

- Finally, to the makers of Lincoln Logs, Legos, and the Errector Set for providing the creative sandbox I pee'd in as a kid.

Contents

Foreword

Handling interrupts in a PC environment has been the bane of computer design engineers since the invention of the microprocessor. Interrupts are extremely important in applications requiring real-time responses to events. The proper handling of interrupts can have a very dramatic effect on a microprocessor-controlled system. A good design handles external events smoothly and with no glitches, a poor or flawed design can have catastrophic, even deadly results.

Various microprocessor families have used differing schemes to process and handle interrupts, each having its own set of advantages and disadvantages. Processors designed for embedded real-time applications tend to have the ability to handle more interrupts than processors used for PC desktop type applications. As engineers try to use these PC centric microprocessors in real-time environments, they find that there is not enough interrupt handling capability. Even most of today's desktop systems run out of interrupt handling capability with the addition of all the readily available peripherals you find on a PC.

Many system I/O bus technologies have evolved over the years to integrate interrupt generating I/O devices into microprocessor buses. These buses tended to evolve with the processor technology and carried many of their traits, good and bad, forward into the next generations. Because of this, it is still an overwhelming challenge for engineers to design the best solution.

PCI bus technology is pervasive in computers of all types. It went from its humble beginnings as a high-speed I/O bus in PCs to its position today as THE bus technology in computers from hand-held PCs to desktop computers to servers. The bus is utilized on a wide variety of form factors in applications of all types. In short, PCI bus is every where.

PCI bus does have its drawbacks but the large economies of scale gained from its acceptance in the PC industry have led many to use the technology despite its drawbacks. Among the most difficult technology hurdles to overcome is the minimal support for interrupts. Design engineers that can overcome this obstacle have the inside track to the most successful designs. Interrupt handling designs are one of the single most challenging areas of PC systems to design properly. Many projects have been delayed or even failed because the designer was not able to solve the interrupt-handling scheme correctly. Microprocessors today are able to handle many more processes much faster than before. Sequencing and coordinating all of the external events that must be processed is a formidable challenge, even with today's design tools.

Future microprocessors and associated I/O buses will hopefully build in better and more robust interrupt support. Until this happens, design engineers will continue their clever use of existing technologies with its limitations.

Joe McGivern has spent a great deal of his career addressing the issues faced by system designers in their use of the bus technologies used in PCs, particularly in the area of interrupt handling. He recognizes the deficiencies and has overcome them. He has shared his knowledge with others via his writings and participation in industry seminars. The sharing of this knowledge has made it easier for countless others to further advance their designs in computer technology.

Jerry Gipper
Director of Marketing,
Embedded Technologies
Technical Products Division
Motorola Computer Group

Introduction

This book is for anyone who wants to use an, ISA, EISA, PCI or MCA based PC system board as the canvas on which their unique interrupt-driven system design will be painted. The Intel 8259 Programmable Interrupt Controller is the primary focal point, since it alone is responsible for resolving contention and maintaining discipline among the many devices starved for processor attention on these platforms. The spirit of this book is to provide the reader with a document that contains the relevant information needed to understand every aspect of the PC's interrupt subsystem and what to do to get the most out of it. For those who want to know how an interrupt is processed at the most basic level, review chapters 3 and 4. If you have always wondered how to write an interrupt service routine properly or have never written one before, Chapter 6 describes the five possible interrupt service routine structures available to the designer, how to program them, and points out the advantages and disadvantages of each. For those who are charged with the task of developing a PCI based systems design, Chapters 9 and 10 will provide the details on how to apply the information gained in earlier chapters to hook the correct interrupt level, develop the PCI device interrupt service routine and customize the PCI platform's IRQ router configuration to optimize the system design.

This book has been organized to serve two primary functions. The first is to provide the reader with a detailed study of the subject matter. The second function is to title the chapters and sections and include Appendix's in such a way as to provide the system designer with a one of a kind Interrupt-driven PC Systems Design *Quick Reference.*

Proven coded examples in C have been provided to expedite the learning process throughout the book. The code is in both source and compiled form to give the designer a head start on any projects pending or in-progress. It is my sincere hope that this document contain information on every aspect of interrupt-driven system design so that not only can new designs be realized with confidence, but problematic older designs can be reviewed, updated and stabilized.

This book does not contain lots of long winded unnecessary filler material for the purpose of making it thicker thereby helping the brain justify the cost. It is a direct and specific document created for the purpose of helping designers master the interrupt-driven aspect of PC systems design and gain confidence in their pursuits.

In preparing the material for the manuscript, I struggled with what information was important and required to thoroughly cover the topic of interrupt-driven system design. So I adopted this approach. I reflected on the time and energy it took to acquire the knowledge base. The days, weeks, months and years of theorizing on how it had to work and the hammering out of various iterations until another tumbler fell into place, led me to one conclusion. Sifting through piles of incomplete, disjointed and sometimes completely irrelevant information in an attempt to fully understand something is not fun. From this premise is derived the criteria with which the elements of this book must meet to be promoted to chapter material. If the information does not pertain, smacks of irrelevance, or is sure to cause unpleasant neural activity it belongs somewhere else.

....**Enjoy.**

1. Interrupt-Driven PC Systems

1.1 Interrupt-Driven Systems

A real time system is one where the success of a process is dependent not only on the accuracy of the computations but also on the timeliness of the results. If the system responds accurately to real time events but fails to deliver the measured response in a timely manner, the system is considered to be in error. *Interrupt-Driven* design principals are fundamental to the majority of real time system design.

There are two methods of data transfer within a PC, *Programmed I/O* and *Direct Memory Access (DMA)*. Programmed I/O is the transfer of data from I/O devices through the processor to memory and from memory through the processor to I/O devices. Direct Memory Access or DMA uses an Intel 8237 DMA controller to bypass the processor and form a direct path between I/O devices and memory through which data transfers are possible in both directions. There are three methods of data synchronization within a PC, *Polling, Interrupt,* and *DMA*. Each is able to initiate data transfers and each has its place in a real time system design. However, of these three methods, interrupt is the single most powerful data synchronization method and is the foundation upon which an *interrupt-driven* real time system design is built.

An *interrupt-driven* system is one in which an application program runs in the *"background"* while the real time events that cause *interrupts* are processed in the *"foreground"*. Other terms used to describe an interrupt-driven system are *foreground-background* and *event-driven*. Interrupt-driven real time systems, in particular data acquisition and control systems, can be found controlling manufacturing processes, at work in telecommunication switching networks, monitoring vital signs, directing aircraft control surfaces (Fly by Wire), and so on... Interrupt-driven systems are capable of handling all but the most complex real time applications.

We find interrupt-driven design principles in the PC, where application programs schedule events and user interface functions in the background while interrupt-driven I/O devices such as the system timer, keyboard, com ports, disk drives, network card, etc. are serviced in the foreground.

PC's are also a powerful, reliable, and inexpensive platform on which to base complex real time systems.

In a real time system design, interrupts fit between the sense and decide phases of the standard control model as shown in Figure 1.1.1.

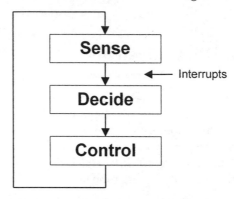

Figure 1.1.1 Control System Model

Any real time event requiring the processor's attention first needs to be recognized or "sensed" before interrupting the processor. Interrupt-driven devices therefore must provide some degree of decision making ability. For example, communication controllers are able to sense when data is in the receive buffer or an error has occurred before interrupting the processor. "Smart" A/D conversion cards are able to monitor environmental conditions and interrupt only when some pre-determined limit has been exceeded and digital I/O boards can interrupt upon sensing a change in the on/off state of a switch and so on. A simple model showing the more common data acquisition and control elements found in a real time PC system design are illustrated in Figure 1.1.2.

Interrupts provide a simple and powerful way to achieve rather complex real time systems design. It is my experience that interrupts, perhaps because of their ability to swiftly lock up a system if the handlers are not properly designed, are avoided out of fear. This book is dedicated to demystifying the design of interrupt-driven PC systems, by revealing the few basic rules required to design solid fault tolerant systems using interrupts and also providing the information and methods that will allow you to achieve the highest performance possible.

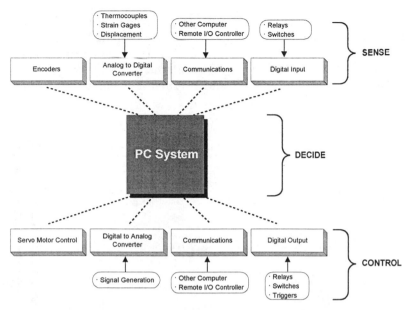

Figure 1.1.2 PC Data Acquisition and Control Model

1.2 Evolution of the PC Interrupt Structure

A computer system's *Interrupt Structure* is defined as the system's hardware and software components that integrate to successfully process interrupt requests. Hardware components include the IRQ bus lines, interrupt controller(s), processor, system BIOS ROM, adapter ROMs and system RAM. Software components include Interrupt Vector Table (Real Mode) or Interrupt Descriptor Table (Protected Mode) entries and the interrupt service routines responsible for handling the device requests.

When the original PC was introduced in 1980, it had to support several interrupt-driven devices such as the keyboard, floppy diskette drive and communication ports to gain acceptance in the emerging PC marketplace. Because the PC would require a more robust interrupt handling scheme than existed in the silicon of processors common to that era, the newly developed *Intel 8259 Programmable Interrupt Controller (PIC)* was incorporated to provide eight unique hardware interrupt levels IRQ[7:0], ordered in priority from IRQ0 (highest) to IRQ7 (lowest). Of the eight IRQs provided, only six (IRQ[7:2]) were made available for use on the PC's 8 bit I/O bus. IRQ0 and IRQ1 were reserved for the *System Timer* which maintains the PC's time of day, and *Keyboard* which at the very least allows access to the system should an errant program lock it up. Following the original PC's introduction, the newer PC/XT maintained the same single PIC interrupt structure as the original PC. This interrupt structure is illustrated in Figure 1.2.1. Device IRQ assignments on the original PC and the PC/XT followed the same standard format as well, and are shown in Table 1.2.1.

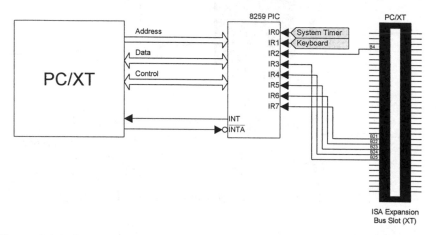

Figure 1.2.1 Original PC & PC/XT Hardware Interrupt Control Structure

IRQ0	- System Timer
IRQ1	- Keyboard
IRQ2	- EGA Video
IRQ3	- Serial Communications Port 2 (COM2)
IRQ4	- Serial Communications Port 1 (COM1)
IRQ5	- Parallel Port (LPT2)
IRQ6	- Floppy Diskette Drive
IRQ7	- Parallel Port (LPT1)

Table 1.2.1 Original PC and PC/XT Standard IRQ Assignments

As technology progressed, the next generation of PCs adopted the Intel 80286 16-bit processor and dropped the PC/XT designator. The new platform which now donned a 16 bit processor and 16 bit I/O bus was called the PC/AT. To accommodate additional interrupt-driven devices introduced with the PC/AT such as the Hard Drive and Real Time Clock, a second 8259 PIC was added to the PC system using the 8259's cascade feature. This new interrupt structure born on PC/AT systems and shown in Figure 1.2.2 provided the system with an additional seven IRQs, bringing the total number to fifteen (IRQ2 was sacrificed to accommodate the second PIC's INT output). Of the fifteen, only 11 were made available for use on the 16-bit AT bus. From this point forward, even as ever more powerful PC platforms including MCA, EISA, and PCI bus technologies were introduced, the interrupt structure given in Figure 1.2.2 remained virtually intact. The only notable difference being the implementation of level triggered IRQs on MCA, EISA and PCI platforms. Although Figure 1.2.2 demonstrates the interrupt structure's connectivity to the AT bus only, refer to Appendix 12.1 XT/ISA/EISA, MCI, and PCI Connector Diagrams with Interrupt Pin Call Outs for connector layouts highlighting the IRQ pins for the XT(ISA), AT(ISA), MCA, EISA and PCI buses as well. A list of all standard device IRQ assignments for the PC/AT is given here in Table 1.2.2.

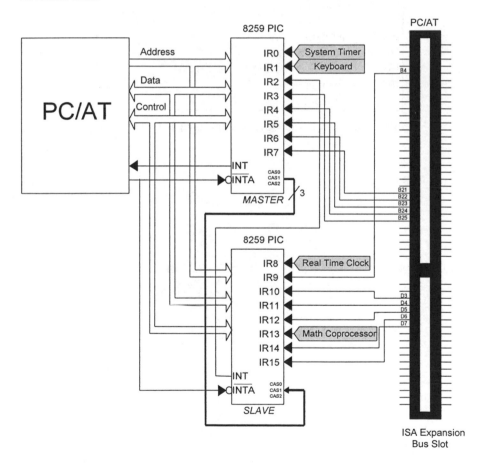

Figure 1.2.2 PC/AT Hardware Interrupt Control Structure

```
IRQ0  - System Timer              Master PIC
IRQ1  - Keyboard
IRQ2  - Cascaded 8295 PIC (Slave)
IRQ3  - Serial Communications Port 2 (COM2)
IRQ4  - Serial Communications Port 1 (COM1)
IRQ5  - Parallel Port (LPT2)
IRQ6  - Floppy Diskette Drive
IRQ7  - Parallel Port (LPT1)
```

```
IRQ8  - Real Time Clock           Slave PIC
IRQ9  - Available
IRQ10 - Available
IRQ11 - Available
IRQ12 - Mouse or Available
IRQ13 - #FERR (Floating Point Error)
IRQ14 - Hard Drive
IRQ15 - Available
```

Table 1.2.2 PC/AT and Beyond Standard IRQ Assignments

2. Data Synchronization

2.1 Polling

When an application program is tasked with having to contact an I/O device periodically to either determine if service is required or to monitor some environmental condition, this process is referred to as *Polling*. Polling a device yields either status indicating whether the device requires service or in the case of a data acquisition cycle, the actual data itself. For instance, polling a communications port to determine if data is available by checking the status of the receive buffer, is an example of polling a device to see if the device requires service. If data is present in the receive buffer, a service routine is called to read and store the information from the receive buffer. Monitoring environmental conditions such as temperature or pressure by polling the device that interfaces to the sensors, is an example where polling a device yields the actual data. For example, each time the A/D converter is read during the polling cycle, the acquired data is immediately made available to an application program for processing.

Polling algorithms take on two basic formats. The first illustrated in Figure 2.1.1 results in all the devices sharing equal priority as each is polled during every polling cycle. The second polling format establishes an implied priority structure with each device having a relative priority among the group of devices being polled. As shown in Figure 2.1.2, the first device found that requires service ends the polling cycle immediately following that device's service routine execution. Therefore the device with the highest priority is the device that is polled first, the device with the lowest priority is polled last. Having a priority among devices being polled is useful when the data transfer rates of some devices are higher than others. By preempting the other lower priority devices, it shortens the polling cycle, and higher data transfer rates are possible.

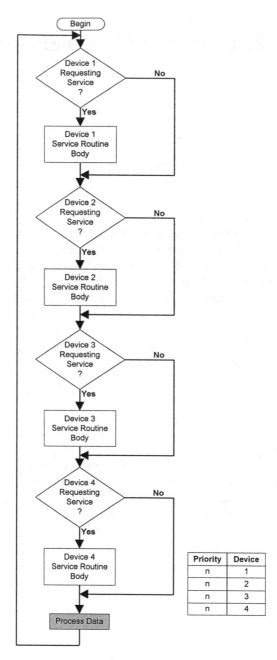

Figure 2.1.1 Equal Priority Polling Format

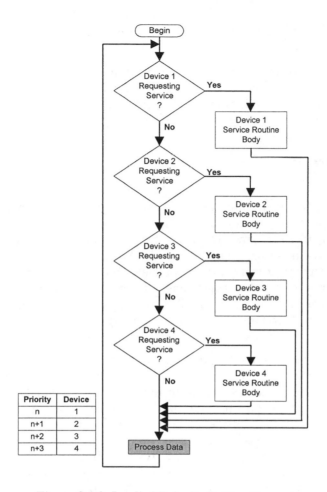

Figure 2.1.2 Implied Priority Polling Format

Polling is the most processor intensive method of device servicing. It requires that nearly all processor time be dedicated to executing the polling loop. Furthermore, data synchronization becomes increasing complex with each new device as the background application is responsible for each of the following areas:

- Polling each device at a rate that allows critical response times to be met.
- Acquiring data from each device at a rate that ensures no data is missed.
- Performing all decide and control operations
- Managing user input and output operations

An intimate knowledge of execution times and device transfer rates are required to coordinate such an effort. The inefficiencies and software complexities involved with polling are simply inhibitive in a real time system of any complexity.

Sometimes however, when the response time requirement of a device is so great as to preclude the use of interrupts as a viable data synchronization method, polling is the only way to ensure that the device is serviced in a timely manner.

2.2 Interrupt

An *interrupt* is a subroutine called asynchronously by external hardware (usually an I/O device) during the execution of the background application. Because the response to interrupts are immediate, an interrupt-driven system can effectively handle many interrupt-driven devices. Interrupts greatly simplify data synchronization as the application can concentrate on the sequencing of operations and user interface functions while the interrupts handle I/O and timing functions. The idea of having to play "Twister" with polling based application code to guarantee data integrity goes away.

Another benefit of interrupts is that devices using a high priority IRQ can interrupt a device using lower priority IRQ. This fact allows those devices with higher data throughput requirements the ability to interrupt devices with lower data throughput requirements, giving those devices with more pressing business more immediate access to processor bandwidth. For a detailed discussion of assigning relative priority to devices refer to Chapter 11.2 "Device Priority Assignment." On ISA, EISA, and MCA systems, the task of assigning priority to devices and choosing the appropriate IRQ is relatively straight forward. PCI systems however assign the IRQ resources for you and it becomes a bit of a trick to order the devices in terms of relative priority within the PC's interrupt structure. Chapter 10 "PCI Interrupt Handling - *Optimizing Performance*" is dedicated to this very subject.

The application of interrupts within any system takes on many forms. First, there are simple *Interrupts* where one device uses an unshared IRQ to request service. Then there are *Periodic Interrupts* (Section 2.3) used to periodically invoke polling cycles, *Shared Interrupts* (Section 2.4) that allow many devices to share the same IRQ resource, and finally *Synchronized Timer Interrupts* used to satisfy complex event timing requirements (Section 11.7).

With regards to data transfer rates, interrupts are not the fastest way to move data in a PC. When data transfer rates are required that exceed what interrupts can reasonable handle, alternative data transfer methods are used. The main benefit of interrupts is founded in data synchronization. In situations where devices with high data transfer rates have some form of on-board memory, a FIFO, dual port memory, etc., the interrupt is often used to effect the block transfer. Once the processor responds to the request, a more sophisticated data transfer technique such as *rep-string* can be used to transfer the data block at high speed. Rep-string transfers are accomplished by using either the INS (input string) or MOVS (move string) instructions combined with the repeat prefix REP. If the port is fast enough, the zero overhead program loop using a rep-string technique moving 16 bit words can yield data transfer rates of up to 4MB/sec on an 8Mhz bus.

It is extremely challenging to propose a reliable maximum data transfer rate for Interrupts because of the many factors that go into it's determination. Unlike DMA, Memory, or I/O access cycles where the bus speed and wait states can be reviewed to determine a definite maximum data transfer rate, the factor that limits the data transfer rate of interrupts is overhead. The operating system, processor speed, refresh rates, the number of nested devices, and the number of registers pushed and popped by the interrupt service routines all have an impact on the maximum data transfer rate achievable using interrupts. Operating systems, in particular, have a major impact on the response time to an interrupt.

When operating under MS-DOS, the time it takes to respond to a request is on the order of a few micro seconds (6 - 15µS). Things get ugly under Windows however. If the service routine has been installed by a device driver implemented as a DLL you can expect latency times to be anywhere from 250 - 1500µS. The excessive latency time results from the fact that the service routine is not called directly but rather the IRQ number is passed first to the VPICD (Virtual Programmable Interrupt Controller Device) maintained by Windows. All other VxD's are then polled to determine if any of them are registered to handle the interrupt. Only after this extensive search will the VPICD look up the starting address in the real mode interrupt vector table and call the service routine. A more efficient approach is to design a VxD. A VxD is capable of telling Windows to send the interrupt requests to it before sending them to the VPICD. A VxD will result in latency times on the order of 20 - 60µS, a definite improvement.

To illustrate the relationships between MS-DOS and Windows 3.1x with regards to relative interrupt throughput rates refer to Figure 2.2.1. The data shown here was the result of profile testing done at Microsoft on a 33Mhz AT compatible machine.

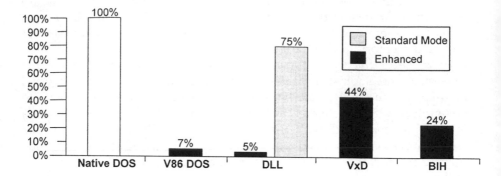

- **Native DOS** - iSR incorporated in MS-DOS application and run in an unvirtualized environment without EMM368 installed
- **V86 DOS** - same application run in virtualized environment (MS-DOS box) in enhanced mode Windows 3.1 environment. Multitasking interference was eliminated by setting *AllVMsExclusive=on* in the System.ini.
- **DLL/Enhanced mode** - iSR was incorporated in a 16 bit Windows DLL following standard rules for iSR design under Windows
- **DLL/Standard mode** - iSR was incorporated in a 16 bit Windows DLL following standard rules for iSR design under Windows
- **VxD** - iSR was incorporated in a 32-bit VxD
- **BIH** - iSR incorporated in a 16 bit DLL was registered as a bimodal interrupt handler

Figure 2.2.1 Relative throughput rates between MS-DOS and Windows[1]

As a reference, the maximum interrupt throughput measured under native MS-DOS denotes 100% of what is possible. In turn each of the interrupt techniques associated with each of the various Windows modes were introduced to an ever increasing interrupt rate until the point where an interrupt was missed. This point marks the maximum interrupt throughput rate. From Figure 2.2.1 it is clear that Windows running in enhanced mode introduces severe interrupt latencies. The best achievable rate among all enhanced mode interrupt handling techniques was realizing using a VxD which managed only 44% of what's possible under native MS-DOS. The worst rate is seen when using an enhanced mode DLL which produces a maximum interrupt rate of only 5% of what's possible under native MS-DOS. Ouch! In Standard Mode however, the situation is quite improved with a standard mode DLL achieving 75%. Although noted that the tests were all designed to minimize extraneous factors which might yield unrealistic results, a different computer system and particularly another device driver will produce slightly different performance ratios than those given in Figure 2.2.1.

2.3 Periodic Interrupt-driven Polling

The method of data synchronization achieved by connecting a periodic interrupt source such as the output of a counter/timer to an IRQ and initiating a polling cycle from within the service routine that runs each time the periodic interrupt occurs is referred to as *Periodic Interrupt-driven Polling (PIDP)*. The benefits of such a method are that the processor is free to perform other tasks in the time between polling cycles and only one IRQ resource is required. This method is perfect for servicing devices with low data transfer rates and monitoring slowly changing environmental conditions or events that require service attempts on the order of milliseconds, seconds, minutes, hours, days, etc... Such applications include, but are not limited to, remote terminal communication, monitoring temperature/pressure/position, or security systems that respond to motion detection or state changes in switch positions.

The polling cycle that executes as part of the iSR invoked each time the periodic interrupt arrives follows the same two basic formats as illustrated in section 2.1 ('Polling"). From the format illustrated in Figure 2.3.1, we see that all the devices share equal priority as each is polled during the periodic interrupt-driven polling cycle. This is the typical format used in conjunction with any periodic polling cycle. A second less common option follows the format given in Figure 2.3.2 to establish an implied priority structure. Each device now has a relative priority among the group of devices being polled. The device with the highest priority being the device that is polled first while the device with the lowest priority is polled last. If one device should require a polling period substantially higher than the others involved in the polling cycle, using an implied priority structure will allow the higher priority device to preempt lower priority devices when requesting service. This shortens the overall polling cycle, opening up processor bandwidth to other system functions.

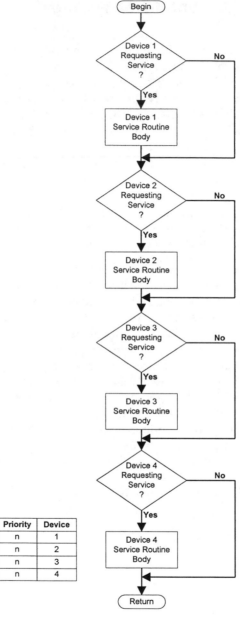

Figure 2.3.1 Equal Priority PIDP iSR Format

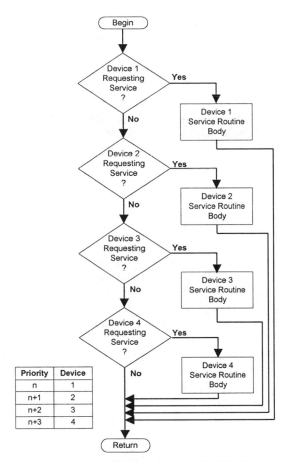

Figure 2.3.2 Implied Priority PIDP iSR Format

For any Periodic Interrupt-driven Polling structure to be successful, the interrupt rate must be chosen carefully to ensure that all the devices are polled fast enough to guarantee service at or above their minimum required rates. At the same time however, you don't want to poll the devices so fast that you wind up unnecessarily wasting processor bandwidth. To illustrate the balance between timer frequency and available CPU time refer to Figure 2.3.3.

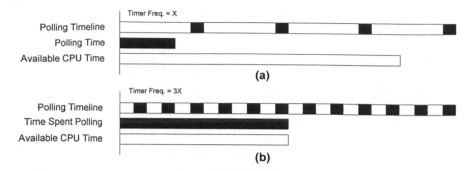

Figure 2.3.3 Available CPU Time Vs. Timer Frequency

When the timer periodically interrupts the processor at some arbitrary frequency X, the processor executes the polling cycle represented by the short black bars in the *Polling Timeline*. When all the polling cycles over a given time base are set side by side, the total *Polling Time* and the total *Available CPU Time* are given as shown in both (a) for a timer frequency = X and in (b) for a timer frequency 3X. By comparing the Available CPU Time in (a) with that shown in (b) we can conclude that increasing the timer frequency i.e. polling period, reduces Available CPU Time. If the timer frequency X was sufficient to poll and service all the devices in this example, then the Available CPU Time shown in (b) clearly demonstrates the negative impact the excessive timer frequency has on processor bandwidth.

To demonstrate the analysis required to determine the most efficient timer frequency for a particular design, consider the following example. Assume 4 devices, device 1 through device 4, all serviced through the use of a Periodic Interrupt-driven Polling structure. The system has a programmable timer whose output is connected to one of the IRQ resources available on either the Master or Slave PIC. A service routine has been installed behind the timer's IRQ to field the periodic interrupt requests and initiate a polling cycle wherein each of the four devices will be polled and serviced if service is requested.

To determine the best operating frequency for the timer, both the upper and lower frequency limits need to be defined. Once a valid operating frequency range has been established, the most efficient operating frequency can be selected. The upper frequency limit is the maximum rate the timer can be operated at before the potential for default IR7 interrupts occur (default IR7 interrupts are the subject of Chapter 8). The upper frequency limit also marks the point where all available CPU time approaches zero. The lower frequency limit is the minimum rate the timer can operate at while still ensuring all four devices are polled and serviced fast enough to guarantee the minimum service rates of each device. If the timer is set too slow, the potential for missed data exists. If set too fast, processor bandwidth is wasted.

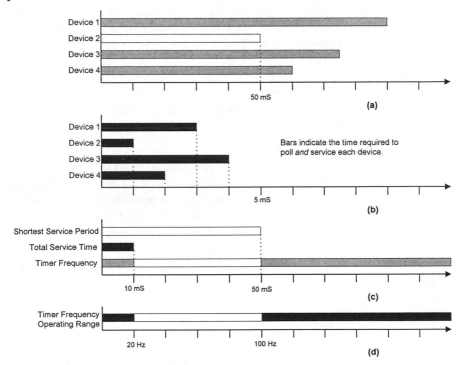

Figure 2.3.4 Optimizing Timer Frequency example

To establish the lower frequency limit, we need to identify the device that requires service most often and note the period. In this example, that would be device 2 which must be polled at least once every 50mS as shown in Figure 2.3.4(a). Inverted, this yields a lower frequency limit of 20 Hz. To establish the upper frequency limit, we add the total time it takes to poll each of the four devices together with the total time it takes to execute each of the four service routines. Adding these times together from the example given in Figure 2.3.4(b) results in the Total Service Time = 10mS. Inverted this yields an upper frequency limit of 100Hz. Figure 2.3.4(c) shows the Shortest Service Period and the Total Service Time just described that are used to define the upper and lower frequency limits. Inverting both times given in (c), results in the Timer Frequency Operating Range for our example shown in Figure 2.3.4(d).

17

Choosing the best operating frequency within the valid Timer Frequency Operating Range is based on limiting processor interrupts as much as possible for the reasons illustrated in Figure 3.2.3. This would lead us to choose the final operating frequency at or just above the lower frequency limit of 20Hz. However, to compensate for the worst case interrupt latency and possible negative timer drift, a couple of final adjustments are required. First, if the worst case latency time in this example has been observed to be 38µS, the operating frequency is adjusted as follows: 1/(50mS - 38µS) = 20.015Hz. Now, assume that the timer in use has a maximum negative drift of 1.5%. To compensate for the drift simply divide 20.015Hz by .985. This yields a final operating frequency of 20.32Hz, which guarantees that all devices and in particular device 2 will be serviced at least once every 50mS.

Two excellent on-board sources for generating periodic interrupts are the PC's own System Timer which operates at 18.2 Hz providing an interrupt every 55mS and the Real Time Clock's periodic interrupt which may be programmed to operate between 2Hz - 8KHz (2^x $1 \leq x \leq 13$). A separate section is devoted to describing each of these on-board periodic interrupt resources in more detail in Chapter 11.5 and 11.6. If more refined frequency resolution is desired, there are many commercially available counter/timer boards on the market.

2.4 Shared Interrupt

Shared Interrupt is the method of data synchronization where more than one device shares the same IRQ resource. This method was first adopted by EISA and is promoted exclusively by MCA and PCI architectures. ISA is strictly an edge triggered IRQ platform. The benefits of sharing interrupts are the seemingly unlimited IRQ resources they provide and the increased number of interrupt-driven devices the system can now entertain.

The *Shared Interrupt* method requires that the 8259's IRx input be configured as level triggered and respond to an active low request signal. This allows any device using an open collector to ground circuit, to generate a interrupt request by simply pulling the IRQ line low. In addition, the open collector to ground approach allows all devices sharing the IRQ to be wire-OR'd and operate simultaneously without conflict. Chapter 3, specifically Sections 3.2 "Edge and Level Triggered IRx Input Signal Specification" and 3.6 "Edge/Level Control Registers" detail the operation of level triggered interrupts for EISA, MCA, and PCI platforms.

Service routines designed to share interrupts differ from single device service routines in a couple of ways. For instance, all the device service routines that share the same IRQ necessarily hook the same interrupt vector. As each service routine loads, it must store the starting address of the service routine that loaded before it. This process creates a linked list or *interrupt chain* where each service routine is able to pass control onto the next service routine in the chain if it's device was not responsible for the request. There are many considerations, variations, and techniques involved in designing service routines that share interrupts. Chapter 7 "Interrupt Chaining - Link Design" is devoted to this subject. For further information related specifically to PCI refer to Section 9.6 "PCI Device Drivers".

---

[1] "Overview of the Interrupt Architecture of IBM PC-Compatibles" , David Long, Microsoft Developer Network Technology Group, http://www.microsoft.com, October 4, 1993

3. The Intel 8259 Programmable Interrupt Controller (PIC)

3.1 The 8259 PIC Overview

The Intel 8259 Programmable Interrupt Controller (PIC) is the heart and soul of an interrupt-driven PC system design. With a plurality of devices in the PC system all competing for processor attention, the 8259 PIC is the device responsible for stacking the incoming requests, alerting the processor to any pending requests of higher priority than any currently in service and deciding which higher priority request will be serviced upon acknowledgement. To any computer system, the interrupt controller is a critical chunk of silicon, and the 8259 despite it's age (a whopping 15+ years), is a credit to it's original designers as it remains a highly effective means of controlling the interrupt process to this day.

Designed for flexibility and power, the 8259 PIC found acceptance in the PC, but has broad application outside of the PC as well. For example, the 8259 can operate as a stand alone PIC with nothing more than read/write capability (i.e. no INT or INTA# connection). It can achieve this by way of the poll command issued through OCW3 which allows the designer to check (poll) for any pending interrupts on the PIC, and retrieve the highest priority IRx level pending service. In the PC however, the 8259 PIC is fully interfaced and has the ability to interrupt the processor and automatically deliver the appropriate interrupt vector byte when acknowledged. The original PC and the XT used only one 8259 PIC to handle system interrupts. Later, starting with the AT, the 8259's cascade feature allowed the INT output of one PIC (Slave) to be connected to the IRx input of another PIC (Master) thereby providing a total of 15 unique IRx levels. This was done to help meet the growing demand for additional IRQ resources. In large systems design, the 8259's cascade feature can be fully implemented to provide a total of 64 IRx levels by connecting a Slave PIC to each of the Master PIC's eight IRx inputs. The cascade feature is covered in detail in section 3.3.

Resolving priority is the 8259's primary responsibility. The priority structure can be fixed as it is in the PC, where IR0 always has the highest priority and IR7 the lowest, or the priority structure can be rotated on-the-fly. Dynamic alteration of the priority structure is an 8259 feature that gives the designer complete control over the assignment of priority. Unfortunately in a PC, the dynamic rotation of the priority structure is not possible because the Non-Specific EOI command(s) embedded in the BIOS, Operating System, and vendor device drivers would no longer be able to identify and reset the correct In-Service bit. This would result in an almost immediate lockup (see Chapter 5.4 for details).

The 8259 supports two modes of triggering on its IRx inputs. The first mode is edge triggering, which requires the IRx input signal to first transition low thereby setting the edge sense latch (see chapter 8.1 for details) before cycling back high where the signal level is then presented to the 8259's Interrupt Request Register (IRR) for consideration. Edge triggered IR inputs can not be reliably shared by two or more devices because of the output characteristics of the device's interrupt signal generation circuitry (see Chapter 8.3 for details). The second mode supported by the 8259's IRx inputs is level triggering, which does allow devices to share an IRx level. The 8259's triggering modes are the topic of the next section.

3.2 Edge and Level IRx Input Signal Specification

The theoretical differences and fundamental timing characteristics of the 8259's two IR input triggering modes are the topic of this section.

3.2.1 Edge Triggered IRx Inputs

To generate a valid request on an edge triggered 8259 IRx input, the requesting signal is required to sustain a low level on the IRx input for a minimum of 100nS. This sets the edge sense latch which in turn arms the request latch. Once armed, the request latch is able to see the IRx input signal. There are eight such request latches, one for each IRx input, these combine to make up the PIC's interrupt request register (IRR). When an active high request signal is asserted on the IRx input, the signal propagates through the request latch and on to the PIC's priority resolver, whose job is to determine if the pending request is of a high enough priority as to warrant an assertion of the PIC's INT line. If the request has priority over all other IRx levels currently pending or in service, the INT line will be asserted and the processor will respond by initiating an interrupt acknowledge sequence. This results in two negative going pulses arriving on the PIC's INTA# line as illustrated in Figure 3.2.1.

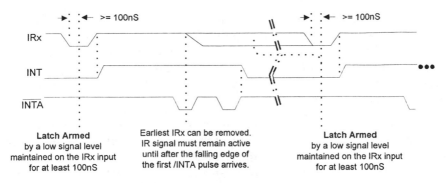

Figure 3.2.1 EDGE Triggered IRx Input Timing Requirements (8086/88 Mode only)

The falling edge of the first INTA# pulse freezes all the request latches in the IRR so the priority resolver will have a static group of logic levels to work with. Once the active request signal has been frozen in the request latch, the priority resolver takes over and determines the highest priority pending request by reviewing the request latches. After the highest priority pending IRx level has been identified, the data bus is driven with the correct interrupt vector byte. The 8259 data sheets indicate that the earliest the request signal being acknowledged can go inactive is just after the falling edge of the first INTA# pulse (see callout in Figure 3.2.1). After the falling edge of the first INTA# pulse, the request latch freezes the active signal level for priority resolution, therefore the asserted request signal is no longer required to complete the interrupt processing cycle. Any other pending requests must remain asserted until they are acknowledged or they will be missed. If the pending request signal falls short of this expectation during it's acknowledgment and deasserts before the falling edge of the first INTA# pulse, a default IR7 will occur. Chapter 8 is devoted to the subject of default IR7s.

When the rising edge of the second INTA# pulse arrives as shown in Figure 3.2.1, the following actions take place:
- The edge sense latch of the acknowledged IRx level is reset thereby disarming and clearing the IRx level's request latch (IRR bitx = 0).
- The acknowledged IRx level's In-Service bit is set.
- The INT line is deactivated.
- The interrupt vector byte is passed to the processor and the interrupt service routine is entered.

As the interrupt service routine completes, the Non-Specific EOI command(s) resets the appropriate IS bit(s) and the IRET instruction is issued, bringing the entire interrupt processing cycle to completion. If the

23

request remained asserted beyond the completion of the interrupt service routine on an edge triggered IRx input, the edge sense latch disarmed by the rising edge of the second INTA# pulse, would prevent the request from being acknowledged a second time. Not until the IRx input signal again cycles low for a minimum of 100nS and rearms the edge sense latch will any additional requests be seen on the IRx input.

The circuit used to generate an interrupt request on an edge triggered IRx input should be the only circuit with an output tied to the IRx input. Edge triggered interrupts were never meant to be shared (See chapter 8.3 for details). There is no industry standard by which edge triggered interrupt request generation circuits are designed. The only requirement is that the circuit be able to sink enough current to defeat the platform's pull-up resistor and pull the IRQx bus line low (INTx# for PCI). Pull-up resistances on the IRQx bus lines vary from platform to platform but are typically 8.2K and above. An example of the device to edge triggered IRx input interface is shown in Figure 3.2.2.

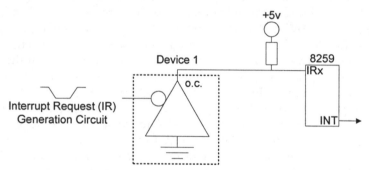

Figure 3.2.2 Edge Triggered Hardware Interface

When designing the circuitry responsible for generating an edge triggered request, the circuit must be able to maintain a low signal level for a minimum of 100nS to set the edge sense latch before asserting the active high request signal. If there is a way to design the circuit such that susceptibility to spurious noise causing false acknowledge cycles on the IRx inputs is minimized, it should be considered. Since noise tends to be additive, noise immunity would be maximized if a high signal level was maintained on the IRx input while inactive. Therefore, a design that makes sense, is a circuit that leaves the IRx input pulled up to 5Vdc by the platform circuitry when idle and generates a negative going pulse of duration just greater than 100nS to assert the request. Maintaining a low level in the idle state would shave 100nS+ from the latency time seen by the request but increases the chance of a transient noise causing an invalid acknowledge cycle.

3.2.2 Level Trigger IRx Inputs

When the 8259's IRx inputs are programmed as level triggered, the edge sense latch is disabled. This means that any IRx inputs programmed as level triggered will have armed request latches at all times. Any active high request signal will therefore immediately propagate through the request latch and be evaluated by the priority resolver. If the priority resolver determines that the request carries the highest priority over all other IR levels pending or in service, the INT line is driven active. An illustrated example describing the level triggered signal timing is shown in Figure 3.2.3.

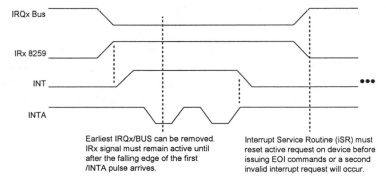

Earliest IRQx/BUS can be removed. IRx signal must remain active until after the falling edge of the first /INTA pulse arrives.

Interrupt Service Routine (iSR) must reset active request on device before issuing EOI commands or a second invalid interrupt request will occur.

**Figure 3.2.3 LEVEL Triggered IRx Timing Requirements
(8086/88 Mode only)**

In response to the PIC's asserted INT line, the processor responds by initiating an interrupt acknowledge sequence that causes two negative going pulses to be generated on the PIC's INTA# line. The falling edge of the first INTA# pulse freezes all the request latches in the IRR for priority resolution. After the priority resolver determines the highest priority pending request level by investigating the request latches, the data bus is driven with that level's interrupt vector byte.

When the rising edge of the second INTA# pulse arrives, the following occurs:

- The acknowledged IRx level's edge sense latch is reset. *
- The acknowledged IRx level's In-Service bit is set.
- The INT line is deactivated.
- The interrupt vector byte is transferred to the processor and the interrupt service routine is entered.

   * Irrelevant - The edge sense latch is disabled in level triggered mode.

When the processor calls the interrupt service routine, the iSR must reset the device's active request signal before issuing the Non-Specific EOI command(s) and enabling interrupts (See Chapter 7 for details on level triggered iSR design). If the request were to remain asserted after the Non-Specific EOI command(s) and the IRET instruction, there would be no reason for the PIC to believe that the still active signal was anything but another valid request, and a second processing cycle would begin in error.

Level triggered IRx inputs promote interrupt sharing by doing away with the edge sense latch. The need for several devices sharing an IRx input to synchronize a low 100nS cycle and set the edge sense latch just so a request can be seen is eliminated. Therefore, devices sharing a level triggered IRx input are free to pull the IRx line low and assert the interrupt request at their leisure.

Devices designed to use level triggered IRx input lines employ circuits with open collector outputs to interface with the IRQx bus line (INTx# for PCI). An example of this is given in the Figure 3.2.4. The open collector outputs allow the devices sharing a common IRx input to be *Wire OR'd.*

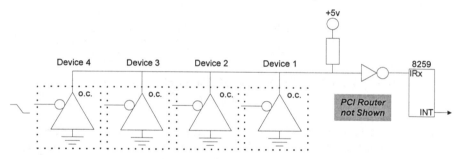

Figure 3.2.4 Shared devices are Wire OR'd using a circuit with O.C. outputs

As such, any of the devices requiring service use the open collector as a means of pulling the IRQx bus line low and assert the request. This configuration is an effective means of sharing the IRx inputs but runs opposite in polarity to the active high specification of the 8259 IRx inputs. To correct the signal polarity, a simple inverter is situated between the IRQx bus lines and the actual level triggered 8259 IRx inputs. Figure 3.2.4 illustrates the industry standard configuration for sharing interrupts on EISA, MCA and PCI platforms. On EISA and PCI platforms, two ELCR registers are used to specify the triggering mode of the 8259 IRx inputs on an input by input basis. ELCR configuration is first handled by the System BIOS, then later by the device drivers as they load (refer to 3.6 for details on ELCR layout and programming).

3.2.3 In Comparison

Edge triggered IR inputs allow interrupt requests to originate from devices that have no means of controlling the request signal via software (i.e. the active request can not be reset by the device's service routine). This includes devices such as counter/timer chips where the request signal remains asserted beyond the resetting of the IS bit(s) by the EOI command(s) and enabling of interrupts (IF=1) by the iSR. In edge triggered mode, the edge sense latch prevents the generation of further requests by requiring the IRx input signal to cycle low for at least 100nS before any further requests can be processed on the input. In level triggered mode however, any request signal that remained asserted would result in another request being processed in error.

Level trigger IRx inputs, in comparison, allow for the sharing of interrupts by disabling the edge sense latch. By removing the edge sense latch and it's 100nS low level requirement at the 8259's IRx input, many devices can assert their requests on the same IRx input simultaneously. The processor will then acknowledge and process each request one after another until all active request signals are reset by their respective service routines. The upside of level triggered IRx inputs is the seemingly unlimited hardware interrupt resource they provide the PC. However, performance issues due to the chaining of interrupts arise. Those issues are covered in Chapter 7.

3.3 Cascading the 8259 PIC

One of the most significant features of the 8259 is it's ability to operate in a cascaded configuration like that shown in Figure 3.3.1. The cascading feature allows a *Slave* 8259 to connect it's INT output line directly to one of the *Master* PIC's IRx inputs. A total of eight Slave PIC's can be added to the Master PIC resulting in a total of 64 distinct IRx inputs. The Master PIC controls the Slave PICs through the use of the cascade lines CAS[2:0], an internal PIC bus of sorts. When a request is initiated on the Slave PIC, the Slave PIC interrupts the Master PIC via one of the Master PIC's IRx inputs. During the acknowledgement cycle the Master PIC will enable the CAS lines and place on them the ID (0-7) of the Slave PIC that initiated the request. The slave PIC, upon recognizing it's ID, resolves priority and releases the interrupt vector byte associated with it's highest priority pending request on to the data bus. The ID corresponds to the Master PIC IRx input the Slave PIC uses (0-7). The Master PIC knows which of it's IRx inputs have Slave PICs attached by referring internally to ICW3 which was initialized by the BIOS to reflect so. Slave PICs on the other hand, use ICW3 as a means of storing their Slave PIC ID.

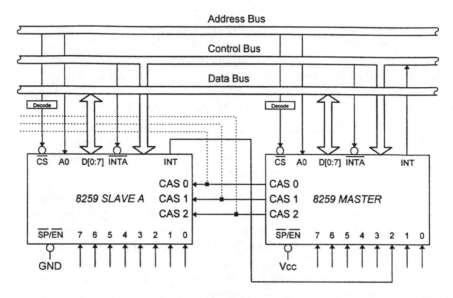

Figure 3.3.1 The PC's 8259 PIC Cascade Arrangement

There are two ways to configure an 8259 as either a Master or Slave PIC. The first way is via the PIC's /SP//EN pin when the 8259's buffered mode feature is disabled (bit3 in ICW4 = 0). When buffered mode is disabled, the /SP side of the /SP//EN pin is in effect and acts as an input used to define the 8259 as either a Slave or Master PIC. When /SP is tied to ground the PIC is a Slave, when tied to +5v, the PIC is a Master. The second way to define a PIC as a Master or a Slave results when buffered mode is enabled (bit3 in ICW4 = 1). If buffered mode is enabled, the /EN side of the /SP//EN pin takes over and acts as an output used to enable an external data bus buffer when the PIC drives the data bus. At that point, the use of the /SP//EN pin to define whether the PIC is a Master or Slave is lost, and the determination is then shifted to the M/S bit in ICW4 (M/S has no meaning when buffered mode is disabled). If M/S = 0 the PIC is a Slave, if M/S = 1 the PIC is a Master. In the PC environment, buffered mode is always disabled on both the Master and Slave PIC's and the /SP//EN pin is used to denote which PIC is the Master and which is the Slave. On the PC's Master PIC, the /SP//EN pin is tied to +5 Vdc and on the Slave PIC the /SP//EN pin is tied to ground as shown in Figure 3.3.1

3.4 Programming the 8259 PIC

The initial set up and overall operation of the 8259 is managed by control words conveyed via the PIC's two I/O ports located at base address + 0 and base address + 1. These control words fall into two categories, Initialization Control Words or *ICWs* and Operation Control Words or *OCWs*. Before the 8259 can begin operation, it must be initialized to define the environment in which it will operate. Items such as processor type, single or cascaded operation, edge or level trigger IRx inputs, etc. must all be defined. There are a total of four ICWs that combine to provide the PIC with a complete profile of the environment it will operate in. Once initialized, three OCW's are available that provide control functions to effectively manage the interrupt process and online status. Control word layout and bit definitions of both ICWs and OCWs and the 8259's somewhat awkward initialization sequence are the focus of this section.

3.4.1 Initialization Sequence

If a command word is written to base address + 0 and bit4 = 1, the 8259 will recognize the data byte as ICW1 and automatically enter the initialization sequence. When the initialization begins, the 8259 will take the following actions:

1. The edge sense latches are reset. This disarms the request latches of edge triggered IRx inputs and forces the input signal to first cycle low for a minimum of 100nS before a request will be recognized. In level triggered mode, the edge sense latches are permanently disabled and therefore have no effect on the IRx input's operation.

2. The Interrupt Mask Register (IMR) is cleared.

3. Priority is assigned IR0 = highest priority level 0 and IR7 = lowest priority level 7.

4. The slave mode address is set to 7.

5. Special Mask Mode is cleared.

6. Status read set in OCW3 is directed to the IRR.

7. If IC4 (bit 0 in ICW1) = 0 then ICW4 is removed from the initialization sequence and all functions within ICW4 will default to 0 (i.e. buffered mode disabled, no Auto EOI, and μP = MCS80/85).

Once the initialization sequence is triggered, the 8259 will follow the sequence flowchart shown in Figure 3.4.1.

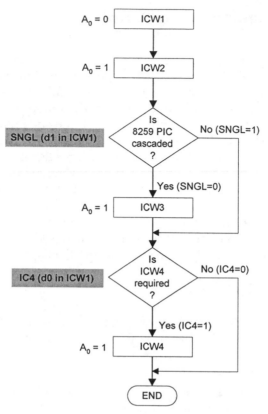

Figure 3.4.1 8259 Initialization Sequence

After ICW1 is issued to base address + 0, the remaining ICWs are issued through base address + 1. ICW1 contains the SNGL (bit1) and IC4 (bit0) parameters that determine if ICW3 and/or ICW4 respectively are included or bypassed during initialization. If the 8259 is part of a cascaded structure as both the Master and Slave PICs are in the PC, ICW3 is required. ICW3 on the Master PIC indicates which IR inputs have a slave PIC connected to them and the Slave PIC uses ICW3 to store the Slave's ID (0-7). Cascade mode is enabled by setting SNGL (bit1) = 1 in ICW1. ICW4 is required during the initialization sequence when the default value of 00h does not accurately represent the environment in which the 8259 is to operate. In the PC environment, ICW4 is required to set the µPM to 8086/8088 Mode (µPM = 1) instead of the default MCS80/85 mode.

The following descriptions detail the purpose and functionality of each of the four 8259's ICWs and three OCWs. Grayed areas in the Figures depict functions and settings irrelevant to the PC.

3.4.2 ICW - Initialization Control Words

ICW1 & ICW2:

$A[7:5]$ in ICW1 combines with $A[15:8]$ in ICW2 to form the *page starting address of service routines* in MCS80/85 Mode. The MCS80/85 system requires that the actual 16 bit vector table address holding the service routine's starting address be transferred during the acknowledgement cycle rather than just the interrupt number as in 8086/88 Mode. During acknowledgement, one of the eight IRx levels will generate a CALL to one of eight locations equally spaced in memory. The spacing of these intervals can be set to 8 or 4 using the *ADI* bit in ICW1. When the interval is set to 8, $A[5:0]$ is calculated by the 8259 and added to the externally programmed $A[15:6]$. When set to 4, $A[4:0]$ is calculated by the 8259 and added to the externally programmed $A[15:5]$. Because vector table addresses are equally spaced in memory, the 8259 calculates the address to call in MCS80/85 Mode as follows:

ADI = 0 – Call Address = Page Starting Address ([A15:A6]) + (8 * IRx level[7:0])

ADI = 1 – Call Address = Page Starting Address ([A15:A5]) + (4 * IRx level[7:0])

LTIM is used to determine whether all eight IRx inputs are level triggered or edge triggered. EISA and PCI platforms render this bit irrelevant and instead use a pair of Edge/Level Control Registers (ELCRs) (see Section 3.6) to individually program each IRx input to use either edge or level triggering.

SNGL indicates that the 8259 is the only PIC in the system, therefore ICW3 has no meaning and is removed from the initialization sequence when SNGL = 1.

IC4 should be set to 1 if any of the ICW4 defaults do not accurately describe the environment in which the PIC is to operate. ICW4 required by the PC to define the µP Mode as 8086/88.

ICW3:

As covered in the Section 3.3, ICW3 is required during initialization by any 8259 PIC acting as either the Master or Slave PIC in cascade structure as both PICs are in a PC. ICW3 is the mechanism by which the Master PIC determines if a Slave PIC is using the IRx level being acknowledged on the Master PIC. The Slave PIC in turn, uses ICW3 to store it's ID ([7:0]) so it can recognize the transfer of responsibility from the Master PIC via the CAS[2:0] lines. In MCS80/85 Mode, bytes 2 and 3 of the call sequence are driven onto the data bus or in 8086/88 Mode, the interrupt vector byte is driven onto the data bus by the responsible party.

ICW4:

SFNM enables or disables *Special Fully Nested Mode.* Special Fully Nested Mode is used when the Master PIC *only* services Slave PIC requests in a cascaded configuration. Normally, the priority resolver will mask the IRx level being acknowledged and all lower priority IR levels. This action locks out any further Slave PIC requests from being processed until the Master PIC IR level in use by the Slave PIC is unmasked via a Non-Specific EOI command. Enabling SFNM resolves this conflict by masking only lower priority IR levels on the Master PIC when the Slave PIC request is acknowledged. This allows higher priority Slave PIC requests to interrupt a lower priority Slave PIC request currently in progress. **PC's do not enable SFNM.**

BUF & M/S - BUF is used to enable Buffered Mode which simply means the /SP//EN pin will act as an output used to enable an external data bus buffer when the PIC drives the data bus. When Buffered Mode is enabled, the /SP//EN pin is no longer able to define the PIC as either a Slave or a Master. As a result the M/S bit is used to make the determination. When Buffered Mode is disabled, M/S has no meaning.

AEOI - When Automatic End Of Interrupt Mode is enabled, it will cause the 8259 to automatically issue a Non-Specific EOI command on the rising edge of the last INTA# pulse. The AEOI can only be enabled in a Master PIC and should be used only when a nested multilevel interrupt structure is not needed. Once initialized, the Automatic End Of Interrupt Mode can be further programmed to automatically rotate the priority structure on-the-fly using OCW2. **This feature is disabled in a PC.**

μPM - This bit determines whether the 8259 should adopt operational characteristics consistent with an MCS80/85 system or an 8086/88 system. **Must be set to 1 (8086/88 Mode) in a PC.**

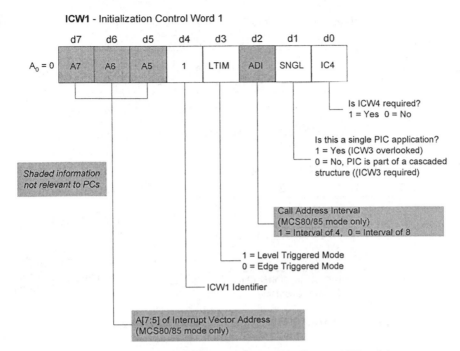

ICW1 - Initialization Control Word 1

Is ICW4 required?
1 = Yes 0 = No

Is this a single PIC application?
1 = Yes (ICW3 overlooked)
0 = No, PIC is part of a cascaded
structure ((ICW3 required)

Shaded information
not relevant to PCs

Call Address Interval
(MCS80/85 mode only)
1 = Interval of 4, 0 = Interval of 8

1 = Level Triggered Mode
0 = Edge Triggered Mode

ICW1 Identifier

A[7:5] of Interrupt Vector Address
(MCS80/85 mode only)

Figure 3.4.2(a) ICW1 - Initialization Control Word 1

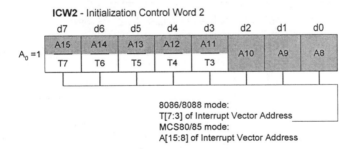

ICW2 - Initialization Control Word 2

8086/8088 mode:
T[7:3] of Interrupt Vector Address
MCS80/85 mode:
A[15:8] of Interrupt Vector Address

Figure 3.4.2(b) ICW2 - Initialization Control Word 2

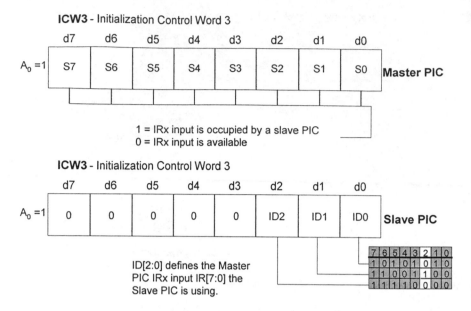

Figure 3.4.2(c) ICW3 - Initialization Control Word 3

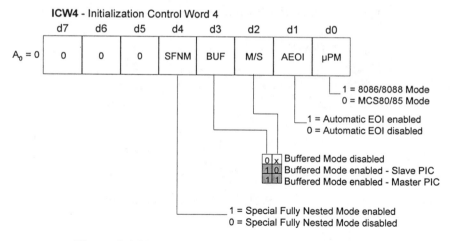

Figure 3.4.2(d) ICW4 - Initialization Control Word 4

3.4.3 OCW - Operational Command Words

OCW1:

Otherwise known as the Interrupt Mask Register (IMR). OCW1 allows each IR input on the 8259 to selectively be turned on (unmasked) or off (masked) by either clearing or setting the IRx levels of the associated bit respectively (refer to Chapter 5.3 for details on programming the IMR).

OCW2:

R, SL, & EOI - The combination of these three bits (**R**otate, **S**elect Level, and **E**nd **O**f Interrupt) define which one of eight possible commands are issued when an OCW2 is written. These commands are listed in Figure 3.4.3(b) and include End of Interrupt and Rotate modes.

L[2:0] - When the SL bit is active, bits L[2:0] indicate the specific IR[7:0] level to be acted upon by the command.

OCW3:

ESMM - This bit is a global enable/disable for Special Mask Mode.

SMM - Special Mask Mode allows the system designer to selectively mask and unmask lower priority IRx levels any time during system operation provided the ESMM bit is set. Setting the SMM bit to 1 causes the PIC's priority resolver to release its mask on all lower priority IRx levels below the highest priority IRx level currently in service. Combine this with the IMR's ability to selectively mask or unmask any IR level, and the result is the ability to selectively enable lower priority IRx levels. For example, if IR3 is currently in service and it has been specified that while IR3 is in service, the device using IR6 should have the ability to interrupt the system, the IR3 iSR will first read and store the current IMR contents, then program the IMR to mask IR[4, 5, 7] and unmask IR6. Next, Special Mask Mode is enabled (SMM=1) and interrupts are enabled. Any pending IR6 requests would now be seen by the processor and acknowledged. Before the IR3 iSR completes, it disables interrupts, disables SMM and restores the IMR to its original value. **Because SMM renders Non-Specific EOI commands ineffective, its use is prohibited in a PC environment.**

P - The Poll Command is used when the 8259 is operated as a stand alone PIC, with no INT or INTA# connections to the system. When the Poll Command is issued (P = 1), the PIC freezes the IRx inputs for priority resolution until the next read from base address + 0. The PIC treats the next read as an interrupt acknowledge, setting the appropriate IS bit and encoding the IRx level to service in the poll data word read. The format of the poll data word returned is as follows:

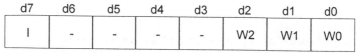

d7	d6	d5	d4	d3	d2	d1	d0
I	-	-	-	-	W2	W1	W0

W[2:0] - Binary code of the highest priority IRx
level currently requesting service.

I - request pending
0 - no request pending

If no IR levels are currently pending service, "I" in the poll data word will = 0, otherwise "I" will be set and W[2:0] will contain the IR[7:0] level to service.

RR & RIS - These bits provide access to the IRR and ISR status registers. When RR is set, the RIS bit determines the register that will be accessed on the next read from base address + 1. On subsequent reads from base address + 0, the 8259 will continue to provide status on the register last pointed to by the RR and RIS bits. Details on reading IRR and ISR status is given in Chapter 5.6.

OCW1- Operational Control Word 1

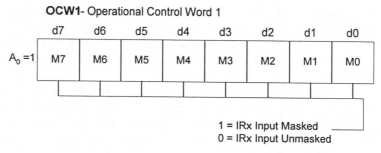

	d7	d6	d5	d4	d3	d2	d1	d0
A_0 =1	M7	M6	M5	M4	M3	M2	M1	M0

1 = IRx Input Masked
0 = IRx Input Unmasked

Figure 3.4.3(a) OCW1 - Operational Control Word 1

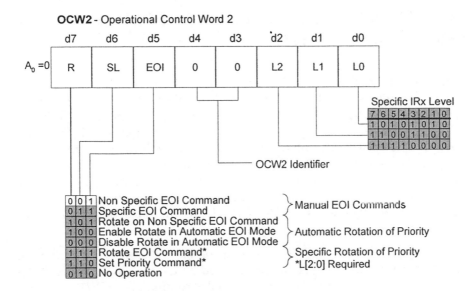

Figure 3.4.3(b) OCW2 - Operational Control Word 2

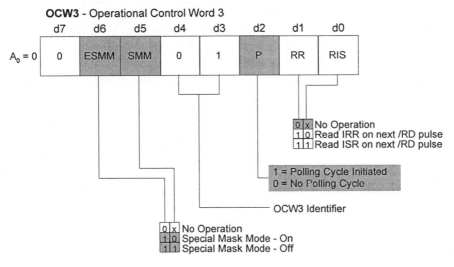

Figure 3.4.3(c) OCW3 - Operational Control Word 3

3.5 BIOS Initialization Routines for PC/XT, PC/AT-ISA, PS/2-MCA, PC/AT-EISA

Knowing the 8259 PIC initialization routines for all the common PC platforms allows the designer flexibility in placing the PIC's hardware interrupts anywhere in the interrupt vector table's first 1K (00000h to 003FFh) of system memory. Because processor exceptions conflict with the Master PIC's hardware interrupt levels (08-0F), reinitializing the Master PIC to use interrupts 50h - 57h and relocating all the service routine's starting addresses to the new table is sometimes desirable (see 11.4). In addition, when working the bugs out of an interrupt-driven design, the ability to initialize the system PIC(s) can be useful in tracking down errant code should interrupts stop processing.

The following examples of 8259 initialization routines for the various PC platforms given in this section are executed by the system BIOS at startup. The only hardware specific variable in the routines is OCW1, the PIC's Interrupt Mask Register. Each system board may or may not possess on-board controller options and therefore the designer, at his/her sole discretion, determines which interrupt levels to mask and which to leave unmasked during the 8259's initialization. As a general rule, IRQs occupied by possible boot devices such as the floppy (IRQ6) and hard drive (IRQ14) and any other devices critical to system operation such as the timer (IRQ0), keyboard (IRQ1), Slave PIC cascade(IRQ2), Real Time Clock (IRQ8), and math-coprocessor (IRQ13) should be unmasked during initialization. All non-system critical IRQs should be masked during initialization to minimize any possible complications resulting from an invalid request being acknowledged before the proper device handler has been installed. Some BIOS manufactures install handlers to deal with erroneous requests which simply include the required Non-Specific EOI command(s) and an IRET instruction. Overall, the platform designer determines the value required for OCW1. Generally, if initialization is required after the system is operational, OCW1 can be omitted from the initialization routine as the Interrupt Mask Registers have already been set up properly.

In Figure 3.5.1, an example in C of the single PC/XT 8259 PIC's initialization is listed. Highlighted comments indicate key points of difference between the PC/XT and other platforms. Specifically, the PC/XT is a single 8259 PIC environment and uses edge triggered IRx inputs. A coded example of this routine can be found in both source **xt_init.c** and executable **xt_init.exe** form on the IDPCSD diskette in the a:\chpt3 subdirectory.

```
/* xt_init.c /*                                                          PC/XT

void main()
{
  disable();

  outportb(0x20, 0x13);  /* ICW1 - Edge Triggered Mode, Single PIC, ICW4 required to define µPM   */
  outportb(0x21, 0x08);  /* ICW2 - Set PIC offset to match the Interrupt Vector Table base Address 08h   */
  outportb(0x21, 0x01);  /* ICW4 - Set PIC operation to 8086/8088 Mode                      */
  outportb(0x21, 0xB8);  /* OCW1 - Mask all but IR0, 1, 2 & 6 (Timer, Keyboard, EGA Video, and Floppy) */

  enable();              Note:  OCW1 value varies based on available platform controllers
}
```

**Figure 3.5.1 Sample BIOS Initialization code
for Original PC and PC/XT Systems**

Like the PC/XT platform, the PC/AT-ISA platform remains edge triggered. However, the PC/AT-ISA adds a second Slave 8259 cascaded on to the Master 8259 using IR2. SNGL bit d1 in ICW1 must be set on both PICs to indicate they are now part of a cascaded configuration. This causes ICW3 to be included in the initialization sequence for both PICs. ICW3 indicates to the Master PIC that IR2 is in use by the Slave PIC and on the Slave PIC, ICW3 indicates what address on the CAS[2:0] lines (010) the Slave PIC should respond to. Figure 3.5.2 demonstrates the initialization of the cascaded Master and Slave PICs. Source and compiled versions of this example (**isa_init.c** and **isa_init.exe**) are included on the IDPCSD disk in the a:\chpt3 subdirectory.

```
/* isa_init.c /*                                                      PC/AT-ISA

  void main()
{ disable()
  ;

  /* Initialize Master 8259 PIC */
    outportb(0x20, 0x11);  /* ICW1 - Edge Triggered Mode, Cascaded PIC, ICW4 required to define  µPM */
    outportb(0x21, 0x08);  /* ICW2 - Set PIC offset to  08h, the PC's Master PIC IVT      base Address   */
    outportb(0x21, 0x04);  /* ICW3 - Slave PIC attached to IR2 Input                            */
    outportb(0x21, 0x01);  /* ICW4 - Set PIC operation to 8086/8088 Mode                        */
    outportb(0x21, 0xB8);  /* OCW1 - Mask all but IR0, 1, 2 & 6 (Timer, Keyboard, Slave PIC and Floppy)   */

  /* Initialize Slave 8259 PIC */
    outportb(0xa0, 0x11);  /* ICW1 - Edge Triggered Mode, Cascaded PIC, ICW4 required to define  µPM */
    outportb(0xa1, 0x70);  /* ICW2 - Set PIC offset to 70h, the PC's Slave PIC IVT base Address   */
    outportb(0xa1, 0x02);  /* ICW3 - Slave PIC ID = 2, the IRx level it occupies on the Master PIC */
    outportb(0xa1, 0x01);  /* ICW4 - Set PIC operation to 8086/8088 Mode                        */
    outportb(0xa1, 0x9E);  /* OCW1 - Mask all but IR8, IR13, and IR14 (RTC, #FERR, and HD)      */

  enable();              Note:  OCW1 values vary based on available platform controllers
}
```

Figure 3.5.2 Sample BIOS Initialization Routine for PC/AT-ISA Systems

Level triggered IRx inputs are the only notable difference between the PS/2-MCA and PC/AT-ISA PIC initializations. From Figure 3.5.3, we see that the LTIM (bit3 in ICW1) is set to 1 during the PS/2-MCA initialization routine. Micro-Channel Architecture specifies that all 15 IRx inputs be configured as level triggered. Both the source (**mca_init.c**) and compiled (**mca_init.exe**) versions of this example are included on the IDPCSD disk in the a:\chpt3 subdirectory.

```
/* mca_init.c /*                                                    PS/2-MCA

void main()
{
    disable();

    /* Initialize Master 8259 PIC */
    outportb(0x20, 0x19);   /* ICW1 -  Level Triggered Mode , Cascaded PIC, ICW4 required to define   µPM  */
    outportb(0x21, 0x08);   /* ICW2 - Set PIC offset to 08h, the PC's Master PIC IV      T base Address        */
    outportb(0x21, 0x04);   /* ICW3 - Slave PIC attached to IR2 Input                                          */
    outportb(0x21, 0x01);   /* ICW4 - Set PIC operation to 8086/8088 Mode                                      */
    outportb(0x21, 0xB8);   /* OCW1 - Mask all but IR0, 1, 2 & 6 (Timer, Keyboard, Slave PIC and Fl   oppy)    */

    /* Initialize Slave 8259 PIC */
    outportb(0xa0, 0x19);   /* ICW1 -  Level Triggered Mode , Cascaded PIC, ICW4 required to define   µPM  */
    outportb(0xa1, 0x70);   /* ICW2 - Set PIC offset to 70h, the PC's Slave PIC IVT base Address               */
    outportb(0xa1, 0x02);   /* ICW3 - Slave PIC ID = 2, the IRx level it occupies on the Master PIC            */
    outportb(0xa1, 0x01);   /* ICW4 - Set PIC operation to 8086/8088 Mode                                      */
    outportb(0xa1, 0x9E);   /* OCW1 - Mask all but IR8, IR13, and IR14 (RTC, #FERR, and HD)                    */

    enable();               Note:  OCW1 values vary based on available platform controllers
}
```

Figure 3.5.3 Sample BIOS Initialization code for PS/2-MCA Systems

One of the advantages of the PC/AT-EISA platform is the ability for each of the fifteen IRx inputs to be defined as either edge or level triggered on an individual basis. The advantage to this comes in the form of maintained compatibility with older ISA devices. Configuring an IRx level as either edge or level triggered is accomplished by the EISA platforms two Edge/Level Control Registers (ELCRs). The initialization sequence including the ELCRs for the PC/AT-EISA platform is shown in Figure 3.5.4. The LTIM bit (bit3 in ICW1), which is normally used to determine the triggering mode of the 8259 PIC IRx inputs, has no meaning on the EISA platform. It is simply a "don't care" bit. Both ELCR's are initialized to indicate edge triggering for all fifteen IRx inputs at startup (ELCRs = 00h). Details regarding ELCRs are discussed in the next section. Both the **eisainit.c** C source file and **eisainit.exe** executable are included on the IDPCSD disk in the a:\chpt3 subdirectory.

```
/* eisainit.c */                                                         F

void main()
{
    disable();

    /* Initialize Master 8259 PIC */
    outportb(0x20, 0x11);   /* ICW1 -  Triggering deferred  , Cascaded PIC, ICW4 required to define    µPM    */
    outportb(0x21, 0x08);   /* ICW2 - Set PIC offset to  08h, the PC's Master PIC IVT    base Address         */
    outportb(0x21, 0x04);   /* ICW3 - Slave PIC attached to IR2 Input                                         */
    outportb(0x21, 0x01);   /* ICW4 - Set PIC operation to 8086/8088 Mode                                     */
    outportb(0x21, 0xB8);   /* OCW1 - Mask all but IR0, 1, 2 & 6 (Timer, Keyboard, Slave PIC and Floppy)      */
    outportb(0x4D0, 0x00);  /* ELCR1 - Edge/Level Control Reg. -   Initialize all IRx Inputs to Edge Triggering   */

    /* Initialize Slave 8259 PIC */
    outportb(0xa0, 0x11);   /* ICW1 -  Triggering deferred  , Cascaded PIC, ICW4 required to define    µPM    */
    outportb(0xa1, 0x70);   /* ICW2 - Set PIC offset to 70h, the PC's Slave PIC IVT base Address              */
    outportb(0xa1, 0x02);   /* ICW3 - Slave PIC ID = 2, the IRx level it occupies on the Master PIC           */
    outportb(0xa1, 0x01);   /* ICW4 - Set PIC operation to 8086/8088 Mode                                     */
    outportb(0xa1, 0x9E);   /* OCW1 - Mask all but IR8, IR13, and IR14 (RTC, #FERR, and HD)                   */
    outportb(0x4D1, 0x00);  /* ELCR2 - Edge/Level Control Reg. -   Initialize all IRx Inputs to Edge Triggering   */

    enable();                        Note:  OCW1 values vary based on available platform controllers
}
```

Figure 3.5.4 Sample BIOS Initialization code for PC/AT-EISA Systems

3.6 AT-EISA Edge/Level Control Registers (ELCRs)

The EISA and PCI platforms are unique in their approach to level vs. edge triggered IRx inputs. To promote compatibility with legacy ISA devices and also realize the unlimited interrupt access derived from interrupt sharing, both platforms allow the designer to individually define each of the 15 IRx inputs as either edge or level triggered through the use of two Edge/Level Control Registers (ELCRs). On the PC/XT, ISA, and MCA platforms, the LTIM bit in ICW1 (bit3) is used to define the triggering mode of *all* the 8259's IRx inputs as either edge or level triggered. On the EISA and PCI platforms however, the LTIM bit is rendered a "don't care" bit in ICW1 and the ELCRs take over responsibility for defining the IRx input's triggering mode. Both the Master and Slave PIC ELCR register definitions are given in Figure 3.6.1.

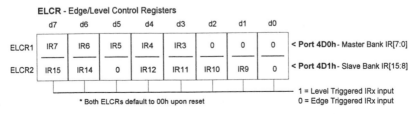

Figure 3.6.1 ELCR - Edge/Level Control Registers

ELCR1 is assigned to the Master PIC and defines the trigger mode for each of the Master PIC's IR[7:0] inputs. It is accessed via port address 4D0h on both the EISA and PCI platforms. The three low order bits d0 - d2 in ELCR1 must be set to 0 to maintain compatibility with edge triggered platform resources.

The Slave PIC IR[15:8] input triggering definitions are managed through ELCR2, accessed via port address 4D1h. Bits d5 and d0 in ELCR2 must be set to 0 for compatibility issues as well. As a rule, only IRx inputs associated with EISA devices or hosting PCI INTx# lines should be programmed to use level triggering.

During the System's BIOS initialization, ELCR1 and ELCR2 are both set to 00h. An example of the ELCR's initialization is given in Figure 3.5.4 (AT-EISA 8259 PIC initialization listing) shown near the end of the previous section. Once initialized, EISA device drivers will conFigure the ELCRs and program the required IRx level to operate in level triggered mode as required. Similarly, the PCI PnP configuration firmware will program the ELCR's when making interrupt routing decisions (details on this process are given in Chapter 10).

If, for some reason, you need to re-initialize either the Master or Slave PIC once the system is up and running (e.g. to redefine the PIC's interrupt vector address in ICW2), do not include the two ELCR registers in the re-initialization routine as they will already reflect the correct triggering mode configuration.

4. The PC's Master and Slave PIC Interrupt Process

4.1 The PC's Master PIC Interrupt Process
- A Step-by-Step Illustration

This section details the events that occur during the servicing of an interrupt request originating on a Master PIC IRx input. On the original PC and XT platforms, the step-by-step process illustrated in Figure 4.1.1 is valid for all eight Master PIC IR[7:0] inputs. In the AT's cascaded configuration however, IR2 on the Master PIC is reserved for Slave PIC requests, therefore Figure 4.1.1 represents the AT's IR[7:3,1,0] only.

Where appropriate, distinctions between level vs. edge triggered IRx inputs and the various PC platforms have been called out.

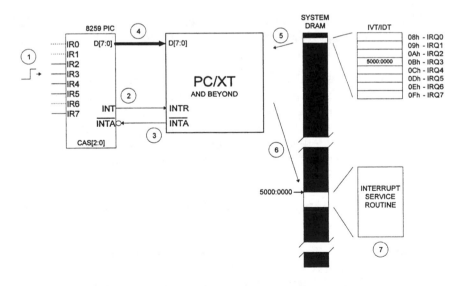

Figure 4.1.1 Master PIC Interrupt Process

1. Interrupt Request Signal is Asserted

Edge Triggered - The device is first required to drive the IRx input low for a minimum of 100nS to set the edge sense latch, then the device asserts the request by driving the IRx input high.

Edge Triggered Application Note: The 8259's initialization sequence resets the edge sense latches.

Level Triggered - The device asserts a request by using an open collector output to pull the IRQx (INTx# for PCI) bus line to ground.

2. The Master PIC Interrupts the Processor

If the request uses an IRx level on the Master PIC that is unmasked and has priority over all other requests pending or in service, the 8259 PIC will assert the INT line and wait for processor acknowledgment.

3. Processor Acknowledges the Request

On each instruction boundary, the processor samples its INTR line checking for an active request signal. When a request is detected, the processor finishes the current task, halts and brings it's W/R#, M/IO#, and D/C# lines low to initiate the interrupt acknowledge sequence.

ISA/EISA & MCA - The expansion bus controller responds by issuing two negative going pulses back on the INTA# pin of both the Master and Slave PIC's simultaneously.

PCI-ISA/EISA/MCA - The host-PCI bridge responds by acquiring the PCI bus and initiating a PCI interrupt acknowledge transaction. The PCI target containing the interrupt controllers (PCI-ISA/EISA/MCA bridge) detects the interrupt acknowledge transaction and claims the transaction by asserting the DEVSEL#. The target (bridge) then generates two negative going pulses on the INTA# pins of both the Master and Slave PIC.

4. Master PIC Transfers the Interrupt Vector Byte to the Processor

The interrupt vector byte is transferred to the processor during the acknowledge cycle. Figure 4.1.2 illustrates this process. To begin, the falling edge of the first pulse freezes the IRx input signal levels for priority resolution. Then, on the rising edge of the second INTA# pulse, the interrupt vector byte *nn* placed on the data bus by the Master PIC, is received by the processor. In addition, the rising edge of the second INTA# pulse resets the IRR bit and sets the ISR bit for the IRx level being acknowledged on the Master PIC which causes the INT line to go inactive.

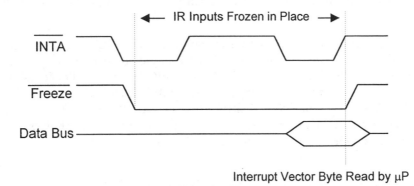

Figure 4.1.2 Acknowledge Cycle Detail

5. Processor Looks up the Starting Address of the Device's iSR

Real mode - The absolute vector table address where the iSR's starting address resides is located at 0:4 * *nn* (*nn* = interrupt vector byte)

Protected mode - The absolute interrupt descriptor table (IDT) address where the iSR's starting address resides is located at 0:8 * *nn*

6. Interrupt Service Routine Executes

The processor pushes the flags, IP, and CS registers, in that order, onto the stack, resets the IF bit (disables interrupts) and makes an indirect jump to the starting address of the iSR.

Edge Triggered - The iSR immediately enters the service routine body and services the device.

Level Triggered - Knowing its device possibly shares the IRx (INTx# for PCI) bus line with other devices, the iSR starts by first reading the pending request status bit on it's companion device. If the iSR detects a pending request, the service routing body is entered and the device is serviced.

PCI Application Note: Reading the pending request status bit by the iSR effectively flushes the posted write buffers before beginning the service routine as required by the PCI specification.

7. Interrupt Processing Cycle Wraps Up

Level Triggered - When the service routine body finishes, the iSR deasserts the active request by resetting the pending request bit on the device.

Non-Specific EOI commands are issued first to the Slave PIC and then to the Master, informing them of the completed service routine. As a result, the ISR bit for IR2 in the Master PIC (Slave PIC IRx level) and the ISR bit for the level just serviced by the Slave PIC are cleared. As the final step, the IRET instruction restores the CS, IP, and flags registers in that order, returning control to the interrupted process. Details on iSR design are covered in Chapter 6.

4.2 The PC's Slave PIC Interrupt Process

- A Step-by-Step Illustration

This section details the events that occur during the servicing of an interrupt request originating on a Slave PIC IRx input. The step-by-step process illustrated in Figure 4.2.1 applies to all eight Slave PIC IR[15:8] inputs. Where appropriate, certain distinctions between level vs. edge triggered IRx inputs and subtle differences among the various PC platforms have been noted.

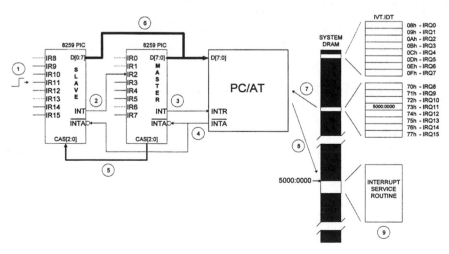

Figure 4.2.1 Slave PIC Interrupt Process

1. Interrupt Request Signal is Asserted

Edge Triggered - The device is first required to drive the IRx input low for a minimum of 100nS to set the edge sense latch, then the device asserts the request by driving the IRx input high.

Edge Triggered Application Note: The 8259's initialization sequence resets the edge sense latches.

Level Triggered - The device asserts a request by using an open collector output to pull the IRQx (INTx# for PCI) bus line to ground.

2. The Slave PIC Interrupts the Master PIC

If the device request is asserted on a Slave PIC IRx level that is unmasked and has priority over all other Slave PIC requests currently pending or in service, the Slave PIC will assert the INT line and interrupt the Master PIC on IR2.

3. The Master PIC Interrupts the Processor

If IR2 (Slave PIC request) is unmasked and has priority over all other requests currently pending or in service on the Master PIC, the Master PIC asserts its INT line and waits for the processor to acknowledge the interrupt.

4. Processor Acknowledges the Request

On each instruction boundary, the processor samples its INTR line checking for an active request signal. When a request is detected, the processor finishes the current task, halts and brings it's W/R#, M/IO#, and D/C# lines low to initiate the interrupt acknowledge sequence.

ISA/EISA & MCA - The expansion bus controller responds by issuing two negative going pulses back on the INTA# pin of both the Master and Slave PIC's simultaneously.

PCI-ISA/EISA/MCA - The host-PCI bridge responds by acquiring the PCI bus and initiating a PCI interrupt acknowledge transaction. The PCI target containing the interrupt controllers (PCI-ISA/EISA/MCA bridge) detects the interrupt acknowledge transaction and claims the transaction by asserting the DEVSEL#. The target (bridge) then generates two negative going pulses on the INTA# pins of both the Master and Slave PIC.

5. Master PIC drives the CAS[2:0] lines with the Slave PIC ID#

The falling edge of the first pulse freezes the IRx input signal levels for priority resolution as shown in Figure 4.2.2. Once priority has been resolved on the Master PIC and it is determined that IR2 holds the highest priority, the Master PIC internally checks ICW3 to see if IR2 is in use by a Slave PIC. It is, so the Master PIC drives the CAS[2:0] lines with the Slave PIC's ID "010", thereby turning the responsibility for driving the data bus with the interrupt vector byte over to the Slave PIC.

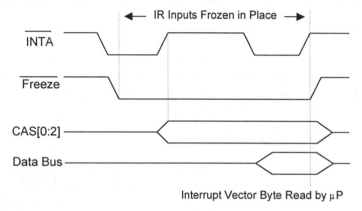

Figure 4.2.2 Acknowledge Cycle Detail

6. Slave PIC Transfers the Interrupt Vector Byte to the Processor

Upon recognizing its ID on the CAS[2:0] lines, the Slave PIC drives the data bus with the interrupt type code for the highest priority request currently pending service. On the rising edge of the second INTA# pulse, the interrupt vector byte *nn* placed on the data bus by the Slave PIC, is received by the processor. In addition, the rising edge of the second INTA# pulse resets the IRR bit and sets the ISR bit for the IRx level being acknowledged on the Master PIC which causes the INT line to go inactive.

7. Processor Looks up the Starting Address of the Device's iSR

Real mode - The absolute vector table address where the iSR's starting address resides is located at 0:4 * *nn* (*nn* = interrupt vector byte).

Protected mode - The absolute interrupt descriptor table (IDT) address where the iSR's starting address resides is located at 0:8 * *nn*.

8. Interrupt Service Routine Executes

The processor pushes the flags, IP, and CS registers, in that order, onto the stack, resets the IF bit (disables interrupts) and makes an indirect jump to the starting address of the iSR.

Edge Triggered - The iSR immediately enters the service routine body and services the device.

Level Triggered - Knowing its device possibly shares the IRx (INTx# for PCI) bus line with other devices, the iSR starts by first reading the pending request status bit on it's companion device. If the iSR detects a pending request, the service routing body is entered and the device is serviced.

PCI Application Note: Reading the pending request status bit by the iSR effectively flushes the posted write buffers before beginning the service routine as required by the PCI specification.

9. Interrupt Processing Cycle Wraps Up

Level Triggered - When the service routine body finishes, the iSR deasserts the active request by resetting the pending request bit on the device.

Non-Specific EOI commands are issued first to the Slave PIC and then to the Master, informing them of the completed service routine. As a result, the ISR bit for IR2 in the Master PIC (Slave PIC IRx level) and the ISR bit for the level just serviced by the Slave PIC are cleared. As the final step, the IRET instruction restores the CS, IP, and flags registers in that order, returning control to the interrupted process. Details on iSR design are covered in Chapter 6.

4.3 Whatever Became of IRQ2?

When the PC-XT evolved into the PC-AT, the IRQ2 bus line (B4 on the ISA bus) was removed from the Master PIC's IR2 input and rerouted to the IR9 input on the Slave PIC as illustrated in Figure 1.2.2. This rearrangement was required to cascade the Slave PIC's INT line to the Master PIC's IR2 input. As a result, device drivers that still hook the original IRQ2 vector (interrupt 0Ah), require an iSR installed behind IRQ9 (interrupt 71H) to redirect the incoming request on IRQ9 to the interrupt vector associated with IRQ2. Normally, PC-AT system BIOS's install the iSR behind IRQ9 during system startup to handle the redirection. A partial C source example is listed in Figure 4.3.1 demonstrating the design of this iSR. The complete C source code file **ir9_ir2.c** and the resulting executable **ir9_ir2.exe** are provided on the IDPCSD disk in the a:\chpt4 subdirectory.

```
/* ir9_ir2.c */

void interrupt NewIr9(void);
void interrupt (*Ir2)(void);
int Seg, Off;

void interrupt NewIr9()
{
    outportb(0xa0, 0x20);    /* Issue Non-Specific EOI command to Slave PIC      */

    Off = peek(0, 0x28);     /* Interrupt 0ah (IRQ2) iSR starting address - Offset    */
    Seg = peek(0, 0x2a);     /* Interrupt 0ah (IRQ2) iSR starting address - Segment */
    Ir2 = ((void interrupt (*)())MK_FP(Seg, Off));
    Ir2();                   /* Far Jump to Interrupt 0ah (IRQ2)                 */
}
```

Figure 4.3.1 IR9 to IR2 Redirection iSR (partial C source)

Unlike the PC/AT, the MCA bus dropped the IRQ2 naming convention and instead, correctly identified the bus line as IRQ9. The MCA bus could do this because a new standard not subject to backward compatibility issues was being created. Today the IRQ2 pin found on the ISA bus is commonly referred to as IRQ2/9 to reflect the pins actual connection to the Slave PIC's IR9 input. Installing an iSR behind IRQ2 (interrupt 0Ah) on the Master PIC or behind IRQ9 (interrupt 71h) on the Slave PIC, will result in the accurate processing of an IRQ2/9 request. However, a Slave PIC iSR installed behind IRQ9 will process an IRQ2 request faster than the equivalent Master PIC iSR using the IRQ2 vector because redirection of the request is not required.

4.4 Interrupt Vector Table (Real Mode)

The *Interrupt Vector Table* or *IVT* is a lookup table used by the processor to identify the starting address of the task or procedure being called. Tasks or procedures called via interrupt are commonly termed *Interrupt Service Routines* (iSRs) or *Interrupt Handlers*, both are synonymous. Interrupt sources capable of invoking interrupt handlers through the IVT fall into the following categories:

- Hardware interrupts: *NMI, IRQ[15:0]*
- Software interrupts: *INTO, INT 3, INT nn* and *BOUND* instructions
- Processor exceptions: *faults, traps, and aborts*

The IVT occupies 1024 bytes (1K) of contiguous address space and consists of 256 entries, each with a unique identifying number (00h - FFh) referred to as a *vector*. Each entry is 4 bytes in length and provides the starting address of the interrupt service routine being called in segment:offset format. Figure 4.4.1 illustrates the IVT's structure (a) and the format of the each entry (b).

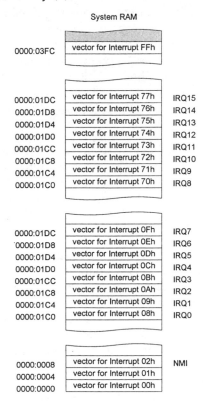

Figure 4.4.1(a) Real Mode Interrupt Vector Table (IVT)

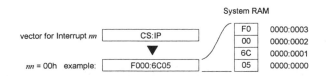

Figure 4.4.1(b) Real Mode Interrupt Vector Table (IVT)

On the 8086, the base address of the IVT is hard-wired at 0000:0000 with a resulting address range of 00000 to 003FFh. Processors starting with the 80286 maintain the original IVT structure as found on the 8086 when operating in real mode, but in addition allow the IVT's base address to be located anywhere in real mode address space and its size defined using the processor's *Interrupt Descriptor Table Register (IDTR)*. On power up or reset, 80286+ processors default to real mode and load the IDTR with 00000000h for the base address and 03ffh for the limit to establish the familiar real mode IVT. Typically, there is no reason to stray from the IDTR's initial defaults when operating in real mode. However if the need arises, the base address and/or size of the IVT in real mode address space can be changed by modifying the IDTR base address or limit values using the LIDT (load IDTR) and SIDT (Store IDTR) instructions. If the limit is changed and an interrupt occurs that is beyond the limit stored in the IDTR, a double-fault exception (Interrupt 08h) will occur. The following Section ("Protected Mode Interrupt Descriptor Table") details the IDTR and the LIDT/SIDT instructions.

The processor uses the IVT to look up the starting address of the handler by first receiving the associated vector from the interrupt source. Next, the processor scales the *vector * 0:4h* to index into the IVT and retrieve the segment:offset of the handler's starting address. On processors which incorporate the IDTR (80286 forward), the IVT's base address is taken into account and the adjusted calculation *baseaddr + (vector * 0:4h)* is used.

During system startup, the system BIOS initializes the IVT by assigning ROM BIOS service routines and IRQ handlers vectors within the IVT. In particular, the system BIOS assigns IRQ0 - IRQ7 vectors 08h - 0fh and IRQ8 - IRQ15 vectors 70h - 77h respectively, as shown in Figure 4.4.1(a). Intel reserved vectors 00h - 1fh for processor use only. This reservation was violated on the original PC design, resulting in a permanent conflict between Intel processor exceptions and the now standard IRQ0 - IRQ7 vector's 08h - 0fh in all PC's. During real mode operation, the problem is minimized because conflicting exceptions rarely if ever occur. In protected mode however, conflicting exceptions and in particular the General Protection fault at vector 0dh are more common. Protected mode operating systems therefore relocate IRQ0 - IRQ7 out of the reserved area. Section 11.4 describes the technique required to relocate IRQ7 - IRQ0 to an alternate block of vectors within the IVT.

4.5 Interrupt Descriptor Table (Protected Mode)

The *Interrupt Descriptor Table* or *IDT* is the protected mode equivalent of the real mode IVT. There are some significant differences however between the two. Instead of the vector entry storing the real mode starting address of the handler in a 4 byte segment:offset format, protected mode IDT entries consist of 8 byte *gate descriptors*. Each gate descriptor in the IDT is referenced by a unique number (00h - ffh) referred to as a *vector*. The IDT can include up to 256 gate descriptors at a maximum size of 2024 bytes (2K). The protected mode IDT may reside anywhere in physical memory as defined by the 32 bit *base address* value stored in the *Interrupt Descriptor Table Register* or *IDTR*. In addition, the IDTR holds a 16 bit *limit* value which defines the IDT's size in memory. If less than 256 IDT entries (limit = 7ffh) are required, the limit value can be set to include only those gate descriptors for which interrupt vectors might occur. For instance, if vector 4eh is the highest vector number for which an interrupt is expected, then calculating the limit value proceeds as follows:

$$limit = (\text{vector} * 08h) + 7$$

$$limit = (4eh * 08h) + 7$$

$$limit = 277h$$

The IDTR is programmable in both real and protected modes using the *LIDT* (Load IDTR) and *SIDT* (Store IDTR) instructions. In protected mode, the LIDT instruction can only be executed when the CPL is 0. It is used primarily by protected mode operating systems to compose the IDT during initialization. An operating system may also use this instruction to switch to an alternate IDT. In contrast, the SIDT instruction copies the values for base address and limit from the IDTR into memory and may be executed at any privilege level. Once initialized, Figure 4.5.1 illustrates how the IDTR is used to locate the IDT in memory.

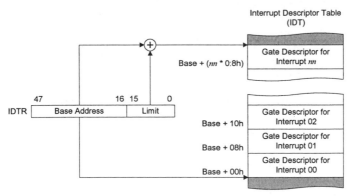

Figure 4.5.1 IDTR Defines IDT in Memory

If an attempt is made to reference a descriptor beyond the limit set in the IDTR, the processor will enter shutdown mode. Only an NMI or reset initialization will inspire the processor to resume its fetch and execute cycle. Default values loaded into the IDTR upon processor reset are

00000000h for the base address and 03ffh for the limit (real mode IVT). When switching into protected mode, the initialization program converts the real mode IVT entries into gate descriptors and loads the IDTR's base address and limit with the appropriate values. In addition, to immediately resolve the conflict that exists between IRQ7 - IRQ0 vectors 08h - 0fh and processor exceptions using those same vectors, the initialization program relocates IRQ7 - IRQ0 to a conflict free block of gate descriptors within the IDT.

There are three possible gate descriptor types allowed to reside in the IDT. They are *Interrupt gates, Trap gates,* and *Task gates.* Of the three, interrupt and trap gates comprise the bulk of the IDT entries. Task gates are generally not used because in most instances, protected mode operating systems handle the task switching in software. Interrupt and trap gates are structured identically as shown in Figure 4.5.2.

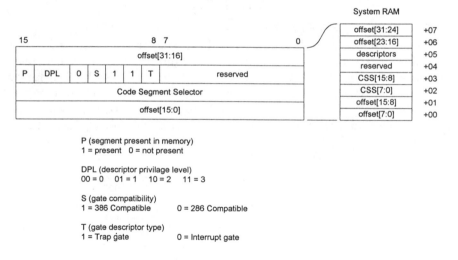

Figure 4.5.2 Interrupt and Trap gate structure

The major difference between interrupt and trap gates is that interrupt gates reset the IF bit in the EFLAGS register (disable hardware interrupts) before passing control to the interrupt handler, trap gates do not. For this reason, interrupt gates are typically used by hardware interrupts IRQ[15:0] to invoke their associated interrupt service routines. Trap gates provide entry into interrupt handlers in a manner consistent with real mode software interrupts. An INT *nn* instruction issued in protected mode however can access both interrupt and trap gates. This gives protected mode software interrupts the option of using an interrupt gate to call procedures that are not subject to interruption by hardware interrupts.

54

In response to an interrupt request in protected mode, the processor scales the *vector * 0:8h* then adds that value to the IDT base address stored in the IDTR (see Figure 4.5.2) to locate the appropriate gate descriptor in physical memory. The interrupt service routine is then indirectly referenced by the interrupt or trap gate as illustrated in Figure 4.5.3.

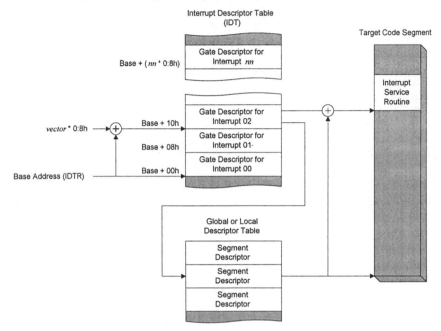

Figure 4.5.3 Protected Mode Interrupt Process

The segment selector value found in the gate descriptor points to a code segment descriptor in either the Global Descriptor Table (GDT) or the current Local Descriptor Table (LDT). The offset defined by the gate descriptor then points to the starting address of the interrupt service routine.

5. Controlling the Interrupt Process

5.1 A Simplified Representation of the Interrupt Processing Hardware

All the methodologies of device interaction described in the previous chapter, with the exception of Polling, evoke an Interrupt Service Routine (iSR) to handle the needs of the device or devices requesting service (The small "i" in the iSR acronym will be reserved from here on out to distinguish between a reference to an Interrupt Service Routine and the 8259's In-Service Register ISR). In fact, to a large extent, interrupt service routines are the workhorses and fundamental design components of interrupt-driven PC systems. This chapter is the starting point for understanding their architecture and the role they play in the PC environment. They are short programs that, somewhere in the middle, contain the service routine body responsible for servicing their respective device or devices. The rest of the iSR is made up of commands that work with and control the flow of the interrupt processing hardware. If the control commands issued by an iSR are issued out of sequence or omitted altogether, the interrupt process will lose its integrity. Also, the system will most likely stop responding to interrupt requests altogether, the keyboard interrupt included. When the keyboard interrupt is undermined, the computer system enters a state commonly referred to as "locked up". It seems then, that thoroughly understanding the flow control aspect of the interrupt process would be key to properly designing interrupt service routines that result in a stable interrupt-driven PC system.

Toward this goal we first need a way to easily visualize the obstacle course an interrupt request signal must navigate before finally being able to tag the processor. It is the obstacles themselves that we are interested in controlling. Fortunately, the 8259 PIC as applied within the confines of a PC system lends itself well to a simplified model. The model is given here in Figure 5.1.1.

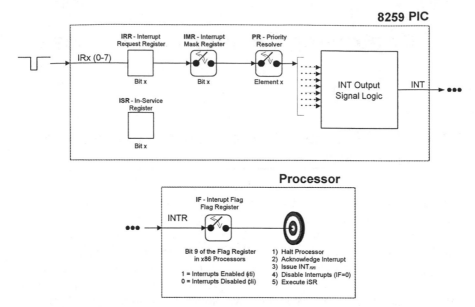

Figure 5.1.1 PC-XT/AT IR0-IR7 Interrupt Request Obstacle Course

The IRR input latch and associated ISR bit are represented here as boxes and are able to provide the status of whether an interrupt request is pending (IRR) or whether an interrupt request has been acknowledged and is currently in service (ISR) for the IRx level of interest. The Interrupt Mask Register (IMR), Priority Resolver (PR) and Interrupt Flag (IF) are all represented here as switches that either block the interrupt request from reaching the processor (open) or allow the interrupt request to advance (closed). These switches are the control elements of the interrupt process. The state of the IMR is at the sole discretion of the designer. Control of the PR and IF switches however, is shared between the designer and the interrupt processing hardware. For example, if all the control element switches (IMR, PR, and IF) shown in Figure 5.1.1 are in the closed position, an interrupt request will pass through the IMR and PR switches causing the INT output logic to assert the INT line. The interrupt request made by the 8259 PIC will then pass through the IF switch (interrupts enabled) and reach its target causing the processor to acknowledge the request. If any of the switches are open, the blocked request will have to wait until the switch is again closed before it can proceed. Expanding Figure 5.1.1 to represent all eight inputs on an 8259 PIC, gives us Figure 5.1.2

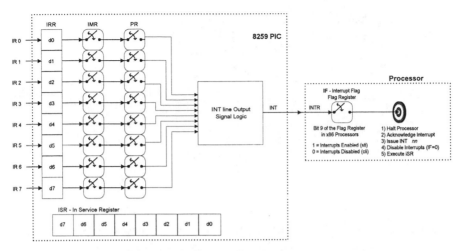

Figure 5.1.2 PC XT/AT Master 8259 PIC Simplified Hardware Representation

Figure 5.1.2 is the simplified hardware representation of the Master PIC found in all PCs from the PC-XT to the present and provides the first complete picture of the elements within the PIC that allow it to control the flow of requests through its interior. In addition, it becomes clear here that the IF bit in the processor's flag register has global repercussions. If the IF bit is not properly controlled, it will impact all requests at all levels. The IMR as mentioned, allows for the designer to selectively turn IRx levels on or off. The PR switches are used by the 8259 PIC when an IRx level is in service to block the equal and lower priority IRs from being acknowledged while passing higher priority IRs on to the processor. The following sections in this chapter cover this in detail.

A simplified hardware model for the cascaded Master/Slave PC/AT interrupt structure is presented here in Figure 5.1.3. Adding a Slave PIC to the system forces Slave PIC interrupt requests IR8 - IR15 to overcome an additional set of IMR and PR switches before reaching the Master PIC. Because of this, Slave PIC interrupt service routines require additional control elements to address the Slave PIC's involvement. The next Chapter, and in particular sections 6.3, 6.5, and 6.6, detail the proper design of Slave PIC iSRs.

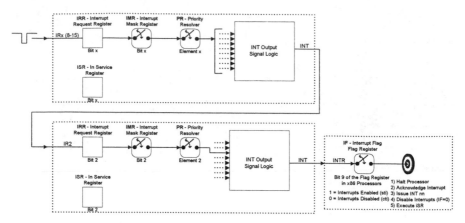

Figure 5.1.3 PC-AT Slave IR8-IR15 Interrupt Request Obstacle Course

The complete simplified hardware representation of the cascaded Master/Slave PIC PC/AT and PS/2 interrupt structure representing all 15 IRx levels is given in Figure 5.1.4. This is a snapshot of the core elements of the interrupt processing hardware in today's PCs that work together to maintain order and resolve contention among a plurality of competing devices. As we begin to develop state diagrams for the purpose of grasping the subtleties of interrupt flow control, Figure 5.1.4 works well as an overall graphical reference. Until the state diagram representations presented next gel, use Figure 5.1.4 as your reference anchor.

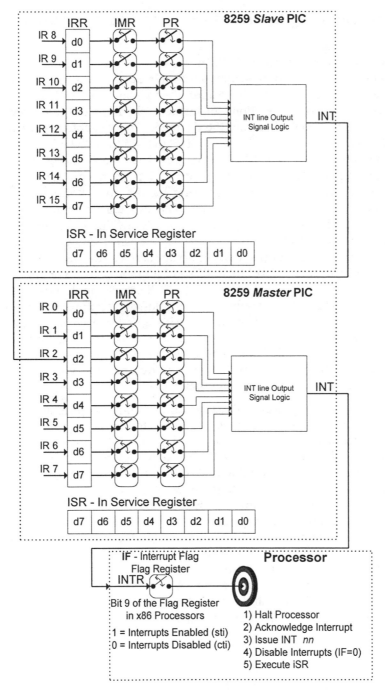

Figure 5.1.4 PC-AT Slave 8259 PIC Simplified Hardware Representation

5.2 Developing Interrupt Process State Diagrams

The simple representations given in section 5.1, and in particular Figure 5.1.4, illustrate the array of switches an interrupt request must navigate in order to be recognized. The disposition of those switches and what controls them is the topic of this section. For instance, the interrupt mask register is under the direct control of you, the designer. The switches represented by the priority resolver are under the control of both the 8259 priority resolver logic and a designer issued EOI command. The disposition of the IF bit in the flags register falls under the control of both the platform processor when the interrupt is acknowledged and the designer there after. The IRR and ISR are status registers only. The IRR can tell us at any given time what IRx levels have pending valid requests awaiting acknowledgment. The ISR tells us what interrupt levels have been acknowledged and are currently being serviced (i.e. their interrupt service routine is in progress). Additionally, the contents of the ISR feed the priority resolver and seed the resolver's decision making process. All of these elements will be broken down and discussed thoroughly in the following sections. Knowing how all of these elements work in concert during an interrupt cycle allows us to gain a mastery over the interrupt process and make informed decisions on the fly during system development. In addition, the answer to why an iSR is not doing what you expected, is easy to determine if you step the iSRs logic through a series of state diagrams.

In order to graphically illustrate the step-by-step analysis of the interrupt process and save trees, we need to create a more convenient model to work from than that given in Figure 5.1.4. Figure 5.1.4 could be used to describe the state of the 8259 PIC at any given time, however it can only show the one state and that ain't gonna fly. So to begin, lets take each element of the process and redefine it graphically. We will start here with the 8259s IRR and ISR status registers. Refer to Figure 5.2.1a. Both the 8259's IRR and ISR can be represented by a set of eight squares stacked up vertically. Let each square represent one of the registers (d0 - d7) bit contents with d0 being the top most square and d7 the lower most. On the Master PIC of a PC-XT, PC-AT or PS/2 system, d0 - d7 represents IR0 - IR7 respectively. On the Slave PIC of a PC-AT or PS/2, d0 - d7 represents IR8 - IR15. In Figures 5.2.1a, b, and c, the bit-to-IRx level association for both the Master and Slave PICs are shown for convenience.

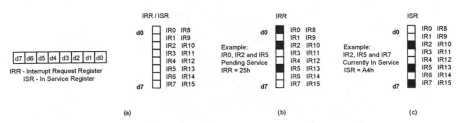

Figure 5.2.1 IRR and ISR as State Diagram Elements

If a high signal level is present at one of the IRR's IRx inputs, the associated square will be solid representing a pending interrupt request at that level. If a low level is present at the IRx input, the representative square will be empty indicating no pending request at that level. Figure 5.2.1b gives an example of what the contents of the IRR will yield for the associated IRR levels pending service. For the ISR, if a bit is set, the square will be solid indicating that an interrupt request at that level has been acknowledged and is currently being serviced. If the bit is reset, the square will be empty indicating no interrupt request is currently in service at that level. Figure 5.2.1c illustrates this concept. Reading the contents of either the IRR or ISR is covered in Section 5.6.

The IMR, Priority Resolver and IF bit act as switches, but just like a bit in the IRR or ISR, they too represent one of only two possible states, open or closed. It follows then that the same graphical representation used with the IRR and ISR can be used here to represent the IMR, Priority Resolver and IF bit in our state diagram. Figure 5.2.2 illustrates how this is accomplished.

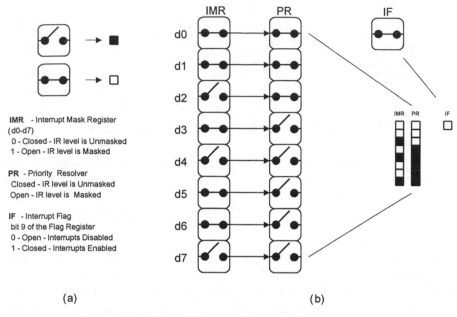

IMR - Interrupt Mask Register
(d0-d7)
   0 - Closed - IR level is Unmasked
   1 - Open - IR level is Masked

PR - Priority Resolver
   Closed - IR level is Unmasked
   Open - IR level is Masked

IF - Interrupt Flag
   bit 9 of the Flag Register
   0 - Open - Interrupts Disabled
   1 - Closed - Interrupts Enabled

(a)   (b)

Figure 5.2.2 IMR, PR, and IF State Diagram Legend

If a switch is open the corresponding box will be solid. When closed the corresponding box will be clear. This has an intuitive feel. Consider a pending interrupt request attempting to advance to the processor. We know the associated squares for closed switch are clear. From this we can make a quick scan of the state diagram and determine the fate of the interrupt request at any state along the logic flow. For example in Figure 5.2.2b, at a glance we see that IR0 and IR1 are not blocked by any solid boxes indicating an open switch, and are therefore free to proceed to the processor for acknowledgment if so desired. Note that a logical 1 in the IMR indicates that the associated interrupt level is Masked. Just the opposite is true for the Interrupt Flag, where a 1 indicates that interrupts are enabled (Unmasked system wide). The Priority Resolver is controlled internally by the 8259 PIC and therefore presenting the indicative logic level is irrelevant. It's either open or closed.

Having given each of the elements in the interrupt process a state diagram equivalent, we can combine them to describe the exact state of the 8259 during any phase of a PC systems interrupt process. The simplified hardware description shown in Figure 5.1.2 and 5.1.4 can now be reduced to the state diagrams shown here in Figure 5.2.3.

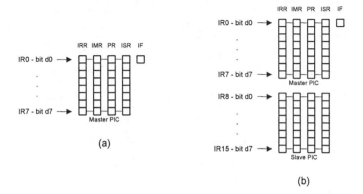

Figure 5.2.3 State Diagram Equivalents of the 8259 Hardware

Figure 5.2.3a is the state diagram for a PC-XT, PC-AT or PS/2 Master 8259 PIC. The top row of squares represent the state of IR0 and are all associated with bit d0 in the IRR, IMR, and ISR respectively. The next row down represents the state of IR1 and so on down to the bottom row representing IR7. The IF square is associated with no particular interrupt level, but instead indicates whether interrupts are enabled or disabled system wide. Figure 5.2.3b is the state diagram for a PC-AT or PS/2 cascaded 8259 PIC interrupt structure. Since any interrupt request originating on the Slave PIC must be passed on to the Master PIC's IR2 input and processed by the Master PIC, both the Slave and Master PIC state diagrams are required for complete representation. With these two state diagrams, we now have the tools needed to explore the operation and control aspects of a PC system's interrupt process.

5.3 Programming the Interrupt Mask Register (IMR)

The Interrupt Mask Register or IMR allows the system designer to selectively enable or disable individual IRx levels. When an IRx level is disabled, the IRx level is referred to as *masked*. If enabled, the IRx level is referred to as *unmasked*. The IMR on the Master PIC controls IR0 - IR7 while the IMR on the Slave PIC controls IR8 - IR15, as shown in Table 5.3.1.

IMR data bits	Associated IR level Master PIC IMR	Associated IR level Slave PIC IMR
d0	IR0	IR8
d1	IR1	IR9
d2	IR2	IR10
d3	IR3	IR11
d4	IR4	IR12
d5	IR5	IR13
d6	IR6	IR14
d7	IR7	IR15

Table 5.3.1 IMR bit Definitions

The IMR has a number of significant uses in designing interrupt-driven systems. As a precautionary measure, the IMR should be programmed to mask all unused IRx levels in the system. This prevents any possible noise glitches on the unused IRx levels from generating default IR7 interrupts. Default IR7 interrupts are explored in detail in Chapter 8, but suffice it to say they subtract from overall system bandwidth. Additionally, if no handlers have been installed in anticipation of an default IR7 interrupt, the PC's interrupt process could lose integrity depending on the reaction of the unsuspecting code installed behind IR7 that will execute. Another use for the IMR is when a group of devices are working together toward achieving one focused objective within a system. The IMR in this instance may be used by one device to preclude another known device or devices from securing any system bandwidth by masking their IRx level(s). Perhaps a device in the group, parked at a lower priority interrupt, has come to the conclusion that unless it can empty its buffer soon, an overflow condition will occur causing the system to destabilize. In this case, the device can tell its partners to hold up by masking their IRx levels long enough to bring its high-water mark down to a safe level. There are a wide variety of creative ways to integrate the IMR into a design.

Programming the IMR is simple, but there is one catch. The IMR is a community register, potentially modified by any code segment executed since the PC was powered on. This dictates that the other bits in the IMR be preserved as we make changes to the IRx levels of interest to us. To do this we must first read the contents of the IMR and then incorporate our changes into the existing IMR contents and write it back to the IMR without disturbing the surrounding bits. The bitwise *OR* and bitwise *AND* functions facilitate this. When masking an IRx level, the bitwise *or* function is used to set the bit desired. When unmasking an IRx level, the bitwise *AND* function is used. Table 5.3.2 demonstrates this procedure.

	Mask IR3		Unmask IR10	
Read IMR contents		0 1 1 0 0 0 1 0b		0 1 1 0 0 1 1 1b
Apply bit pattern	OR	0 0 0 0 1 0 0 0b	AND	1 1 1 1 1 0 1 1b
Write back result		0 1 1 0 1 0 1 0b		0 1 1 0 0 0 1 1b

Table 5.3.2 Programming the IMR

In the first example, it is desired to mask IR3. From Table 5.3.1 we see that bit d4 in the Master PIC IMR is associated with IR3. When developing a mask bit pattern, set all the bits associated with the IRx levels you wish to mask to logic 1. In this example we only want to mask IR3 so we set d4 to logic 1 and set all remaining bits to 0. We then *OR* our bit pattern with the current contents of the Master PIC IMR and write the result back to the Master PICs IMR register. This effectively masks IR3 without disturbing any of the surrounding bits. Likewise, to unmask an IRx level, set the bits corresponding to the IRx levels you desire to unmask to logic 0 and set all the remaining bits to logic 1. In this example it is desired to unmask IR10, to do this we set bit d2 corresponding to IR10 in the Slave PIC IMR to logic 0 and the remaining bits to logic 1. Then *AND* the bit pattern with the current contents of the Slave PIC IMR and write the result back to the Slave PIC IMR.

The PIC's I/O Base Address+1 always points to the PIC's IMR. Reading the IMR requires no read register command to be issued first as with the IRR and ISR. For the Master PIC, the IMR can be read or written to at I/O address 21h. The Slave PIC IMR is located at I/O address A1h. Realizing the examples given in Table 5.3.2 in coded form is demonstrated in Figure 5.3.3a and 5.3.3b.

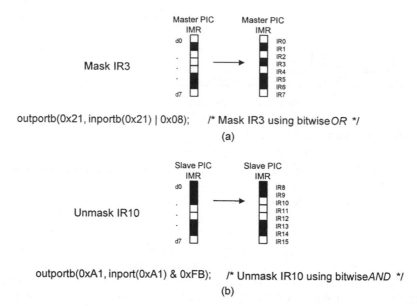

outportb(0x21, inportb(0x21) | 0x08);   /* Mask IR3 using bitwise*OR* */

(a)

outportb(0xA1, inport(0xA1) & 0xFB);   /* Unmask IR10 using bitwise*AND* */

(b)

Figure 5.3.3 Programming the IMR (C examples)

The state diagram representation of the IMR is shown here as well. When a bit is masked such as IR3 in the 5.3.3a example, the IMR switch for that IRx level is opened preventing the request from proceeding. An open switch is represented in the state diagram as a solid box. The example given in Figure 5.3.3b shows the IR10 level being unmasked. The associated box for IR10 is cleared indicating a closed IMR switch for IR10. Additional examples on IMR programming for Microsoft C and iAPX assembly are provided in Appendix 12.2 "Programmers Toolkit".

5.4 Issuing End of Interrupt (EOI) Commands

The End of Interrupt or EOI command is issued by a devices' interrupt service routine to let the 8259 PIC know that the requesting device has been attended to. The class of EOI command issued to both the Master and Slave 8259 PICs within a PC system is of the *Non-Specific* variety. A Non-Specific EOI command, unlike the Specific EOI command, does not require the programmer to specify the IRx level when the command is issued, hence the name *Non-Specific*. The reason the IRx level can be omitted from the EOI command, is that the associated IRx level is already known to the 8259 PIC in a PC system by way of the In-Service Register (ISR). The highest priority IRx level set in the ISR is necessarily the IRx level who's interrupt service routine is currently executing. A Non-Specific EOI operates based on this assumption. In the PC, the interrupt structure is rigid, that is IR0 has the highest priority level 0 and IR7 has the lowest priority level 7 always. Therefore, the condition the Non-Specific EOI relies on to accurately associate with the correct IRx level is always present in a PC. If you look into the 8259 data sheets, you will find features such as the ability to rotate the priority structure or selectively enable lower priority IRx levels using Special Mask Mode. Unfortunately, you can't use these features in a PC because they would disturb the interrupt structure and screw up the Non-Specific EOI's ability to associate with the correct IRx level. This in turn would cause all on board interrupt-driven resources and any other resources using unfamiliar iSRs to fail shortly after the interrupt structure was first modified.

By understanding how the 8259 PIC responds to the Non-Specific EOI command, we gain valuable insight into how the PIC successfully controls the interrupt process. This is important to understanding the proper development of the flow control aspects of interrupt service routine design. Here is what happens. The 8259 PIC responds to the Non-Specific EOI command by resetting the highest priority bit in the ISR. Remember, this bit is always accurately associated with the IRx level issuing the EOI command in a PC system. The 8259 PIC also responds to the Non-Specific EOI command by unmasking the IRx level of the associated device and all lower priority IRx levels via the Priority Resolver's control logic. The Priority Resolver contains an internal mask register that it uses to carry out its decisions. The set of eight PR switches, as illustrated in Figure 5.2.2(b), make up this mask register. To understand the dynamics of the PR's switches and the role the Non-Specific EOI command plays in the interrupt process, example Figure 5.4.1 steps through a typical interrupt processing cycle for a Master 8259 PIC IRx input using a state diagram representation.

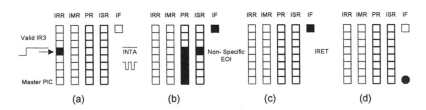

Figure 5.4.1 EOI Command's Function within the Interrupt Process

In this example it is assumed no interrupts are masked (IMR is clear) and no IRx levels are currently in service (ISR is clear). We can determine this quickly, by scanning the IMR and ISR for any solid boxes at the starting point represented by Figure 5.4.1a. In Figure 5.4.1a, a valid IR3

69

request arms the IR3 input latch in the IRR. Since no other interrupts of equal or higher priority are in service and the IR3 level is unmasked (IMR), the processor recognizes the request and issues the interrupt acknowledge pulses back to the Master 8259 PIC on INTA#. When the 8259 PIC receives the INTA# signals, it provides the processor with the vector table address associated with the recognized IRx level and masks the IRx level currently being acknowledged and all other lower priority IRx levels. The ISR bit associated with the acknowledged IRx level is set and the processor automatically disables interrupts after receiving the vector data by resetting the IF bit in the flags register and enters the interrupt service routine. This is exactly what we see happen in Figure 5.4.1b. When the interrupt service routine completes, it issues the Non-Specific EOI command to the Master PIC, resulting in the state diagram shown in Figure5.4.1c. The ISR bit was reset for the associated IRx level and all IRx levels of equal or lower priority were unmasked by the Priority Resolver. Interrupts remain disabled until the IRET is issued. This action enables interrupts by restoring the CS, IP, and specifically the flag register thereby setting the IF bit back to logic 1 (interrupts enabled).

The sequence of events just described shows how the 8259 PIC manages the PR switches to allow only interrupts of a higher priority than the IR xlevel currently in service to interrupt the processor. The sequence of events presented in Figure 5.4.2 also shows the impact a Non-Specific EOI command has on an 8259 PIC when no other requests are currently in service (ISR is clear when the request is made). This is not always the case though. Several IRx levels can be in service at the same time. How is it possible for two or more IRx levels to be in service at the same time? Good question. The concept of nested interrupt service routines is not presented until the next Chapter, but trust me for now, it is entirely possible and in most instances preferred. Knowing more than one IRx level can be in service at the same time presents us with the second question we need to ask to complete our understanding of the effect the Non-Specific EOI has on the 8259 PIC. What happens to the PR mask register after a Non-Specific EOI command is issued while other IRx levels are currently in service? Below in Figure 5.4.2(a), the answer to this question is illustrated for us. In Figure 5.4.2(a), a valid IR3 appears while IR5 is currently in service as indicated by the state of the ISR bit d5. Since interrupts are enabled and the IMR, PR and IF pose no barrier, the IR3 request is acknowledged and the resulting state diagram illustrated in Figure 5.4.2(b) show the set ISR bit for IR3, the PR's mask of IR3 and all lower priority IRx levels and interrupts disabled by the processor (solid IF box). The iSR is then entered.

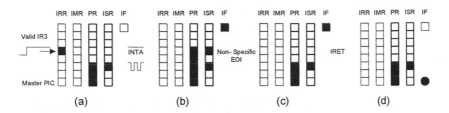

Figure 5.4.2 EOI Command's effect when another IR level is In Service

When the Non-Specific EOI command is issued as illustrated in Figure 5.4.2(c), the PR does in fact unmask IR3 and all lower priority level interrupts, but since IR5 is still registered with the ISR as in service, the PR mask register maintains the mask on IR5 and all lower levels as it should. An IRET instruction then returns the 8259 PIC to the original state it was in before being interrupted by IR3, and the IR5 service routine proceeds.

The Non-Specific EOI is quite important to the interrupt process, and all interrupt service routines are required to issue it. If the interrupt service routine is servicing a device using IR0-IR7 on the Master PIC, a Non-Specific EOI need only be issued to the Master PIC. If a Interrupt Service Routine is servicing a device using IR8 - IR15, a Non-Specific EOI must be issued to both the Slave and then the Master PIC. **The Non-Specific EOI commands must by issued to the Slave and then the Master PIC in that order.** If the interrupt service routine were to issue the Non-Specific EOI command to the Master PIC first and then the Slave PIC, any pending requests on the Slave PIC would have to race through the Slave PIC's PR logic and activate the Slave PIC's INT line before a lower priority pending IR3 - IR7 request on the Master could accept the acknowledgement of the processor that rightly belonged to the pending Slave PIC's IR level. Essentially a condition would exist whereby lower priority IR3-IR7 interrupts pending on the master PIC could "cut in line". The speed of the processor, the bus speed, and the 8259's logic technology all enter into this equation. So for sanity's sake, issue the EOI commands to the Slave and then the Master PIC in that order always.

Example code is provided here in Figure 5.4.3 and in Appendix 12.1 on how to issue a Non-Specific EOI command to both the Slave and Master 8259 PICs.

```
outportb(0xA0, 0x20);    /* Non-Specific EOI Slave PIC     */
outportb(0x20, 0x20);    /* Non-Specific EOI Master PIC    */
```

Figure 5.4.3 Issuing Non-Specific EOI commands (Borland C examples)

r a Non-Specific EOI command is 20h and is issued through)CW2 is written to the 8259 PIC's base I/O Address+0. st always be disabled before issuing any OCWs. For further V2 command format, refer to Section 4 in Chapter 3.

5.5 Enabling and Disabling Interrupts System Wide

The focus of this section is on the Interrupt Flag (IF), which occupies bit 9 of an x86 processor's flag register. The state of the Interrupt Flag determines whether interrupts are enabled or disabled system wide. It is essentially a system wide interrupt mask bit. If the state of the IF is not controlled properly, bad things can happen very fast. For instance, if interrupts are left disabled (IF switch open) by an improperly programmed interrupt service routine or are inadvertently disabled by the application program, the time of day interrupt (IR0), the keyboard interrupt (IR1) and all other IRx levels would be unable to reach the processor for acknowledgment as Figure 5.1.4 bears out. Time, relative to the PC would stand still, which isn't such a bad thing I guess, but we would lose the keyboard as an input device, all communications, and disk access. As mentioned earlier, we sometimes refer to a PC that experiences these symptoms as "locked up".

Controlling the IF is a cooperative effort between the processor and the interrupt service routine. From the processor's perspective, it must disable interrupts before passing control over to the requesting device's iSR. The reason is that it can't presume to know what's best for the interrupt service routine's device. Some service routines simply can't afford to be interrupted (refer to Chapter 11.1). The disabling of interrupts by the processor lends flexibility to the iSR's design by giving the iSR the option of completing without interruption by leaving the IF bit alone (*Locked* iSR) or enabling interrupts via the enable interrupts command thus allowing itself to be interrupted by a higher priority request (*Nested* iSR). Both the locked and nested iSR design methods will be formally presented and reviewed in the next chapter. The interrupt service routine's ability to control the IF comes in the form of three instructions - STI (enable interrupts), CLI (disable interrupts) and IRET. STI sets the IF to 1 which closes the IF switch enabling interrupts and the CLI instruction sets the IF to 0 which opens the IF switch and disables interrupts. The STI and CLI instructions are strait forward and there C counterparts enable(); and **disable();** even more so. The IRET instruction needs a little more explanation though. When the processor acknowledges an interrupt, it pushes the Flag, CS, and IP registers, in that order, on to the stack. The complementary action taken by the iSR is to issue its final instruction, the IRET. The IRET instruction pops the IP, CS, and Flag registers off the stack, thereby restoring them to there original values. Since interrupts were necessarily enabled (IF = 1) when the processor acknowledged the interrupt, the IF will again assume the value of logic 1 (interrupts enabled) when the IRET pops the Flag Register.

How all this stuff works itself into the interrupt process is described in the step-by-step state diagram shown in Figure 5.5.1 (boy these state diagrams sure are useful!). A valid interrupt request appears in Figure 5.5.1(a), in this case IR3. The processor responds by acknowledging the request, pushing the Flag, CS, and IP registers, disabling interrupts, and passing control on to the requesting IRx level's interrupt service routine. When interrupts are disabled, the IF is set to 0, closing the IF switch as represented by the solid box now present in Figure 5.5.1(b). At this point the iSR could maintain the status quo with regards to the IF and leave interrupts disabled, rendering the (c) and (d) states inapplicable. In this example however, to get an idea of how the enable and disable interrupt commands pertain, we will assume that our example describes the flow of a Nested ISR, that is one that is designed to allow itself to be interrupted by higher priority IRx levels. To allow other higher priority IRx levels to interrupt its execution, the Nested iSR issues the enable interrupts command STI before entering the service routine body. Figure 5.5.1c shows how the enable interrupts command clears a pathway for the higher priority IR0, IR1, and IR2 in this example.

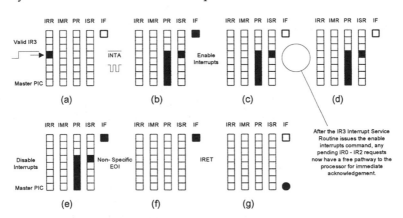

**Figure 5.5.1 Enabling and Disabling of Interrupts
During the Interrupt Process**

The interrupt process remains in the state shown in Figure 5.5.1(d) as the service routine body proceeds until the disable interrupts command is issued by the IR3 interrupt service routine. The disable interrupts command is not an option in any ISR that enables interrupts. As we learned in section 5.1, **Interrupts must be disabled at the processor before issuing an ICW or an OCW to the 8259 PIC.** The Non-Specific EOI is issued through OCW2. Therefore, relative to our example, a disable interrupts command must be issued prior to the Non-Specific EOI command. The Non-Specific EOI is then issued leaving only the IF switch open (f). The IRET command completes the iSR's responsibility to the interrupt process, by restoring the IP, CS, and Flag Registers thereby enabling interrupts. The enabled interrupts condition that resulted from the IRET command is represented by the clear IF box in Figure 5.5.1(g).

The syntax required to enable and disable interrupts is given here in Table 5.5.1 and is available in Appendix 12.2 "Programmers Toolkit".

	Borland C	Microsoft C	iAPX
Enable Interrupts	enable();	_enable();	STI
Disable Interrupts	disable();	_disable();	CLI
IRET	Compiler automatically adds IRET when the Interrupt keyword is used to define the function. See Section 9.2 for details.		IRET

Table 5.5.1 Interrupt Flag (IF) Control Instructions - Syntax Examples

5.6 Reading the 8259 PIC's IRR or ISR Status

To read either of the status registers on the 8259 PIC you must first issue a read register command. The read register command is issued via an OCW3. It indicates to the 8259 PIC which of the two status registers, IRR or ISR, you wish to read. Once a read register command has been issued, you can then read the contents of the 8259 PIC status register by reading the same Base I/O Address+0 back. Again the bit definitions for the IRR and ISR are as follows: A logic 1 in the IRR indicates an IRx level currently latched and pending service. A logic 0 indicates no request is present at the IRx input. A logic 1 in the ISR means a request has been acknowledged and is currently being serviced for the associated IRx level. Logic 0 indicates the IRx level's service routine is not currently in progress. The following Table 5.6.1 lists the IRR and ISR data bit to IRx level equivalents for the Master and Slave PICs.

IRR and ISR data bits	Associated IR level - Master PIC	Associated IR level - Slave PIC
d0	IR0	IR8
d1	IR1	IR9
d2	IR2	IR10
d3	IR3	IR11
d4	IR4	IR12
d5	IR5	IR13
d6	IR6	IR14
d7	IR7	IR15

Table 5.6.1 IRR and ISR Register Definition

To read the Interrupt Request Register's (IRR) status, first write 0Ah to the 8259's Base I/O Address+0, then read the same Base I/O address back. For the Master PIC the Base I/O Address is 20h. For the Slave PIC, the Base I/O address is A0h. To read the contents of the In Service Register (ISR), first point to the ISR by writing a 0Bh to the 8259s Base I/O Address+0, then obtain ISR status by reading Base I/O Address+0 back. Figure 5.6.1 below shows two code examples on how to read the 8259 PIC status registers.

```
outportb(0x20, 0x0A);   /* Issue read IRR command to the Master 8259 PIC   */
IRR = inportb(0x20);    /* Read IRR status                                 */
```

(a)

```
outportb(0xA0, 0x0B);   /* Issue read ISR command to the Slave 8259 PIC   */
ISR = inport(0xA0)      /* Read ISR status                                 */
```

(b)

Figure 5.6.1 Reading the IRR or ISR (Borland C example)

The first example (a) shows how to attain the Master PIC's IRR status. The second example (b) shows how to read the Slave PIC's ISR. The 8259 "remembers" the last register pointed to, and all successive reads to Base I/O Address+0 will yield the contents of that status register until the read register command instructs the 8259 PIC otherwise. In the PC environment, the 8259 PIC is contacted by many different pieces of software. Because of this, it is always recommended that you don't rely on the 8259 PIC to yield the contents of the status register on successive reads. **Always issue a read register command immediately before reading the contents of the IRR or ISR**. Additional examples on attaining the IRR or ISR status using Microsoft C and iAPX assembly can be found in Appendix 12.2 "Programmers Toolkit".

6. Interrupt Service Routine Structures and Development

6.1 Interrupt Service Routine (iSR) Anatomy

Armed with the understanding of all the control elements involved in the interrupt process, this chapter will use the state diagram representations and programming examples given in Chapter 5 to construct the four basic interrupt service routine models available to us in a PC system environment. We will begin our journey into the construction of fully functioning iSRs by first reviewing the anatomy of an iSR shown here in Figure 6.1.1.

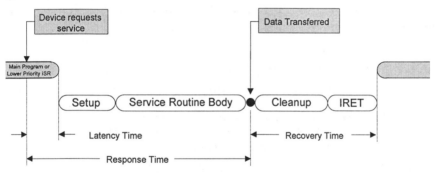

Figure 6.1.1 iSR Anatomy

Figure 6.1.1 represents the fundamental structure of any PC based iSR. First, prior to entering the *Service Routine Body* where the relevant work of the iSR is performed, the *Setup* segment saves the state of the machine and performs any additional application specific duties required for the iSR to operate successfully within the PC environment. Next, the *Service Routine Body* is responsible for servicing the device. This may be anything from incrementing a variable or transferring of a single piece of data, to acting as a self contained data acquisition and control element. The *Service Routine Body* completes when the programmed task is done updating variables and/or transferring data. The *Cleanup* segment of the iSR is next. It is responsible for issuing Non-Specific EOI commands, restoring the state of the machine, and performing any additional application specific tasks as needed. The last segment in an iSR returns control back to the interrupted process by issuing an IRET command (RFI for a Power PC) as the final instruction.

There are three iSR timing elements shown in Figure 6.1.1 relevant to any interrupt-driven system design effort. The first is the *latency time*. The latency time describes the time it takes for the device iSR to begin execution after the IR signal is asserted by the device. The *response time* is defined as the elapsed time between when the IR signal was asserted by the device and the time marking the completion of the service routine body. The time it takes for the iSR to return control to the interrupted process after the device is serviced is known as the *recovery time*. The three timings just mentioned can be used to predict maximum interrupt rates for the various IRx levels in a PC system design. The topic of how the timings relate to application development will be tabled until Chapter 11 as both Chapters 7 and 8 are required reading before the topic will have any relevance.

From the fundamental iSR structure illustrated in Figure 6.1.1, the four basic iSR structures specific to the PC can be derived. All four PC based iSR structures share the following four properties:

1. The iSR must save the state of the machine before proceeding with the service routine body. (Setup)

2. Once the service routine body performs the actual device service, the iSR must let the 8259 PIC know that the request has been serviced by issuing a Non-Specific EOI command. This allows further requests pending at the current IRx level and all lower priority IRx levels a chance of being acknowledged by the processor. (Cleanup)

3. The state of the machine must be restored. (Cleanup)

4. The iSR must issue as it's final command, an IRET instruction. (IRET)

To arrive at the four basic iSR structures we first note there are PC specific conditions that eliminate the possibility for a "One Size Fits All" iSR. A Master PIC iSR (IR[0:7]) differs from a Slave PIC iSR (IR[8:15]) because at a minimum, an additional Non-Specific EOI command is required to satisfy the Slave PIC (refer to section 5.4 Issuing End Of Interrupt (EOI) commands). For this reason, separate iSR structures for the Master and Slave PICs are needed. Deciding whether or not an iSR should allow itself to be interrupted while in progress is an additional variance in the basic iSR model. This option is available to us in the PC environment and applies to both Master and Slave PIC iSRs. If an iSR can be interrupted by a higher priority IRx level, it is referred to as *Nested*. To design an interrupt service routine as nested, you simply make it the iSR's first order of business to enable interrupts (set the IF bit in the x86 flags register or the EE bit in the MSI register of a Power PC to one) and after the service routine body has executed, disable interrupts at the beginning of the cleanup segment before proceeding.

If an interrupt service routine maintains the disable interrupts condition (IF = 0) throughout the duration of its execution, the iSR is referred to as *Locked*. A locked iSR starts and completes without allowing interruption by any higher priority IRx levels pending service. Locked iSRs are generally avoided as they have a tendency to add to the latency time seen by higher priority requests. They do have a place though under certain conditions, as discussed in Chapters 11.1. I've seen it argued that a locked iSR may cause the system clock to lose time by holding the system hostage long enough to cause the timer tick interrupt IR0 to miss interrupt cycles. This would be the case if the total Locked iSRs processing time from acknowledgement to IRET exceeded the IR0's 55mS periodic interrupt time minus the IR0 handler's execution time ($\approx 100\mu S$). That's equivalent to roughly 90,000+ I/O operations! Locked or Nested iSRs typically never approach this length.

To illustrate how a *Nested* iSR operates within a system environment versus that of a *Locked* iSR, refer to the interrupt request processing example given in Figure 6.1.2. In this example we will assume three IRx levels successively requesting service in the order of lowest to highest priority. Figure 6.1.2(a) shows how the three successive requests are processed if all three iSRs are designed as *Nested*. From 6.1.2(a), we can see how each successive request is able to interrupt the service routine already in progress. Figure 6.1.2(b) describes the exact same situation, but shows how the system will process the requests when all three iSRs are *Locked*. In Figure 6.1.2(b) we see how the latency time seen by higher priority pending requests is lengthened by a Locked iSR's operation. Specifically, IR2's unwillingness to enable interrupts during its execution in this example increases the latency time seen by IR0. Additionally, we observe the processing cycle may be shortened slightly when using Nested iSRs, but only when the requests arrive in a *low to high* priority order. In this case, each Nested iSR will return to the lower priority iSR it interrupted upon completion and not to the main program where the processor will execute an additional instruction before the INTR line is again sampled and the next request recognized. If the requests arrived in a high to low priority order (i.e. IR0 then IR1 then IR2), a timing chart similar to Figure 6.2.1(b) where a processor instruction was executed before the next Nested iSR was acknowledged would be generated.

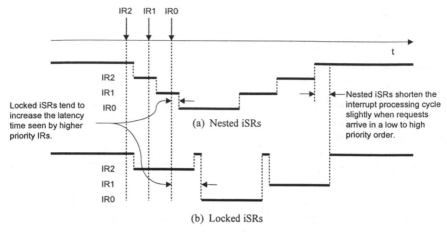

Figure 6.1.2 Locked and Nested iSR Processing Cycle Example

The distinction between the Master PIC and Slave PIC iSRs and the option of operating either as locked or nested results in the four basic iSR structures common to PC systems. The four basic iSR structures are:

1.   *Locked Master PIC iSR*

2.   *Locked Slave PIC iSR*

3.   *Nested Master PIC iSR*

4.   *Nested Slave PIC iSR*

If there are only four basic iSR structures available within the PC system environment, why are there five iSR structures presented in this chapter? As we will discover, the Nested Slave PIC iSR, if approached by simply enabling interrupts in the iSR's Setup segment, results in a half-locked, half-nested iSR thing. Further steps are required to fully nest a Slave PIC iSR. This modified Nested Slave PIC iSR results in the fifth iSR structure.

As each of the five iSR types are discussed, a flowchart, source code example, state diagram, and system flow diagram will be presented. The flowchart is there to help you port the iSR design to whatever language you prefer. As C is one of the most commonly used languages for realizing PC application designs, the source code examples are given in C and allow you to immediately roll the iSR design into your application. A few notes on the C's compiler operation when designing an iSR:

1.   The "interrupt" keyword causes the compiler to save the entire machine state at beginning of the iSR and restore the entire machine state just prior to exiting the iSR. To optimize the iSR's performance, work with the assembler source to remove unnecessary register Pushes and Pops.

2. The compiler adds the IRET instruction to the end of the iSR automatically and sets the data segment to that of the main program so that global variables can be accessed.

3. Because the compiler places the machine state save at the beginning of the iSR, the enable interrupts command required by both the Nested Master PIC and Nested Slave PIC iSR's is not the first command issued by the iSR. Edit the assembler source and place the enable interrupts command before the machine state save to reduce the *latency time* of higher priority requests.

The state diagrams presented along with each iSR structure track the iSR's progress through the PC's interrupt structure and help familiarize you with the various aspects of iSR flow control. The state diagrams become progressively important as the complexity of the iSR designs increase. The system flow diagram illustrates how the iSR structures behave within the PC when challenged by higher priority requests.

6.2 Locked Master PIC iSR

We begin our review of the basic iSR structures with the least complicated iSR of them all, the *Locked Master PIC iSR*. Back in Chapter 3, it was discovered that when acknowledging a request, the x86 processor automatically disables interrupts by resetting the IF flag in the flags register (EE flag in the MSR on a PowerPC) before entering the iSR. After interrupts are disabled, it is the iSR's responsibility to then re-enable interrupts before returning control to the interrupted process. A locked iSR always maintains the disabled interrupts condition (IF=0) throughout its processing and only enables interrupts when returning control to the interrupted process. This means that a locked iSR owns the PC's interrupt structure for the duration of its execution. No requests of higher priority are allowed to interrupt a locked iSR in progress.

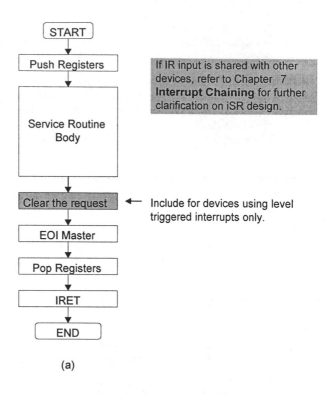

(a)

```
/* lmp_isr.c */

void interrupt  LockedMPICiSR(void);
setvect(0x0d,  LockedMPICiSR);          /* iSR installed behind Interrupt 0dh (IRQ5)        */

void interrupt  LockedMPICiSR()
{
    /*Service Routine  Body*/
    /*Reset device request if level triggered*/

    outportb(0x20, 0x20);               /* issue Master PIC Non-Specific EOI                */
}
```

(b)

Figure 6.2.1 Locked Master PIC iSR

The flowchart and C source code example for a *Locked Master PIC iSR* are shown here in Figure 6.2.1. A complete C source code example **lmp_isr.c** is provided on the IDPCSD diskette in the a:\chpt6 subdirectory. The locked iSR's Setup segment consists of nothing more than saving the machine state. In C, the compiler adds the machine state save to the beginning of the iSR when the "interrupt" keyword is encountered as shown in Figure 6.2.1(b). After this, the Service Routine Body responsible for performing the actual work required by the device is processed. If the device generating the request is level triggered, the interrupt request is cleared on the device. After the Service Routine Body, the Cleanup segment is entered where the Non-Specific EOI command is issued to the Master PIC to alert it to the fact that the request was serviced. This clears the In-Service bit associated with the request. The state of the machine is then restored, marking the end of the Cleanup segment and the IRET instruction issued. The IRET instruction enables interrupts and returns control to the background program by restoring the CS, IP, and flags registers in that order. Both the restoration of the machine state and the IRET instruction are added by the C compiler.

Referring now to the state diagram given for the Locked Master PIC iSR in Figure 6.2.2, we can see how a request is processed by the PC's interrupt processing hardware from start to finish.

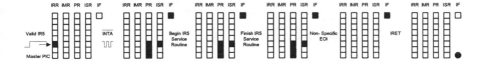

Figure 6.2.2 Locked Master PIC iSR State Diagram

First, a request arrives at IR5 input and immediately appears on the Master PIC's INT line. The processor acknowledges the request by disabling interrupts (opening the IF switch) and setting the IR5 in-service bit in the Master PIC. The IR5 level and all lower priority IR levels are then masked by the priority resolver as a result of the IR5 in-service bit being set. The IF switch is maintained in the open position (IF = 0) throughout the execution of a locked iSR. This is characteristic of locked iSRs in general. At the end of the IR5 iSR, a Non-Specific EOI is issued to the Master PIC. As a result, the IR5 in-service bit is reset, causing the priority resolver to unmask IR5 and all lower priority levels. The IRET command ends the processing cycle by enabling interrupts. As more complex iSR designs are encountered, the state diagram will prove to be a valuable tool in the verification of the iSR's design.

The *Locked Master PIC iSR* system flow example given in Figure 6.2.3 shows how a pending higher priority IR3 request is forced to wait until the IR5 iSR completes. After the IR5 iSR completes, control is returned to the interrupted process (background application). The processor will then fetch and execute one instruction before reaching the next instruction boundary where the pending IR3 request is seen and acknowledged.

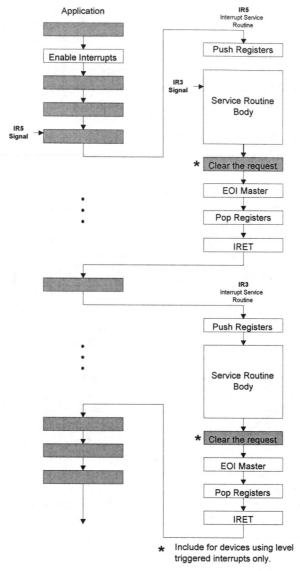

Figure 6.2.3 Locked Master PIC iSR System Flow

Although a Locked iSR adds to the latency time and consequently the response time seen by higher priority pending requests, as covered in Chapter 11.1, the Locked iSR is useful in certain situations.

6.3 Locked Slave PIC iSR

The *Locked Slave PIC iSR* is almost identical to the Locked Master PIC iSR with the exception of one additional Non-Specific EOI command required to satisfy the Slave PIC. Figure 6.2.1 gives the flowchart and C source code for a *Locked Slave PIC iSR*. A complete C source code example **lsp_isr.c** is provided on the IDPCSD diskette in the a:\chpt6 subdirectory.

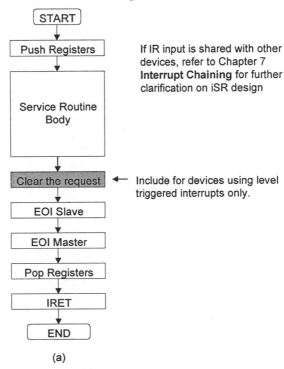

(a)

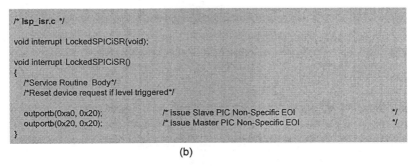

(b)

Figure 6.3.1 Locked Slave PIC iSR

The *Locked Slave PIC iSR* begins by saving the state of the machine and servicing the requesting device. Next, if the device generating the request is level triggered, the interrupt request is cleared on the device before proceeding with the Cleanup segment. A Non-Specific EOI command is issued to the Slave PIC and then to the Master PIC. The state of the machine is restored and the iSR returns control to the background program. The order in which the Non-Specific EOI commands are issued is important. Refer to Section 5.4 "Issuing End Of Interrupt (EOI) commands" for details.

The state diagram given in Figure 6.3.2 now includes both Master PIC (top) and Slave PIC (Bottom) representations. From this diagram we can trace how a request originating on the Slave PIC moves through both PICs during the interrupt processing cycle.

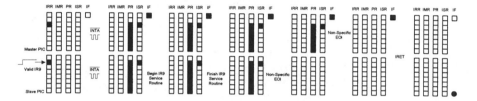

Figure 6.3.2 Locked Slave PIC iSR State Diagram

In this example, an active request arrives at the Slave PIC's IR9 input and propagates through the Slave PIC's interior, appearing on the INT line. IR2 on the Master PIC sees the Slave PIC request and the Master PIC's INT line is asserted. The processor then acknowledges the request. The IF switch is opened (IF=0) during the acknowledgment and remains so throughout the processing of the *Locked Slave PIC iSR*. As the iSR enters the Cleanup segment, it first issues a Non-Specific EOI to the Slave PIC to clear the In-Service bit for that IR level and release the mask on that and all lower priority IR levels. A Non-Specific EOI is then issued to the Master PIC which unmasks IR2 and all lower priority levels on the Master PIC. As its last instruction, the iSR issues the IRET, thereby enabling interrupts and returning control to the background program. The cycle is complete.

The behavior of the *Locked Slave PIC iSR* with regards to processing by the system is the same as that of the Locked Master PIC iSR. From the system flow diagram given in Figure 6.3.3, we see that IR15's iSR could care less about the higher priority IR9 request currently pending.

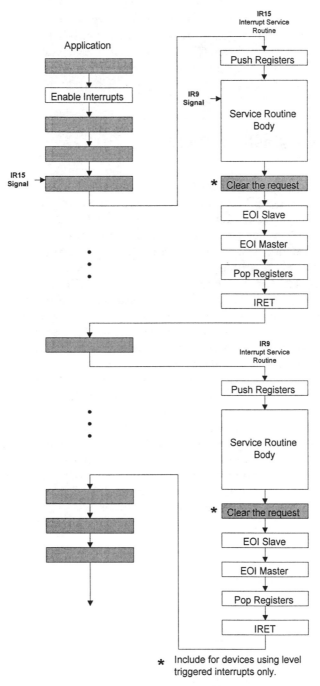

Figure 6.3.3 Locked Slave PIC iSR System Flow

87

The IR9 request must wait until interrupts are enabled by the IR15 iSR's IRET instruction before the processor can acknowledge it. Because the disabled interrupts condition (IF=0) effects all 15 IR levels in a PC, the IR15 iSR will also force the higher priority Master PIC IR levels IR0 and IR1 to wait for acknowledgment, the same as IR9 had to in the Figure 6.3.3 example.

6.4 Nested Master PIC iSR

The *Nested Master PIC iSR* is the most commonly used Master PIC iSR structure. A nested iSR minimizes the latency time, and hence the response time seen by pending higher priority requests. This is why the *Nested Master PIC iSR* is preferred over its locked counterpart. Locked iSRs increase the latency time seen by higher priority interrupts and is reserved for use only when absolutely necessary (see Section 11.1 "Locked Vs. Nested iSRs" for details). The *Nested Master PIC iSR* is able to minimize the response time experienced by higher priority requests by immediately enabling interrupts upon entry. The flowchart and C source code example for a *Nested Master PIC iSR* given in Figure 6.4.1 illustrates this point. Refer to the **nmp_isr.c** file on the IDPCSD diskette in the a:\chpt6 subdirectory for a complete C source code example. Once the PC's interrupt structure has been made available to higher priority IRx levels, the iSR is then free to save the state of the machine. No ill effects will result from enabling interrupts prior to saving the machine state because enabling interrupts only effects the flags register. The flags register was saved by the processor prior to the iSR's entry. The enable interrupts and machine state save operations together comprise the nested iSR's Setup segment. In C, the compiler will place the machine state save at the beginning of the iSR. To place the enable interrupts command ahead of the machine state save, edit the assembler source generated by the compiler.

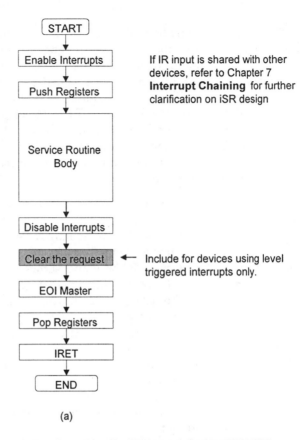

If IR input is shared with other devices, refer to Chapter 7 **Interrupt Chaining** for further clarification on iSR design

Include for devices using level triggered interrupts only.

(a)

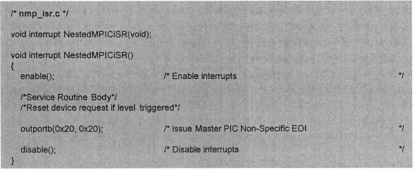

(b)

Figure 6.4.1 Nested Master PIC iSR

The Service Routine Body then follows and services the request. Next, as the nested iSR enters the Cleanup segment, it prepares to issue the Non-Specific EOI command (OCW2) by first disabling interrupts. As mentioned in Chapter 3.4, interrupts must be disabled before issuing an ICW or an OCW to the 8259 PIC. Before the Non-Specific EOI is issued, the interrupt request will be cleared on the device if the device generating the request is level triggered. The Non-Specific EOI is then sent to the Master PIC and the state of the machine is restored, marking the end of the Cleanup segment. The IRET instruction then enables interrupts and passes control back to the calling process.

While interrupts are enabled during the iSR's processing cycle, the possibility exists for a higher priority pending request to interrupt the nested iSR. The mechanics of how the hardware processes nested iSRs on the Master PIC is demonstrated in Figure 6.4.2. The state diagram given here describes the Master PIC only and shows how the enable interrupts command closes the IF switch and makes it possible for higher priority pending requests to be acknowledged. The cycle begins when a request appears on IR5, causing the processor to halt operation and acknowledge the interrupt. The first instruction issued by the iSR enables interrupts by setting the IF bit in the flags register to one (IF switch closed). As the IR5 iSR enters it's Service Routine Body, we observe a higher priority IR3 request being asserted. With no other higher priority requests currently in service (IR2, IR1, or IR0) and interrupts enabled (IF switch closed), the path is clear through the PC's interrupt processing hardware for the IR3 request to be acknowledged by the processor.

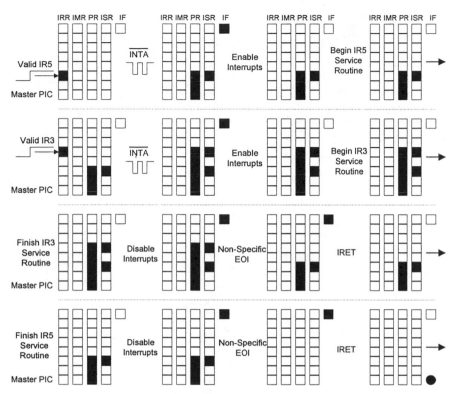

Figure 6.4.2 Nested Master PIC iSR State Diagram

Figure 6.4.2 now shows both the IR3 and IR5 In-Service bits set in the ISR. The priority resolver reacts to the IR3's In-Service bit being set by masking IR3 and all lower priority IR levels. The IR3 iSR in this example then enables interrupts and processes the Service Routine Body without incident. Interrupts are then disabled and the IR3 iSR issues a Non-Specific EOI to the Master PIC. The IR3 in-service bit is reset as a result of the Non-Specific EOI and the priority resolver releases the mask on IR3 and all lower priority IR levels. Because the IR5's in-service bit remains set however, the priority resolver maintains the mask on IR5 and all lower priority IR levels. The IR5 iSR ends its processing cycle by disabling interrupts and issuing its Non-Specific EOI and IRET commands.

The Nested Master PIC iSR system flow example given in Figure 6.4.3 shows how nested iSRs are processed by the system. The improved response time seen by the higher priority IR3 iSR is evident as the IR5 iSR immediately enabled interrupts, making the PC's interrupt structure accessible to higher priority requests.

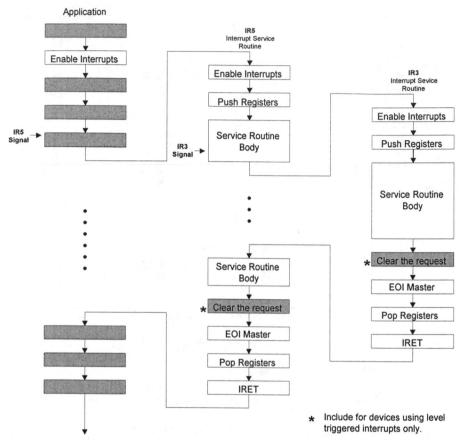

Figure 6.4.3 Nested Master PIC iSR System Flow

6.5 Nested Slave PIC iSR

With the exception of the additional Non-Specific EOI command required to let the Slave PIC know the request was serviced, the structure of the *Nested Slave PIC iSR* given in Figure 6.5.1 is identical in structure to that of the Nested Master PIC iSR covered in the last section. Operationally however, there are significant differences. To compliment this discussion, you will find a complete C source code example **nsp_isr.c** provided on the IDPCSD diskette in the a:\chpt6 subdirectory.

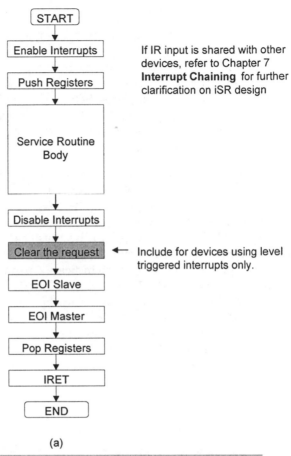

If IR input is shared with other devices, refer to Chapter 7 **Interrupt Chaining** for further clarification on iSR design

Include for devices using level triggered interrupts only.

(a)

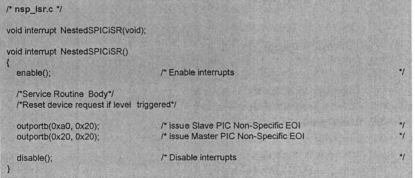

```
/* nsp_lsr.c */

void interrupt NestedSPICiSR(void);

void interrupt NestedSPICiSR()
{
    enable();                        /* Enable interrupts                          */

    /*Service Routine Body*/
    /*Reset device request if level triggered*/

    outportb(0xa0, 0x20);            /* issue Slave PIC Non-Specific EOI           */
    outportb(0x20, 0x20);            /* issue Master PIC Non-Specific EOI          */

    disable();                       /* Disable interrupts                         */
}
```

(b)

Figure 6.5.1 Nested Slave PIC iSR

We observe the *Nested Slave PIC iSR* enabling interrupts immediately upon entry. This allows higher priority requests if present, to interrupt the *Nested Slave PIC iSR*, or so you would think. In reality, only IR0 and IR1 on the Master PIC have the ability to interrupt a *Nested Slave PIC iSR*. All pending higher priority IRx levels on the Slave PIC must wait until the *Nested Slave PIC iSR* completes before acknowledgement is possible. In other words, the *Nested Slave PIC iSR* structure appears nested to IR0 and IR1 on the Master PIC and locked to all higher priority IRx levels on the Slave PIC. Why? Good question.

The answer becomes clear as we analyze the state diagram example for a Nested Slave PIC iSR given in Figure 6.5.2. The example begins when a request is presented to IR12 on the Slave PIC with no higher priority requests currently in service. As the request propagates, the Slave PIC asserts it's INT line connected to the Master PIC's IR2 input. The Master PIC recognizes the active request on IR2 and asserts it's INT line causing the INTR pin on the processor to indicate a pending request. The processor samples the active INTR line on the next instruction boundary and dispatches the acknowledge pulses to the PICs. The priority resolvers on both the Master and Slave PICs respond and mask the requesting level and all lower priority IRx levels respectively. Interrupts are disabled by the processor and the IR12 iSR is entered. Upon entry, the IR12 iSR immediately enables interrupts (IF=1).

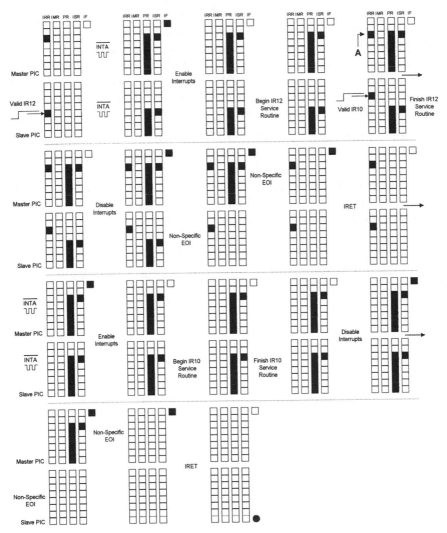

Figure 6.5.2 Nested Slave PIC iSR State Diagram

Sometime during IR12's processing while interrupts are still enabled, a higher priority request is presented to the Slave PIC's IR10 input. The IR10 request has a clear shot through the Slave PIC, but when the Slave PIC attempts to interrupt the Master PIC on IR2, the new request finds IR2 still masked because of the IR12 Slave PIC request currently in service. In Figure 6.5.2, the state illustrating this point is indicated by the bold "A". The IR10 request must wait until the IR12 iSR completes before the IR10 will ever be recognized by the processor. Therefore, the Master PIC's IR2 level is responsible for the Nested Slave PIC iSR appearing locked to higher priority Slave PIC requests. If the request was an IR0 or an IR1 on the Master PIC instead of IR10, the request would have been acknowledged as there are no open switches (nothing masked) standing in the way. Beyond this point, the state diagram is relatively uneventful. When the IR12 iSR completes, the IR10 request is acknowledged and IR10's Nested Slave PIC iSR proceeds normally without further interruption.

Because of the *Nested Slave PIC iSR's* dual personality, two system flow diagrams are required to describe its behavior within a PC. Figure 6.5.3 accurately illustrates how the PC will process a higher priority Slave PIC request attempting to interrupt a *Nested Slave PIC iSR* already in progress. As expected, the higher priority Slave PIC request (IR10) is unsuccessful in convincing the IR12 iSR that it really is "with the band."

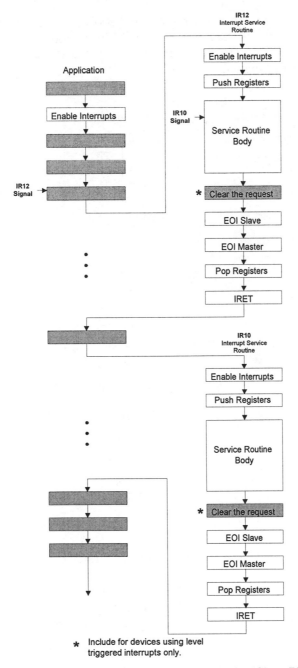

Figure 6.5.3 Nested Slave PIC iSR - Appears Locked to Slave PIC Requests

Figure 6.5.4 illustrates how the PC will process a Master PIC IR0 or IR1 request that arrives while a *Nested Slave PIC iSR* is in progress. The higher priority Master PIC levels are unaffected by the IR2 mask and have no problem interrupting the IR12 iSR.

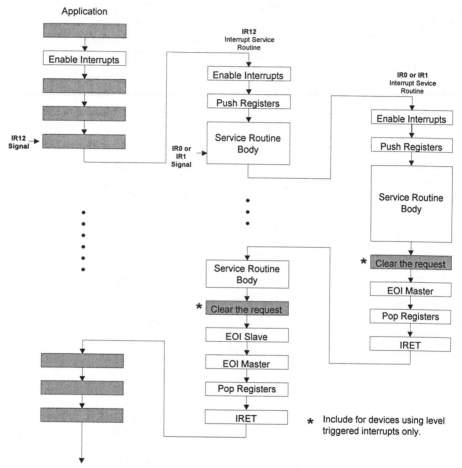

Figure 6.5.4 Nested Slave PIC iSR - Appears Nested to Master PIC Requests

There is a way to fully nest a Slave PIC iSR such that all higher priority IR levels, including those on the Slave PIC, are able to interrupt a Slave PIC iSR in progress. The technique is the subject of the next section.

6.6 Nested Slave PIC iSR / SFNM

This section is dedicated to designing a Nested Slave PIC iSR that gives higher priority requests on both the Master and Slave PICs the ability to interrupt a Nested Slave PIC iSR in progress. As we saw in the last section, simply enabling interrupts when the Nested Slave PIC iSR is entered, does not release the Master PIC priority resolver' s mask on IR2. The designers of the 8259 PIC saw this as a potential issue with regards to the Master/Slave PIC configuration and compensated for it by providing the SFNM feature. SFNM stands for Special Fully Nested Mode. SFNM is a feature available on all 8259 PICs and when enabled on the Master PIC, allows higher priority Slave PIC requests the ability to interrupt a lower priority Slave PIC request already in service. The 8259's SFNM accomplishes this feat by directing the Master PIC's priority resolver to mask all lower priority IRx levels but leave the IRx level used by the Slave PIC itself unmasked when a Slave PIC request is acknowledged by the processor. In a PC environment, this means the Master PIC's priority resolver would mask IR[3:7] but leave IR2 unmasked every time a Slave PIC request was acknowledged. This would clearly allow the system to see and acknowledge higher priority Slave PIC requests when a lower priority Nested Slave PIC iSR was in progress. It would seem then, that simply enabling the 8259's SFNM on the PC's Master PIC would resolve the problem of higher priority Slave PIC requests not being able to interrupt a lower priority Slave PIC request already in service. Unfortunately, the 8259's SFNM effects all the IRx levels on the 8259 PIC when enabled. There is no way to selectively enable or disable SFNM for a particular IRx level. If the SFNM feature were enabled on the Master PIC, an iSR installed behind any of the Master PIC IRx levels would be able to interrupt itself. Only lower priority IRx levels are masked when a request is acknowledged when SFNM is enabled. Each time the iSR was re-entered, the state of the machine would again be saved and with no limit on how many times the iSR could interrupt itself, the threat of a stack overflow is always present.

Since system stability can not be guaranteed when the Master PIC's SFNM feature is enabled, is there a way to use the principal on which it is based and emulate it with minimal overhead in software? Yup. The iSR structure capable of emulating the SFNM and providing higher priority Slave PIC requests with the ability to interrupt a Slave PIC iSR already in progress is referred to as a *Nested Slave PIC iSR / SFNM*. The first key to emulating SFNM is finding a way to successfully unmask IR2 before enabling interrupts during the *Nested Slave PIC iSR / SFNM's* Setup segment. Since IR2's mask is maintained by the priority resolver, the only way to unmask it would be to clear the IR2 In-Service bit in the Master

PIC's ISR. The only way to clear IR2's In-Service bit is to issue a Non-Specific EOI to the Master PIC. The Non-Specific EOI command will cause the priority resolver to unmask IR2, but it will also cause IR[3:7] to be unmasked as well (refer to section 5.4 "Issuing End Of Interrupt (EOI) Commands"). Since IR[3:7] are lower priority IRx levels compared to the Slave PIC's IR2, releasing their mask while a Slave PIC iSR is in progress would throw the priority structure into anarchy. Furthermore, if lower priority IRx levels are allowed to interrupt higher priority IRx levels, the stack will overflow in short order. To counter this undesired fallout, we first use the Master PIC's IMR to manually mask IR[3:7] before issuing the Non-Specific EOI. Because we will be using the Master PIC's IMR in this way, it is important that the original state of the IMR be preserved for restoration after all the Nested Slave PIC iSRs have processed. The flowchart and C source code required to realize a *Nested Slave PIC iSR / SFNM* iSR is shown in Figure 6.6.1. Refer to the **nsp_sfnm.c** file on the IDPCSD diskette in the a:\chpt6 subdirectory for a complete C source code example.

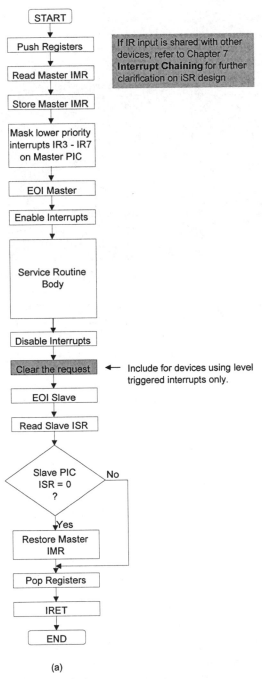

(a)

Figure 6.6.1(a) Nested Slave PIC iSR / SFNM

```
/* nsp_sfnm.c */

void interrupt (NestedSPICiSR_sfnm)(void);

void interrupt NestedSPICiSR_sfnm()
{
    int oldMPIC_IMR;
    oldMPIC_IMR = inportb(0x21);              /* store Master PIC IMR                               */
    outportb(0x21, oldMPIC_IMR | 0xf8);       /* mask IR[3:7]                                       */
    outportb(0x20, 0x20);                     /* issue Non-Specific EOI to Master PIC               */

    enable();                                 /* enable Interrupts                                  */

    /* Service Routine Body */
    /* Reset device request if level trigger */

    disable();                                /* disable Interrupts                                 */
    outportb(0xa0, 0x20);                     /* issue Non-Specific EOI to Slave PIC                */

    outportb(0xa0, 0x0b);                     /* point to Slave PIC In-Service Register             */
    if (inportb(0xa0) == 0) {                 /* any lower priority Slave PIC requests still in service? */
        outportb(0x21, oldMPIC_IMR);          /* No - restore Master PIC IMR                        */
    }
}
```

Figure 6.6.1(b) Nested Slave PIC iSR / SFNM

After the state of the machine is saved, the first order of business is the preservation of the Master PIC's IMR. Once the IMR contents are stored and IR[3:7] are masked, the Non-Specific EOI command is issued and the interrupts are enabled. No assembler source edit is required to rearrange the C compiler's placement of the machine state save before the enable interrupts at the beginning of the iSR, as the order provided by the compiler is required in this instance. After the Service Routine Body executes, interrupts are disabled in preparation for the Non-Specific EOI command (OCW2). When the Non-Specific EOI command is issued to the Slave PIC, the in-service bit for the IR level currently being serviced is reset. The iSR then checks the Slave PIC's in-service register to determine if any more lower priority Slave PIC iSR's are still in service. A check of the Slave PIC ISR is required, as the iSR may have interrupted one or more lower priority requests also using Nested Slave PIC iSR(s) / SFNM on the Slave PIC. If any other Slave PIC requests are still in service, the mask held on IR[3:7] remains valid and the restoration of the Master PIC IMR is not this iSR's responsibility. If on the other hand, the Slave PIC ISR indicates no further Slave PIC requests currently in service (ISR=0), the Master PIC IMR will be restored. Regardless of the decision, the state of the machine is restored and the IRET instruction issued. The Special Fully Nested Mode emulation has been successfully achieved.

Visualizing the dynamics of how the SFNM emulation is able to maintain control over the PC systems nested priority structure is best captured by reviewing the State Diagram example illustrated in Figure 6.6.2.

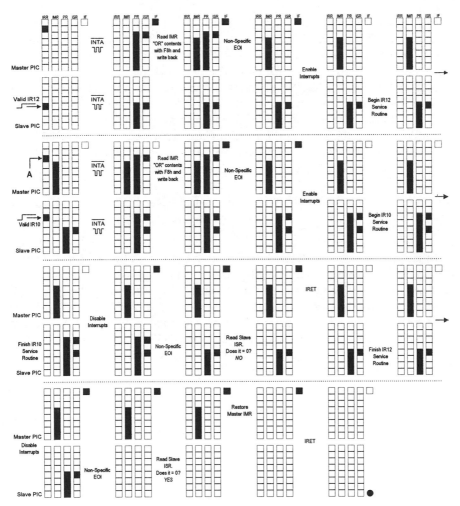

Figure 6.6.2 Nested Slave PIC iSR / SFNM State Diagram

In this example, we will assume that a *Nested Slave PIC iSR / SFNM* is installed behind both IR12 and IR10. The example begins when an IR12 request arrives and is acknowledged by the processor. The IR12 iSR then saves the Master PIC IMR contents, masks IR[3:7], issues a Non-Specific EOI to release the priority resolvers mask on IR2 and enables interrupts. Shortly after the IR12 iSR has enabled interrupts, an IR10 request arrives. Unlike the simple Nested Slave PIC iSR, the Nested Slave PIC iSR / SFNM has convinced the priority resolver that it is in it's best interest to release the mask on IR2 and allow the processor to see and acknowledge the IR10 request. The location state diagram marking the critical spot where IR2 has been successfully unmasked, granting IR10 a pathway to the processor, is indicated in Figure 6.6.2 by a bold "**A**". The IR10 iSR repeats the initial SFNM emulation steps performed by IR12's iSR and proceeds with the Service Routine Body. Interrupts are disabled and the Non-Specific EOI is issued to the Slave PIC. Now, the IR10 iSR checks the Slave PIC's In-Service Register for any lower priority iSRs still in service. In this example, IR12 is still in service, so the IR10 iSR does not restore the Master PIC IMR, it simply restores the state of the machine and issues an IRET. The IR12 iSR Service Routine Body then completes, interrupts are disabled and the Non-Specific EOI command issued to the Slave PIC. This time, when the Slave PIC ISR is checked by the IR12 iSR, no Slave PIC IRx levels remain in service. Therefore, the IR12 iSR restores the Master PIC IMR, allowing lower priority IRx levels on the Master PIC (IR[3:7]) a crack at the processor.

In Figure 6.6.3, we see how the PC is able to process the *Nested Slave PIC iSR / SFNM* in a manner consistent with the concept of nesting. Again, note that when the IR10 service routine checks the Slave PIC ISR for any remaining requests in service at the end of the iSR, it finds the IS bit for IR12 still active an refrains from restoring the Master PICs IMR. When the IR10 iSR finishes, control is passed back to the IR12 iSR. The IR12 iSR then checks the Slave PIC ISR for other Slave PIC iSRs still in service. Finding none, it restores the original Master PIC IMR. That's how it works.

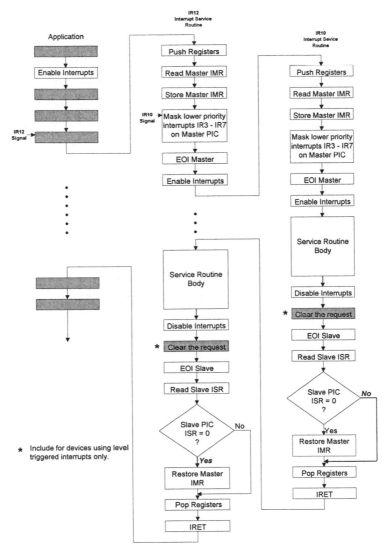

Figure 6.6.3 Nested Slave PIC iSR / SFNM System Flow

The advantage of this technique over the standard Nested Slave PIC iSR without any SFNM emulation, is that the *latency time* seen by pending higher priority Slave PIC requests is reduced, thereby increasing the potential throughput.

7. Interrupt Chaining - Link Design

7.1 Interrupt Chains

When two or more devices share a hardware IRx level, the method by which the device iSRs are able to install themselves and successfully provide the required service to the shared devices is known as interrupt chaining. Interrupt chains are created as each of the device iSRs install behind the same IRx level in successive order. The device iSRs that combine to make up an interrupt chain, are commonly referred to as *links*. As each *link* hooks the IRx level, it stores the starting address of the previously installed link found at the IRx levels interrupt vector table address. Once hooked to the chain, the newly installed link's awareness of the former link's starting address allows the newly installed link to pass control on to the previously installed link. In general, a link will pass control onto the next link in the chain when the device it represents was not responsible for the request. As Figure 7.1.1 illustrates, the first order of business for any link, is determining if its associated device is requesting service.

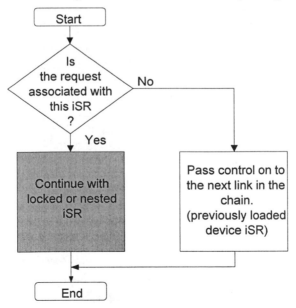

Figure 7.1.1 Interrupt Chain Link - Flowchart

If the link discovers its associated device is requesting service, the device will be serviced. If the device is not currently pending service when the chain is entered, the link will restore the machine state less the CS, IP, and flags register and use the starting address of the previous link to make a direct jump to the next link in the chain. Figure 7.1.1 shows the basic model for the link design most commonly used to realize an interrupt chain in the PC environment, but as we will discover shortly, there are powerful variations on this theme.

The goal in this chapter is to fully understand the dynamics of interrupt chaining in all its forms as it relates to devices sharing a common IRx level on the MCA, EISA, and PCI platforms. To help us in the study of interrupt chaining, the following example will be used throughout this chapter. This model will assume there are four devices, device1, device2, device3, and device4. All four devices share a common IRx level. Each device iSR or *link*, will then by definition hook the same interrupt vector table address, creating a linked list comprised of the four device links. There are three ways for a device link to hook an IRx level within a PC. The first way is to install the links via adapter ROM. The adapter ROM is commonly found on the device itself. The adapter ROM on the device holds the device's iSR and installs it when the system scans for adapter ROMs during system boot. This is a common practice in Plug-and-Play environments such as PCI. The adapter ROM method of link installation is very limiting when designing custom applications, as the designer has no say on how the links are designed and only limited control over the load order and IRx level used.

Secondly, the links might be put in place by installable device drivers or TSRs via the autoexec.bat or config.sys files at system startup as described in Table 7.1.2. This method provides the designer with full authority over the chain's link design and load order (provided the driver is not supplied by a vendor). Once the chain has been constructed (all links installed), an example application called backgrnd.exe executes to provide the software interface to each of the device iSRs in order to give the Table 7.1.2 example some real world meaning.

Autoexec.bat	Config.sys

`cls`
`c:\dev1.exe`
`c:\dev2.exe`
`c:\dev3.exe`
`c:\dev4.exe`
`c:\backgrnd.exe`
	`device = c:\dev1.sys`
	`device = c:\dev2.sys`
	`device = c:\dev3.sys`
	`device = c:\dev4.sys`

Table 7.1.2 iSR Installation Example

The third way of installing the device links is via the application itself. During the initialization phase of the application, the links are installed one after the other until the chain is fully constructed. The application then enables interrupts and enters the background processing loop. By installing the links from within the application program, the designer is able to decide on the chains overall design by retaining control over the individual link designs and link load order. For the purpose of demonstrating all the interrupt chaining techniques given in this chapter, the example links for device1 - device4 are installed via the application.

As mentioned earlier, each device iSR that hooks an IRx level and possesses the ability to pass control onto the previously installed iSR is referred to as a *link*. How a chain processes a request is the direct result of how the links within that chain are designed. Essentially, there are two ways to go about it. One method of link design results in an *Implied Priority Chain* or *IPC*. Implied Priority Chain's are the standard for Plug-and-Play environments such as PCI. The second method results in an *Equal Priority Chain* or *EPC*. The Equal Priority Chain is not currently an option in any of today's Plug-and-Play environments .because the Plug-and-Play specification does not afford adapter card manufactures any flexibility in the area of link design. When designing outside the Plug-and-Play environment however, an Equal Priority Chain is attainable and offers powerful characteristics not available when designing with IPCs. An overview of the various interrupt chaining techniques discussed throughout this chapter is given section 7.5 "Designing with Chains".

Software examples offered in this chapter have been tested under MS-DOS versions 3.3+ and have been found to work under both Windows 95 and NT DOS boxes as well. Program stability under protected mode Operating Systems however, is not guaranteed. **Note: NT will not allow the programmable RTC interrupt rate to exceed 1K.**

7.2 The Implied Priority Chain (IPC)

The method of link design that results in the *Implied Priority Chain (IPC)*, is the standard method implemented on MCA, EISA, and PCI Plug-and-Play shared IRx level platforms. If you are designing PCI Plug-and-Play adapter card device drivers, this section provides the flowchart for the IPC link and provides C source code examples that detail the link's design and load procedure. Throughout the remainder of this chapter, the following definitions will be used. The link directly responsible for servicing a particular device is referred to as that device's *companion link*. The device serviced by a particular link in a chain is referred to as that link's *companion device*.

To demonstrate how an IPC is constructed and processes a request, we begin here by assuming the four device model introduced in the last section. First, the IPC is constructed as each device link successively hooks the IRx level. As the device1 link is installed, it stores the double word found occupying the interrupt vector table address. The device1 link then stores its starting address in the vector table. Device2 follows by repeating the same procedure. Device2 now holds the starting address for device1's link. Device3 then device4 follow accordingly, each storing the starting address of the previously installed link. The linked list is now complete and the IPC constructed.

When a request is detected on the line, the processor will perform its required acknowledge procedure and make the indirect jump to the starting address of the service routine found at the vector table address associated with the IRx level. To help understand what will happen next refer now to Figure 7.2.1.

Implied Priority	n	$n+1$	$n+2$	$n+3$
Load Order	4th	3rd	2nd	1st

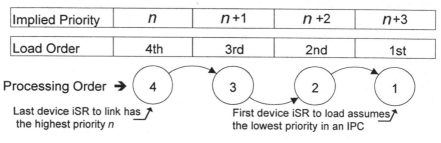

Processing Order → (4) (3) (2) (1)

Last device iSR to link has ↗ the highest priority *n*   First device iSR to load assumes↗ the lowest priority in an IPC

Figure 7.2.1 Implied Priority Chain (IPC) - "Find and Finish"

Figure 7.2.1 describes the devices in the order they were loaded and the implied priority each carries; 1 being the first link loaded and *n* representing the highest priority. The chain is entered and is processed in the order shown. Since the device4 link was the last to install, it's starting address occupies the vector table address and therefore marks the starting point for processing the IPC. Once a request is acknowledged and the IPC entered, a determination is made by the device4 link as to whether or not device4 was responsible for the request. This is accomplished by interrogating a status register on device4, and known to the device4 link, that indicates whether a device4 request is pending or not. If a request is not pending on device4, the device4 link will make a direct jump to the starting address of the link installed just before it. In this example, device3's link. The process of checking each link's companion device for a pending request and jumping to the next link in the chain if no request is found pending, continues on down the chain until the device responsible for the request is located and serviced. To demonstrate how the IPCs process a request, we will assume for the moment that device4 was responsible for the request. When the device4 companion link determines a request is pending, it services the device, proceeds with the Cleanup segment and issues the IRET instruction. When the IRET instruction is issued, the processing of the IPC processing cycle abruptly ends. An IPC essentially operates on a "Find and Finish" principal. Ending the processing of a chain when the first device (device4 in this example) with a pending request is discovered and serviced implies that device4 has priority over any other device whose companion link hooked the IRx level before it, as the device3, device2, and device1 companion links did in the this example (see Figure 7.2.1). If all four devices in our example were to request service at the same time, four complete interrupt cycles would be necessary to service all four devices. The first interrupt cycle would service device4, the next device3, the next device2 and the last device1. In an IPC, the load order determines the relative priority of each of the devices. As you can see, if things get busy on a specific IPC's IRx level, the first link to load will be the last link in the chain, rendering it hard pressed to get a word in edgewise. The preemption of lower priority requests by higher priority requests can be frustrating when designing with IPCs, especially when the required devices all have similar throughput requirements. To illustrate how implied priority levels created by IPCs fit into the overall PC's interrupt structure, refer to Table 7.2.2. Here we see the priority assignments realized by a system using IPC's installed behind IR9, IR10 and IR11.

8259 PIC IRx Input	Priority Level	Native IRx level	Priority Level	First Implied IRx level	Priority Level	Second Implied IRx level
IR0	0	Timer				
IR1	1	Keyboard				
IR8	2	RTClock				
IR9	3	device7	4	device6	5	device5
IR10	6	device4	7	device3		
IR11	8	device2	9	device1		
IR12	10	Mouse				

Table 7.2.2 IPC Priority Assignment Example

Notice how the IPC installed behind IR9 adds two additional implied IR levels. Device6 carries a system priority of 4 and device5 carries a system priority of 5. The IPCs installed behind IR10 and IR11 each add one implied IRx level. Implied IRx levels act in the same manner as any one of the PC's 15 native IRx levels do by preventing lower priority IRx levels, implied or native from occurring out of turn. An IPC adds to the problem of preemption already inherent in the PC's fixed priority structure. Any iSR or chain residing at a lower IRx level sees an increased number of higher priority IRx levels it must compete with when IPCs are present at higher priority IRx levels. To illustrate, the Slave PIC's IR12 occupied by the mouse in this example, usually carries a system priority level of 6. With three IPC's added to the system at the higher priority IR9, IR10, and IR11 levels, the mouse priority level is lowered from 6 to 10. This may not have an adverse effect on the operation of the mouse, but any throughput intensive device using IR12 could experience diminished performance.

Even with the inherent preemption issue, IPCs do work. In most instances, the design does not begin to approach the maximum bandwidth of the system. In other cases though, where the designer would shove a MAC truck through the PC if given the opportunity, the preemption issue resulting from the PC's rigid priority structure is further aggravated by the additional implied priority levels introduced by IPCs. In the coming sections, techniques that equalize the priority assignments given to devices sharing a common IRx level are presented. From here on we'll stick with the industry standard IPC method of link design, compatible with the current Plug-and-Play system design specification.

Figure 7.2.3(a) shows the flowchart for realizing an IPC compliant link. The IPC link begins by pushing all the required registers. Next, it politely queries its companion device as to whether a request is pending or not. If not, registers are restored and a direct jump is made to the starting address of the next link in the IPC. If a request is pending, the device is serviced and the processing of the IPC terminated by the issuance of the IRET instruction. With the exception of the Push Registers process which is handled by the link frame, the proper locked or nested iSR design (as detailed in Chapter 6) can be directly inserted into the links framework as illustrated in Figure 7.2.3(a). A discussion on whether to use a locked or nested iSR is the subject of Chapter 9.1. If a link does not meet the criteria for a locked iSR, then design it for nested operation because long chains with a full compliment of locked links will extend the response time seen by higher priority requests and diminish their otherwise attainable throughput rates.

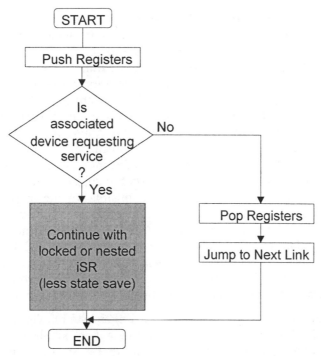

Figure 7.2.3(a) Implied Priority Chain (IPC) Link - Flowchart

```
/* ipc_link.c */

void interrupt ipc_link(void);
void interrupt (* Original_iSR)(void);
int ourDevicePending;

 void interrupt ipc_link()
{
    if (ourDevicePending) {              /* Is companion device pending service?    */

        /*Service Routine Body*/
         /*Reset device request if level triggered*/

        outportb(0x20, 0x20);            /* issue Master PIC Non-Specific EOI        */

    } else {

        Original_iSR();                  /* Far Jump to next link in the chain       */
    }
}
```

Figure 7.2.3(b) Implied Priority Chain (IPC) Link - Source Code

The question might arise, "What happens if control is passed to the last link in the chain but the last link's companion device doesn't require service?" Wouldn't the direct jump in this case, send the system into a brick wall? No. The reason is that at least one link in the chain necessarily has a device requiring service. If all the links prior to the last link found no active service requests pending on their respective companion devices, then the last link's device is necessarily the one requesting service and the direct jump into Oz will never be taken. Of course this is assuming the world is round. Two anomalies exist that can cause this model to fail. The first is a default IR7 which is specific to chains installed behind IR7 or IR15. The default IR7 feature of the 8259 PIC is the subject of the next chapter. The second results when the device responsible for the request gives its companion link a false indication with regards to its interrupt pending status by claiming no pending request. Either of these conditions will allow a jump to unfamiliar code if no other devices sharing the IRx level are requesting service. Section 7.5 "Designing with Chains" covers the techniques required to safely return control to the background program should one or both of these conditions befall an IPC occupied IRx level.

The C source code for realizing an IPC link is listed in Figure 7.2.3(b). In this example, the link is designed around a Locked Slave PIC iSR. Of particular interest, is the way the link stores the starting address of the previously loaded link and jumps to it if the link's companion device is not responsible for the request. This is what makes a link a link and not a simple iSR. The example application given next, will use this conceptual building block to construct a fully functioning IPC using the four device model given in section 7.1.

To demonstrate an IPC's construction and overall operation once live, the example program **ipc.exe** is now presented. This program and source code file are found on the IDPCSD disk in the a:\chpt7 subdirectory. The partial source code listing shown in Figure 7.2.4 highlights the relevant **ipc.exe** code segments. Here we see the procedure required to install all four device links successfully and the four IPC link designs themselves. In this example, a common structure is assigned to each IPC device link that defines all the link's operational variables and pointers (see common.h on the IDPCSD disk). The extra step of equating each link's starting address with its structural counterpart (devLink[n].iSR in this example) was done for completeness. This extra step can be eliminated without repercussion from the compiler. Just remember to update the setvect(); statements to reflect the original link name. The load order, which defines the IPC's processing order and consequently the implied priority each device carries, is a function of where the IPC link hooks the IRx level in the source file. The first link to hook the IRx level encountered by the compiler's top to bottom scan of the source file will be the first link to load. This fact is apparent if you observe how the order of the setvect statements listed in Figure 7.2.4 result in the 4⇨3⇨2⇨1 processing order. Although the links in this example are designed around the Locked Slave PIC iSR format, either the Nested Slave PIC iSR or Nested Slave PIC iSR / SFNM could easily be substituted.

```
/* ipc.exe */

/* define device links */
void interrupt(dev1Link)(void);
void interrupt(dev2Link)(void);
void interrupt(dev3Link)(void);
void interrupt(dev4Link)(void);

/* assign common structure to each device link (see common.h) */
deviceLink devLink[LiNK_TOTAL];

/* add starting addresses to device link structure */
devLink[0].iSR = dev1Link;
devLink[1].iSR = dev2Link;
devLink[2].iSR = dev3Link;
devLink[3].iSR = dev4Link;

/* link load order - top to bottom (top first to load) */
devLink[0].oldiSR = getvect(IRQ_8);     /* remember previously loaded iSRs starting address */
setvect(IRQ_8, devLink[0].iSR);         /* install device 1 links starting address behind IR8   */

devLink[1].oldiSR = getvect(IRQ_8);     /* remember previously loaded iSRs starting address */
setvect(IRQ_8, devLink[1].iSR);         /* install device 2 links starting address behind IR8   */

devLink[2].oldiSR = getvect(IRQ_8);     /* remember previously loaded iSRs starting address */
setvect(IRQ_8, devLink[2].iSR);         /* install device 3 links starting address behind IR8   */

devLink[3].oldiSR = getvect(IRQ_8);     /* remember previously loaded iSRs starting address */
setvect(IRQ_8, devLink[3].iSR);         /* install device 4 links starting address behind IR8   */

/* device links */
void interrupt dev1Link()               /* device 1 service routine                */
{
    if (devLink[0].irPending) {         /* is device 1 requesting service?         */
        devLink[0].counter++;           /* Yes - service device 1                  */
        /* Reset device request */
        outportb(0xa0, 0x20);           /* issue Slave PIC Non-Specific EOI        */
        outportb(0x20, 0x20);           /* issue Master PIC Non-Specific EOI       */
    } else {
        lvt[lvtidx[0]]();               /* jump to next link in the chain          */
    }
}

void interrupt dev2Link()               /* device 2 service routine                */
{
    if (devLink[1].irPending) {/* is device 2 requesting service?                  */
        devLink[1].counter++;           /* Yes - service device 2                  */
```

```
        /* Reset device request */
        outportb(0xa0, 0x20);          /* issue Slave PIC Non-Specific EOI     */
        outportb(0x20, 0x20);          /* issue Master PIC Non-Specific EOI    */
    } else {
        lvt[lvtidx[1]]();              /* jump to next link in the chain       */
    }
}


void interrupt dev3Link()              /* device 3 service routine             */
{
    if (devLink[2].irPending) {        /* is device 3 requesting service?      */
        devLink[2].counter++;          /* Yes - service device 3               */
        /* Reset device request */
        outportb(0xa0, 0x20);          /* issue Slave PIC Non-Specific EOI     */
        outportb(0x20, 0x20);          /* issue Master PIC Non-Specific EOI    */
    } else {
        lvt[lvtidx[2]]();              /* jump to next link in the chain       */
    }
}


void interrupt dev4Link()              /* device 4 service routine             */
{
    if (devLink[3].irPending) {        /* is device 4 requesting service?      */
        devLink[3].counter++;          /* Yes - service device 4               */
        /* Reset device request */
        outportb(0xa0, 0x20);          /* issue Slave PIC Non-Specific EOI     */
        outportb(0x20, 0x20);          /* issue Master PIC Non-Specific EOI    */
    } else {
        lvt[lvtidx[3]]();              /* jump to next link in the chain       */
    }
}
```

Figure 7.2.4 IPC.exe - Partial Source Code Listing

The IPC represented at the beginning of this section in Figure 7.2.1 comes to life in this example. The 4⇨3⇨2⇨1 processing order is achieved by successively loading device1 - device4's companion links in that order behind IR8 (PC's Real Time Clock interrupt). Chaining to the RTC's IR8 level, gives our example an unlimited source of interrupts. The RTC also offers a programmable interrupt rate as well as allowing us to observe the IPC in action at interrupt rates ranging from 2Hz to 8KHz. Details on the programming and general use of the RTC's periodic interrupt is the subject of Chapter 11.6.

The **ipc.exe** screen output is shown here in Figure 7.2.5. As you can see, each device link has an associated counter and interrupt pending status represented and aligned vertically on the screen. The RTC's periodic interrupt rate is also displayed.

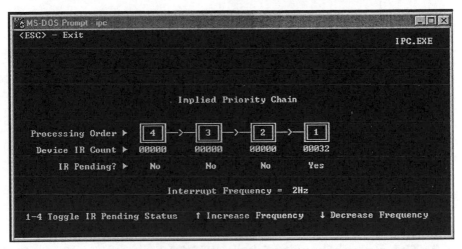

Figure 7.2.5 IPC.exe - Output Screen (DOS)

Since none of the four example devices actually exist, an interrupt pending status bit for each will be simulated by a virtual device status register maintained by the **ipc.exe** program itself. To toggle the interrupt pending status "ON" or "OFF" for any of the 4 devices, press one of the following keys:

Press "**1**"   Toggle Device1's interrupt pending status bit

Press "**2**"   Toggle Device2's interrupt pending status bit

Press "**3**"   Toggle Device3's interrupt pending status bit

Press "**4**"   Toggle Device4's interrupt pending status bit

What you can expect to observe:

The device with its interrupt pending status bit activated and carrying the highest implied priority will see its counter increment with each periodic interrupt signal received from the RTC at the displayed rate. Lower priority devices pending service will not see their counters increase until all higher priority devices indicate an inactive pending status.

After running the **ipc.exe**, you may want to rearrange the link's load order and recompile to see what happens. Be sure to edit the ScreenLocation = x variable for each of the device links shown in the complete source code listing on the disk, to maintain the 0 to 3, top to bottom order. Otherwise, the counters will operate properly but the processing order of the links will not appear in the correct order on the display.

Because one of the four devices must have asserted its IR signal for the IPC to have been entered, the **ipc.exe** example program ensures that at least one device's interrupt pending status is active at all times. The last remaining active pending status can not be toggled inactive.

To slow the interrupt rate down, press the down arrow. To increase it, press the up arrow. Press "Esc" to quit.

Press "↑"   Double the Interrupt Rate (2Hz - 8KHz)

Press "↓"   Half the Interrupt Rate (8KHz - 2Hz)

Press "ESC"   Remove IPC, Restore RTC functions, and End Program

The **ipc.exe** program will leave no trace of its presence upon exit.

7.3 The Equal Priority Chain (EPC)

The *Equal Priority Chain* or *EPC* is capable of maintaining equal priority among a plurality of devices. Equal priority is established when each link in the EPC is designed to pass control on to the next link, regardless of whether its associated device has a pending request or not. A link designed in this manner is referred to as an EPC link. This allows every device represented by an EPC link the opportunity to be serviced each and every time the chain is invoked. If two devices represented by companion links in the same EPC were to request service at the same time, both devices would be serviced with just one pass of the EPC. For the MCA, EISA, and PCI interrupt sharing platforms, this is a tremendously powerful technique. By providing equal priority among a plurality of devices, the EPC offers PC's packed with several devices sharing a common purpose a way to alleviate the unbalanced access to the processor bandwidth resulting from the PC's rigid priority structure. An example where an EPC would be used might be an array of modems in a BBS or internet slip connection system. Figure 7.3.1 describes the processing order of an EPC after our four example devices load. Notice how the link load order has no bearing on the priority of the devices represented by their companion links.

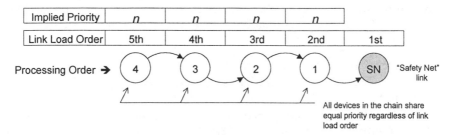

Figure 7.3.1 Equal Priority Chain - "Polling Loop"

In theory, the EPC operates similar to a *Polling Loop*. The difference between a simple polling loop and the EPC however, is that the EPC guarantees at least one device requires service each time the chain is processed whereas a simple polling loop can not make that claim. After each EPC link passes control on to the next link in the chain, eventually the end of the chain is reached. When the last device link in the chain makes its jump, a special link at the end of the chain is needed to accept the transfer of control and end the EPC's processing cycle by issuing the required Cleanup commands and IRET instruction. That link is referred to as the *Safety Net*. The Safety Net is fundamental to the successful processing of an EPC. Unlike the device links, the Safety Net link is load order specific and must be the first link to load making it the last link in the chain as shown in Figure 7.3.1. If the Safety Net is missing from the end of the chain, the last device link in the EPC will jump to the unfamiliar address it found in the interrupt vector table when it loaded. If that happens there is no way to predict the outcome, however the word **CRASH!** comes to mind.

How the PC system's priority structure is effected by the installation of EPCs is illustrated here in Table 7.3.2.

8259 PIC IRx Input	Priority Level	1st link processed	Priority Level	2nd link processed	Priority Level	3rd link processed
IR0	0	*Timer*				
IR1	1	*Keyboard*				
IR8	2	*RTClock*				
IR9	3	device3	3	device2	3	device1
IR10	4	device2	4	device1		
IR11	5	device2	5	device1		
IR12	6	*Mouse*				

Table 7.3.2 EPC Priority Assignment Example

We immediately observe that no implied priority levels are added, hence the priority levels normally associated with the PC's 15 native IRx levels remain intact.

The general flow of an EPC link and C source example are shown in Figure 7.3.3. The EPC link design given here is referred to as Method 1. As we will discover shortly, two additional methods exist that can result in an EPC. The Method 1 EPC link starts out by saving the machine state. Next, the link determines if its associated device was responsible for the request by reading the pending interrupt status on its companion device. If the device is requesting service, the Setup segment (less the state save) and the Service Routine Body will process. The device request is then reset. On some adapter cards, simply reading the pending status register on the device resets the active request signal. For simplicity sake, the device request reset process will be considered part of the Service Routine Body from here on out. Whether the companion device is requesting service or not, the link will always pass control on to the next link in the EPC by first restoring the machine state and then jumping to the next link.

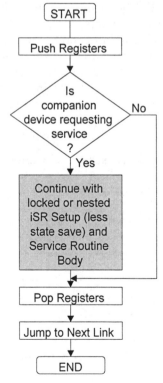

Figure 7.3.3(a) Method 1 EPC Link - Flowchart

```
/* epc1_lnk.c */

void interrupt epc1_link(void);
void interrupt (*Original_iSR)(void);
int ourDevicePending;

void interrupt epc1_link()
{
    if (ourDevicePending) {       -    /* Is companion device pending service?    */

        /*Service Routine Body*/
        /*Reset device request if level triggered*/

        outportb(0x20, 0x20);        /* issue Master PIC Non-Specific EOI          */

    }

    Original_iSR();                  /* Far jump to next link in the chain          */
}
```

Figure 7.3.3(b) Method 1 EPC Link - Source Code

From Figure 7.3.3(a) we observe that no Cleanup commands are issued by the EPC link. Method 1 device links are not responsible for the Cleanup commands, that task is reserved for the last link in the EPC, the *Safety Net*. Since the Safety Net is always the last link processed, it has no need to store the address found at the vector table address when it loaded. Therefore a Safety Net gets installed as a simple iSR. The general flowchart and C source for realizing the Safety Net is given in Figure 7.3.4. It is a good idea to add the disable interrupts command to the Safety Net as indicated in Figure 7.3.4(b) as one or all of the device links in the EPC will most likely be designed as nested. Once a nested EPC link enables interrupts, it is the responsibility of the Safety Net to disable interrupts before issuing the Non-Specific EOI commands (OCW2's).

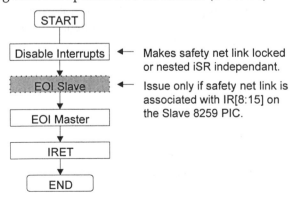

Figure 7.3.4(a) Safety Net - Flowchart

```
/* snet_lnk.c */

void Interrupt(snet_link)(void);

void Interrupt snet_link(void);
{
    disable()                  /* disable interrupts if iSR nested                        */
    outportb(0xa0, 0x20);      /* issue Non-Specific EOI to Slave PIC if IRQ[15:8] request */
    outportb(0x20, 0x20);      /* issue Non-Specific EOI to Master PIC                     */
}
```

Figure 7.3.4(b) Safety Net - Source Code

Some PC system BIOSs install Safety Nets behind unused IRx levels at system startup to handle any unexpected IR signal anomalies should they occur. In this instance, a Safety Net link supplied by the designer is not required. In general however, PC system BIOSs have no set standard on what default code will be loaded behind unused IRx levels at system startup. To remain as platform hardware independent as possible, it is strongly recommended that you install the Safety Net links yourself. In open system architectures, adapter card manufacturers sometimes use adapter ROM's as the vehicle for trucking the device links into place. This is certainly the case in Plug-and-Play systems such as PCI. Installing Safety Nets requires a little more ingenuity when staring down the barrel of an adapter ROM. The reason is that the firmware scans and executes adapter ROM code prior to loading device drivers via the config.sys or autoexec.bat. The only way then to install the Safety Nets, would be to design and install custom adapter ROM that would load the Safety Nets behind available IRx levels at system startup before any of the other adapter ROMs were discovered. If a custom adapter ROM is not an option, then an EPC is best realized on hardware platforms (motherboards) where the PC's system BIOS does in fact provide default Safety Nets behind available IRx levels at startup. In systems that do not load any device links via adapter ROM, Method 1 EPCs are easily reachable on any one of the MCA, EISA, or PCI platforms. Here, installing the Safety Net first is a simple matter of organizing the load order of the system startup files in the config.sys and autoexec.bat or correctly arranging the link load order in the application source code. A key benefit to using Method 1 is that it allows for the links to be programmed using a generic format, thus making their load order irrelevant. All you need to remember is that Method 1 requires the Safety Net to be installed first, before any of the EPC links load. An example application program (**epc1.exe**) demonstrating the design and operation of a Method 1 EPC is presented at the end of this section.

As mentioned, there are two additional methods available to the designer for successfully achieving an EPC. The second method for achieving an EPC also has possibilities in the open architecture environment. In this method, referred to as Method 2, the ability to complete the EPC processing cycle by issuing the cleanup commands lies within all of the EPC links. In other words, each Method 2 EPC link has a built in Safety Net. The last link processed by the EPC will be responsible for activating its Safety Net and ending the EPC processing cycle. Since Method 2 EPC links are able to remain load order independent by design, the placement of a particular link in the EPC's processing order is arbitrary. Therefore, it is required that all Method 2 EPC links also possess the ability to determine if they are the last link in the chain. This will allow the last link to correctly activate the resident Safety Net, thereby ending the processing cycle by issuing the required Cleanup commands and IRET instruction. To make the "last link" determination requires a reliable piece of information that can unerringly indicate to each Method 2 EPC link whether or not it currently resides at the end of the chain. That piece of information is known as the *End Of Chain* code or *EOC*. Since each EPC link stores the value it found in the vector table when it loaded, if the EOC occupied that vector table address before any of the Method 2 EPC links loaded, the first link to load would pick it up and store it. Each successive link loaded, would pick up the starting address of the previously installed link and not the EOC. The EOC code would be in the possession of the first link to load only, and by comparing the address picked up and stored as each link loaded with the EOC, a determination as to whether a link was the last in the chain would be a snap. To illustrate how a Method 2 EPC link is designed, refer to Figure 7.3.5(a).

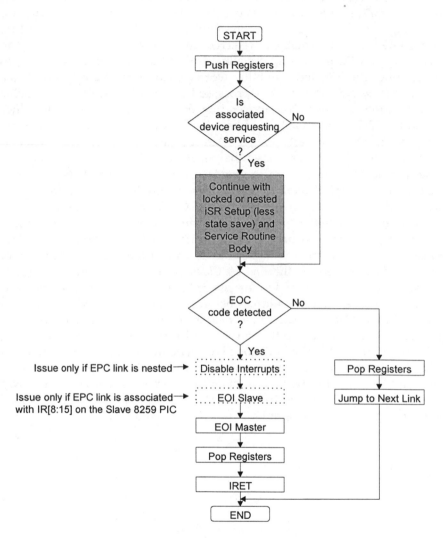

Figure 7.3.5(a) Method 2 EPC Link - Flowchart

```
/* epc2_lnk.c */

void interrupt epc2_link(void);
void interrupt (* Original_iSR)(void);
int ourDevicePending;
int eoc;

void interrupt epc2_link()
{
    if (ourDevicePending) {              /* Is companion device pending service?           */

        /*Service Routine  Body*/
        /*Reset device request if level   triggered*/

    }
    if (eoc) {                           /* Last link in chain?                            */

        disable();                       /* Yes - disable interrupts if  iSR nested        */
        outportb(0xa0, 0x20);            /* issue Non-Specific EOI to Slave PIC if IRQ[15:8] request  */
        outportb(0x20, 0x20);            /* issue Non -Specific EOI to Master PIC           */

    } else {

        Original_iSR();                  /* No - Far jump to next link in the chain        */
    }
}
```

Figure 7.3.5(b) Method 2 EPC Link - Source Code

The flowchart is straight forward with only one exception. The locked or nested iSR that is inserted into the Method 2 EPC link framework is split at the point where the Service Routine Body ends and the Cleanup commands are issued. Here, the EOC test is inserted.

A recognizable EOC code needs to be installed at the interrupt vector table address before any of the EPC links load. The value stored at the associated IRx levels vector table address by the system BIOS could be used if you logged all the values for each IRx level and then custom programmed every link associated with that particular EPC to look for that specific code. Of course that would make your EPC design platform-hardware specific. A better way is to choose a standard EOC value yourself and install it behind the PC's available IRx levels before any of the EPC links get loaded. That way, the EPC design is no longer tied to a specific hardware platform. The EOC code value should be chosen so that it has no chance of actually being a valid EPC link's starting address which would cause the model to fail. 0000:0000 is a good example of an EOC code that will work. Figure 7.3.5(b) is the source code listing for a Method 2 EPC link designed around a Locked Slave PIC iSR. This link design will be combined with other Method 2 EPC link's in an example application program given at the end of this section.

The up side of Method 2 is that along with Method 1, the EPC links are programmed using a generic format making their load order irrelevant. This makes Method 2 a good candidate for Plug-and-Play environments such as PCI. The Method 2 EPC execution time is slightly longer than the Method 1, as the "last link?" conditional shown in Figure 7.3.5(a) is added to each of the links in the chain.

The last method used to implement an EPC is Method 3, *Custom last link*. This method requires that you customize the last link to automatically end the EPC processing cycle by issuing the necessary cleanup commands. There is no need to load an EOC code or install a Safety Net first. Simply program the last link in the EPC to include the necessary clean up commands and make sure it gets loaded first before any of the Method 1 EPC links.

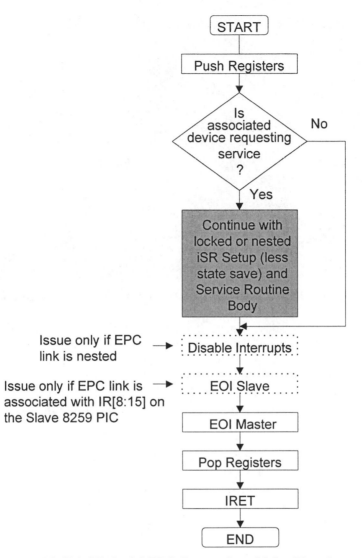

Figure 7.3.6(a) Method 3 EPC Custom Last Link - Flowchart

```
/*  epc3_lnk.c */

void interrupt epc3_link(void);
void interrupt (* Original_iSR)(void);
int ourDevicePending;

void interrupt epc3_link()
{
    if (ourDevicePending) {        /* Is companion device pending service?              */

        /*Service Routine Body*/
        /*Reset device request if level triggered*/

    }

    disable();                    /* disable interrupts if iSR nested                  */
    outportb(0xa0, 0x20);         /* issue Non-Specific EOI to Slave PIC if IRQ[15:8] request  */
    outportb(0x20, 0x20);         /* issue Non-Specific EOI to Master PIC              */

}
```

Figure 7.3.6(b) Method 3 EPC Custom Last Link - Source Code

Figure 7.3.6(a) shows what a custom last link flowchart looks like. Notice how the last link is still required to query its device as to whether service is pending or not. This is necessary because of the way an EPC works. Remember, all devices in an EPC are given the chance to be serviced on any given pass of the chain. Therefore the last link's device was not necessarily responsible for the request, but the link will always process anyway. All EPC links loaded after the custom last link are programmed as Method 1 EPC links relative to the flowchart given in Figure 7.3.3(a). Method 3 is the most efficient method for processing an EPC, but honestly it only beats Method 1 by a single jump instruction. It does stand out as the least involved method of the three just described. If you are in complete control of all the EPC link designs and their load order, this method is the most attractive for achieving an EPC design. Figure 7.3.6(b) lists the source code needed to realize a Method 3 EPC custom last link.

To demonstrate the construction and operation of an Equal Priority Chain for each of the three methods covered in this section, the programs **epc1.exe, epc2.exe,** and **epc3.exe** are now presented. These programs and complete source code files are found on the IDPCSD disk under the a:\chpt7 subdirectory. Partial source code listings for each of the three example programs are also presented in this section to highlight relevant code segments.

We begin the overview of the example programs with **epc1.exe.** The partial source code listing is shown in Figure 7.3.7.

```
/* epc1.c */

define# LINK_TOTAL 4

/* define Safety Net and device links */
void interrupt(SafetyNet)(void);
void interrupt(dev1Link)(void);
void interrupt(dev2Link)(void);
void interrupt(dev3Link)(void);
void interrupt(dev4Link)(void);

/* assign common structure to each device link (see common.h) */
deviceLink devLink[LINK_TOTAL];

/* add starting addresses to device link structure */
devLink[0].iSR = dev1Link;
devLink[1].iSR = dev2Link;
devLink[2].iSR = dev3Link;
devLink[3].iSR = dev4Link;

/* link load order - top to bottom (top first to load) */
setvect(IRQ_8, SafetyNet);               /* install Safety Net */

devLink[0].oldiSR = getvect(IRQ_8);   /* remember previously loaded iSRs starting address */
setvect(IRQ_8, devLink[0].iSR);       /* install device 1 link's starting address behind IR8   */

devLink[1].oldiSR = getvect(IRQ_8);   /* remember previously loaded iSRs starting address */
setvect(IRQ_8, devLink[1].iSR);       /* install device 2 link's starting address behind IR8   */

devLink[2].oldiSR = getvect(IRQ_8);   /* remember previously loaded iSRs starting address */
setvect(IRQ_8, devLink[2].iSR);       /* install device 3 link's starting address behind IR8   */

devLink[3].oldiSR = getvect(IRQ_8);   /* remember previously loaded iSRs starting address */
setvect(IRQ_8, devLink[3].iSR);       /* install device 4 link's starting address behind IR8   */

/* Safety Net and device links */
void interrupt SafetyNet()
    disable();                        /* disable interrupts                      */
    outportb(0xa0, 0x20);             /* issue Slave PIC Non-Specific EOI         */
    outportb(0x20, 0x20);             /* issue Master PIC Non-Specific EOI        */
}

void interrupt dev1Link()             /* device 1 service routine - custom last link */
{
    if (devLink[0].irPending) {       /* is device 1 requesting service?          */
        devLink[0].counter++;         /* Yes - service device 1                   */
        /* Reset device request */
    }
    devLink[0].oldiSR();              /* jump to next link in the chain           */
}

void interrupt dev2Link()             /* device 2 service routine                  */
{
    if (devLink[1].irPending) {       /* is device 2 requesting service?          */
        devLink[1].counter++;         /* Yes - service device 1                   */
        /* Reset device request */
```

129

```
      }
      devLink[1].oldiSR();              /* jump to next link in the chain     */
}

void interrupt dev3()                   /* device 3 service routine           */
{
      if (devLink[2].irPending) {       /* is device 3 requesting service?    */
         devLink[2].counter++;          /* Yes - service device 1             */
         /* Reset device request */
      }
      devLink[2].oldiSR();              /* jump to next link in the chain     */
}

void interrupt dev4Link()               /* device 4 service routine           */
{
      if (devLink[3].irPending) {       /* is device 4 requesting service?    */
         devLink[3].counter++;          /* Yes - service device 1             */
         /* Reset device request */
      }
      devLink[3].oldiSR();              /* jump to next link in the chain     */
}
```

Figure 7.3.7 epc1.exe - Partial Source Code Listing

Of particular interest is the installation of the Safety Net first, before any of the device links load. The individual device link's are designed as locked in this example. To design the links as nested, add the enable interrupts instruction just before the Service Routine Body and rebuild the executable. Disabling interrupts before issuing the Cleanup commands is always the responsibility of the Safety Net.

The relevant source code for **epc2.exe** is listed in Figure 7.3.8. Here we are most interested in both the installation and the value chosen for the EOC. In this example, a value of 0000:0000 was selected because it meets the EOC's number one criteria of having absolutely no chance of being a device link starting address.

```
/* epc2.exe */

define# LINK_TOTAL 4

/* set EOC code = 0000:0000 */
#define EOC ((void interrupt (*)(void))0)

/* install the EOC code behind IR8 */
setvect(IRQ_8, (void interrupt (*)())EOC);

/* define device links */
void interrupt(dev1Link)(void);
void interrupt(dev2Link)(void);
void interrupt(dev3Link)(void);
void interrupt(dev4Link)(void);
```

```
/* assign common structure to each device link (see common.h) */
deviceLink devLink[LINK_TOTAL];

/* add starting addresses to device link structure */
devLink[0].iSR = dev1Link;
devLink[1].iSR = dev2Link;
devLink[2].iSR = dev3Link;
devLink[3].iSR = dev4Link;

/* link load order - top to bottom (top first to load) */
devLink[0].oldiSR = getvect(IRQ_8);    /* remember previously loaded iSR's starting address */
setvect(IRQ_8, devLink[0].iSR);        /* install device 1 link's starting address behind IR8    */

devLink[1].oldiSR = getvect(IRQ_8);    /* remember previously loaded iSR's starting address */
setvect(IRQ_8, devLink[1].iSR);        /* install device 2 link's starting address behind IR8    */

devLink[2].oldiSR = getvect(IRQ_8);    /* remember previously loaded iSR's starting address */
setvect(IRQ_8, devLink[2].iSR);        /* install device 3 link's starting address behind IR8    */

devLink[3].oldiSR = getvect(IRQ_8);    /* remember previously loaded iSR's starting address */
setvect(IRQ_8, devLink[3].iSR);        /* install device 4 link's starting address behind IR8    */

/* device links */
void interrupt dev1Link()
{
    if (devLink[0].irPendingBit) {     /* is device 1 requesting service?                 */
        devLink[0].counter++;          /* Yes - service device 1                          */
        /* Reset device request */
    }
    if (devLink[0].oldiSR != EOC) {    /* is this the last device link in the chain?      */
        devLink[0].oldiSR();           /* No - Jump to the next link                      */
    } else {                           /* Yes - issue the Cleanup commands                */
        disable();                     /* disable interrupts here if link is nested       */
        outportb(0xa0, 0x20);          /* issue Slave PIC Non-Specific EOI                */
        outportb(0x20, 0x20);          /* issue Master PIC Non-Specific EOI               */
    }
}

void interrupt dev2Link()
{
    if (devLink[1].irPendingBit) {     /* is device 2 requesting service?                 */
        devLink[1].counter++;          /* Yes - service device 2                          */
        /* Reset device request */
    }
    if (devLink[1].oldiSR != EOC) {    /* is this the last device link in the chain?      */
        devLink[1].oldiSR();           /* No - Jump to the next link                      */
    } else {                           /* Yes - issue the Cleanup commands                */
        disable();                     /* disable interrupts here if link is nested       */
        outportb(0xa0, 0x20);          /* issue Slave PIC Non-Specific EOI                */
        outportb(0x20, 0x20);          /* issue Master PIC Non-Specific EOI               */
    }
}

void Interrupt dev3Link()
{
    if (devLink[2].irPendingBit) {     /* is device 3 requesting service?                 */
        devLink[2].counter++;          /* Yes - service device 3                          */
```

```
        /* Reset device request */
    }
    if (devLink[2].oldiSR != EOC) {   /* is this the last device link in the chain?        */
        devLink[2].oldiSR();           /* No - Jump to the next link                        */
    } else {                           /* Yes - issue the Cleanup commands                  */
        disable();                     /* disable interrupts here if link is nested         */
        outportb(0xa0, 0x20);          /* issue Slave PIC Non-Specific EOI                  */
        outportb(0x20, 0x20);          /* issue Master PIC Non-Specific EOI                 */
    }
}


void Interrupt dev4Link()
{
    if (devLink[3].irPendingBit) {    /* is device 4 requesting service?                   */
        devLink[3].counter++;          /* Yes - service device 4                            */
        /* Reset device request */
    }
    if (devLink[3].oldiSR != EOC) {   /* is this the last device link in the chain?        */
        devLink[3].oldiSR();           /* No - Jump to the next link                        */
    } else {                           /* Yes - issue the Cleanup commands                  */
        disable();                     /* disable interrupts here if link is nested         */
        outportb(0xa0, 0x20);          /* issue Slave PIC Non-Specific EOI                  */
        outportb(0x20, 0x20);          /* issue Master PIC Non-Specific EOI                 */
    }
}
```

Figure 7.3.8 epc2.exe - Partial Source Code Listing

The EOC must also be in place before any of the device links load. Because device 1 is the first device link to load, it stores the value currently residing in the interrupt vector table, in this case the EOC code. From Figure 7.3.8, we observe all the device links have been programmed to test for the 0000:0000 value. As the chain processes a request, all the device links will compare their stored value with the EOC, but only device 1 will find a match. Device 1 then activates its resident Safety Net and the EPC processing cycle ends.

The custom last link found in Method 3 EPCs must be the first link installed. After the custom last link is in place, the designer is free to load as many Method 1 EPC links as needed in whatever order desired. The custom last link will always invoke the Safety Net regardless of whether its companion device requires service or not. This is clear from the source code listing shown in Figure 7.3.9.

```
/* epc3.c */

define# LINK_TOTAL 4

/* define device links */
void interrupt(custom_dev1Link)(void);
void interrupt(dev2Link)(void);
void interrupt(dev3Link)(void);
void interrupt(dev4Link)(void);

/* assign common structure to each device link (see common.h) */
deviceLink devlink[LINK_TOTAL];

/* add starting addresses to device link structure */
devLink[0].iSR = custom_dev1Link;
devLink[1].iSR = dev2Link;
devLink[2].iSR = dev3Link;
devLink[3].iSR = dev4Link;

/* link load order - top to bottom */
devLink[0].oldiSR = getvect(IRQ_8);   /* remember previously loaded iSRs starting address */
setvect(IRQ_8, devLink[0].iSR);       /* custom last link is always first to load           */

devLink[1].oldiSR = getvect(IRQ_8);   /* remember previously loaded iSRs starting address */
setvect(IRQ_8, devLink[1].iSR);       /* install device 2 links starting address behind IR8   */

devLink[2].oldiSR = getvect(IRQ_8);   /* remember previously loaded iSRs starting address */
setvect(IRQ_8, devLink[2].iSR);       /* install device 3 links starting address behind IR8   */

devLink[3].oldiSR = getvect(IRQ_8);   /* remember previously loaded iSRs starting address */
setvect(IRQ_8, devLink[3].iSR);       /* install device 4 links starting address behind IR8   */

/* device links */
void interrupt custom_dev1Link()      /* device 1 service routine - custom last link        */
{
    if (devLink[0].irPending) {       /* is device 1 requesting service?                    */
        devLink[1].counter++;         /* Yes - service device 1                             */
        /* Reset device request */
    }
    disable();                        /* disable interrupts here if link is nested          */
    outportb(0xa0, 0x20);             /* issue Slave PIC Non-Specific EOI                   */
    outportb(0x20, 0x20);             /* issue Master PIC Non-Specific EOI                  */
}

void interrupt dev2Link()             /* device 2 service routine                           */
{
    if (devLink[1].irPending) {       /* is device 2 requesting service?                    */
        devLink[1].counter++;         /* Yes - service device 1                             */
        /* Reset device request */
    }
    devLink[1].oldiSR();              /* jump to next link in the chain                     */
}

void interrupt dev3()                 /* device 3 service routine                           */
{
    if (devLink[2].irPending) {       /* is device 3 requesting service?                    */
```

```
        devLink[2].counter++;          /* Yes - service device 1            */
        /* Reset device request */
    }
    devLink[2].oldiSR();              /* jump to next link in the chain     */
}

void interrupt dev4Link()             /* device 4 service routine           */
{
    if (devLink[3].irPending) {       /* is device 4 requesting service?    */
        devLink[3].counter++;         /* Yes - service device 1            */
        /* Reset device request */
    }
    devLink[3].oldiSR();             /* jump to next link in the chain     */
}
```

Figure 7.3.9 epc3.exe - Partial Source Code Listing

Method 3 is the leanest method code wise. Because this method is load order specific and the links can not be programmed using a generic format, it really has no chance of being adopted as a Plug-and-Play standard. If, however, you are in control of all device link designs and their load order, this method is the least complicated and most efficient.

With the exception of the specific link design and load order of the EPC method being represented, all three sample programs are similar in operation. Remaining consistent with the four device model given in section 7.1, each program preserves the device 1 thru device 4 load order and each EPC is installed behind IR8 (Real Time Clock). By enabling the RTC's periodic interrupt, the example programs are provided with an unlimited source of interrupts. Additionally, the RTC's periodic interrupt offers a programmable interrupt rate. This allows us to observe the EPC's operation at frequencies ranging from 2Hz to 8KHz. Details on the programming and general use of the RTC's periodic interrupt is the subject of section 11.6.

Each program displays the individual device links comprising the EPC in the order they are processed. Accompanying each device link is a counter and interrupt pending status. The program name is indicated in the upper right corner of the screen. Figure 7.3.10(a) is a screen capture of the **epc1.exe** program. **epc2.exe** and **epc3.exe** generate screens almost identical to **epc1.exe**. The variation in method however, calls for slightly different EPC representations. Figure 7.3.10(b) and 7.3.10(c) illustrate the subtle differences between the EPC representations.

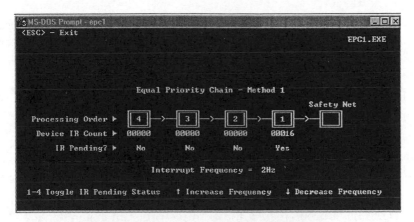

Figure 7.3.10(a) epc1.exe - Output Screen

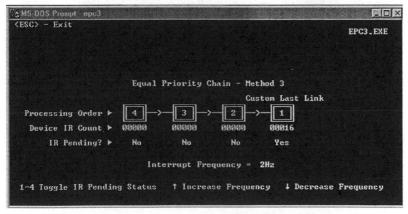

Figure 7.3.10(b) epc2.exe - Output Screen (chain only)

Figure 7.3.10(c) epc3.exe - Output Screen (chain only)

Since none of the four example devices actually exist, an interrupt pending status for each will be simulated by a virtual device status register maintained by the program itself. To toggle the interrupt pending status "ON" or "OFF" for any of the 4 devices, press one of the following keys:

Press "**1**"   Toggle Device1's interrupt pending status bit

Press "**2**"   Toggle Device2's interrupt pending status bit

Press "**3**"   Toggle Device3's interrupt pending status bit

Press "**4**"   Toggle Device4's interrupt pending status bit

Because one of the four devices must have asserted its IR signal for the EPC to have been entered, the example program ensures that at least one device's interrupt pending status is active at all times. The last remaining active pending status can not be toggled inactive.

What you can expect to observe:

Any of the four devices that indicate an active pending interrupt status bit will see their counter increment with each periodic interrupt signal received from the RTC at the displayed rate.

Method 1 and Method 2 EPC links are load order independent. If you rearrange the load order of the Method 1 or Method 2 links in the source code file and rebuild the executable, you should observe no difference in the EPC's operation. Also, be sure to reflect the new screen positions by preserving the link's .screenLocation variable in a 0 to 3/top to bottom order.

To slow the interrupt rate down, press the down arrow. To increase it, press the up arrow. Press "Esc" to quit.

Press "↑"   Double the Interrupt Rate (2Hz - 8KHz)

Press "↓"   Half the Interrupt Rate (8KHz - 2Hz)

Press "ESC" Remove the EPC, Restore RTC functions and End Program

Neither the epc1.exe, epc2.exe, or epc3.exe will leave any trace of its presence upon exit.

7.4 IPC Link Rotation

The EPC just discussed in section 7.3 is a sound method of equalizing the priority among a plurality of devices sharing the same IR input. What an EPC offers in balanced priority over an IPC is counteracted by slightly diminished throughput rates seen by all the EPC devices. The diminished throughput results from the polling characteristic of the EPC dictates that all device links process each time the chain is entered. An EPC link positioned at the front of the chain experiences a minimal response time but loses this advantage in the recovery time, as the remaining EPC links continue to process. An EPC link near the back of the chain sees a lengthy response time and a short recovery time. The combination of response and recovery together is the same for all the links in the EPC and dictates the balanced throughput experienced by all EPC links.

The IPC method discussed in section 7.2 provides devices with IPC companion links positioned toward the front of the chain, quick response times, and a recovery time consisting of nothing more that the required Cleanup commands. This results in higher possible throughput rates for those devices with links positioned near the front of the IPC. Unfortunately, the IPC's implied priority structure forces device links positioned toward the back of the chain to struggle uphill, through snow, in minus 40°F to get serviced when traffic is heavy on devices with companion link's positioned near the front of the chain.

To recap, EPC's offer balanced priority with a slightly lower possible throughput rates than an IPC. IPC's offer improved throughput, but add to the number of priority levels and further exaggerate the preemption issue. The *IPC link rotation method* is capable of both balancing the priority and providing the maximum throughput rates possible in a shared interrupt environment. The way this is accomplished is by allowing the links within an IPC to be dynamically rearranged, or more specifically *rotated*, each time the chain processes a request. In this section, we will introduce two rotate strategies, each capable of satisfying differing application requirements.

7.4.1 Strategy 1

Strategy 1 provides each device with a companion link in the IPC equal opportunity for service. The principal on which this strategy operates is based on the simple rule that once service has been rendered, the device link that just serviced its companion device is rotated to the end of the chain and assumes the lowest priority. This strategy guarantees that no device will be serviced twice before all other devices with pending requests are serviced at least once. This rule equalizes the priority among competing devices. Figure 7.4.1 illustrates this concept of device link rotation using strategy 1. After the device 2 request is processed, the chain rotates such that device 2's companion link now occupies the last position in the IPC.

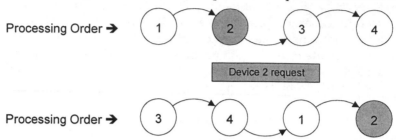

Figure 7.4.1 Strategy 1 - Device Just Serviced Rotates to the End of the IPC

To realize the IPC link rotation method in software, the application needs to be aware of the starting addresses of each of the device links so that it can rotate their order. The IPC device links are no longer responsible for storing the starting address of the previously installed link. The application will assemble and maintain all of the starting addresses in a *Local Vector Table* (LVT). It is not necessary to hook the IRx level and retrieve the starting address in order to build the LVT. As covered later in this section and demonstrated in a source code example, you can simply equate the link's starting address to the correct LVT entry. It is worth noting that the IPC link rotation method is only possible if all the device links are programmed in and installed by the application. If the device links are installed via adapter ROM or by TSR via one of the systems startup files (autoexec.bat or config.sys), there is no easy method of retrieving the device link starting address from the system's interrupt vector table and assembling the required Local Vector Table.

The flowchart for an IPC link used to realize the IPC link rotation method is shown here in Figure 7.4.2.

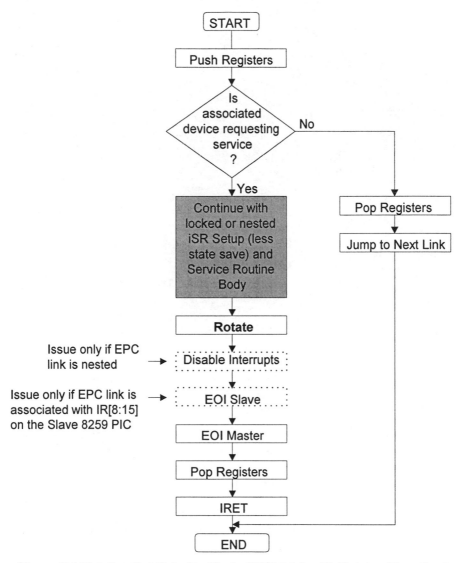

Figure 7.4.2(a) Implied Priority Chain (IPC) Link with Rotate - Flowchart

```
/* ipc_link.c */

void interrupt ipc_link(void);
void interrupt (*Original_iSR)(void);
int ourDevicePending;

void interrupt ipc_link()
{
    if (ourDevicePending) {              /* Is companion device pending service?  */

        /*Service Routine Body*/
        /*Reset device request if level triggered*/

        rotate_strategy1(1);             /* rotate the device links              */

        outportb(0xa0, 0x20);            /* issue Slave PIC Non-Specific EOI     */
        outportb(0x20, 0x20);            /* issue Master PIC Non-Specific EOI    */

    } else {

        Original_iSR();                  /* Far Jump to next link in the chain   */
    }
}
```

Figure 7.4.2(b) Implied Priority Chain (IPC) Link with Rotate - Source Code

This is a standard IPC link design with the addition of a call to a rotate procedure. Once the Service Routine Body completes, a rotate procedure is called that carries out the rotation of the device links per the strategy specified.

The design of the rotation procedure and the application that demonstrates the IPC link rotation method will be based on the four device model presented in section 7.1. To remain consistent with that model, we will assume the four devices load in the order of device 1 thru device 4. The load order as it applies to the IPC link rotation method is irrelevant however, as the application has complete control over the placement of all the device link starting addresses within the Local Vector Table and the order in which those addresses are called. We will use this fact and initialize our example application to realize an IPC processing order of 1⇨2⇨3⇨4. This will help simplify the learning process as we begin to develop the rotate procedure for strategy 1 and the working example application program.

To achieve a rotatable IPC, some new concepts are required. First, when the chain is entered, the link positioned at the front of the IPC is not a device link, but rather a link known as the *director*. The director link is always the first link processed by the IPC and is used to immediately jump to the device link currently defined as having the highest priority, in this example device 1. The IPC device link currently positioned as the last device link in the IPC always points to the Safety Net link. The Safety Net link was included in the development of our rotatable IPC example because it is easier to remove the Safety Net from the design than it is to try and add it in later. The next section and on into Chapter 8 discuss how the Safety Net link is sometimes desired when designing with IPCs. Although in theory, the IPC should never pass control to a Safety Net, possible system anomalies could occur within a PC that would cause the IPC model to fail without it. The director and Safety Net links never rotate, only the device links do. The director is always the first link to process and resides permanently at the front of the IPC. The Safety Net resides permanently at the end. Figure 7.4.3 models the rotatable IPC with the device link processing order remaining consistent with our example.

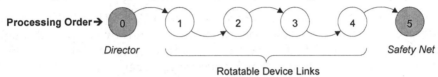

Figure 7.4.3 Rotatable IPC Model

Another procedure unique to the IPC link rotation method is the inclusion of an index table into the Local Vector Table defined as LVTIDX[] in this example. To minimize the overhead involved in the rotation process, the LVT[] entries are not modified during the rotate procedure. Instead, the indexes into the LVT[] located in the LVTIDX[] table are updated to reflect the new processing order. The LVTIDX[] provides an efficient means of rotating the IPC device links through the use of a procedural algorithm we will develop shortly for Strategy 1.

IPC entry point	LVTIDX[00] = 01	LVT[01] = device 1 link's starting address
Device 1 link's jump index	LVTIDX[01] = 02	LVT[02] = device 2 link's starting address
Device 2 link's jump index	LVTIDX[02] = 03	LVT[03] = device 3 link's starting address
Device 3 link's jump index	LVTIDX[03] = 04	LVT[04] = device 4 link's starting address
Device 4 link's jump index	LVTIDX[04] = 05	LVT[05] = Safety Net's starting address
	*LVTIDX[] table entries are updated to rotate the processing order	* LVT[] Table entries remain constant after initialization.

Figure 7.4.4 LVT[] and LVTIDX[] Initialization Example

Figure 7.4.4 illustrate how the LVT[] and LVTIDX[] are initialized to realize the 1⇨2⇨3⇨4 processing order. As the chain is entered, the *director* looks up the starting address of the first device link to be processed by using the contents of LVTIDX[00] to index into the LVT[] entry holding the starting address. In this example, LVTIDX[00] = 1. The director therefore will jump to the address held by LVT[1], which according to Figure 7.4.4 is the device 1 link's starting address. Just as the director is permanently assigned LVTIDX[00], each of the device links are also assigned an LVTIDX[] entry and use the value stored there to look up the starting address in the LVT[] of the next link to jump to if their companion device was not responsible for the request. For example, the device1 link will jump to the device2 link starting address held by LVT[LVTIDX[01]], the device2 link will jump to the device3 link starting address found at LVT[LVTIDX[02]] and so on. By tracking the progress of each device link, we can manually map the processing order. In this example, the director jumps to the device 1 link, device1 ⇨ device2, device2 ⇨ device3, device3 ⇨ device4 and device4 ⇨ Safety Net. The last device link to process in the IPC (device4 in this example) always points to the Safety Net link.

Developing the algorithm that works on the LVTIDX[] and allows us to achieve the Strategy 1 method of link rotation begins by stepping through the rotation process. In Figure 7.4.5 we can observe the effects of two different device requests on the processing order per the Strategy 1 specification.

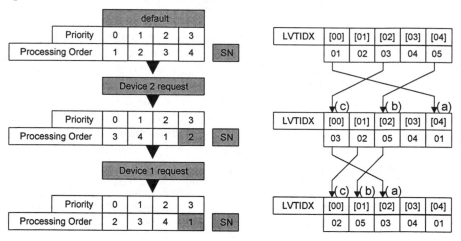

Figure 7.4.5 Strategy 1 - Rotation

After device2 is serviced, the device2 link assumes the lowest priority by rotating to the end of the device link portion of the IPC. The director and Safety Net links always remain the first and last links in the chain respectively. From the updated LVTIDX[] table, we observe that the IPC is now set up to realize the correct 3⇨4⇨1⇨2 processing order. Next, after the device1 request is processed, the device1 link assumes the lowest priority among the device links in the chain and the LVTIDX[] reflects the expected 2⇨3⇨4⇨1 processing order. What falls out of these two examples, is that in order to rotate the device links in an IPC, only three distinct modifications to the LVTIDX[] are required. The following three rules are given here and are labeled in Figure 7.4.5 as well.

(a) The old high priority device link pointed to by the LVTIDX[00] entry must be returned to the LVTIDX[] entry associated with the device that normally calls it.

(b) The newly determined low priority device link must now point to the Safety Net link.

(c) The IPC entry point held in LVTIDX[00] must now point to the new high priority device link's starting address.

These three rules lead directly to the strategy 1 rotate procedure. This procedure is called by the device link whose companion device was responsible for the request. The algorithm in procedural form as it exists in the C source code file for RotateS1.exe on the IDPCSD disk, is listed here in Figure 7.4.6.

```
/* rotates1.c */

/* calling_link =    device link's local identifier, used to store and access the link's starting address
                     LVT[calling_link] = link's starting address. Also used by the link to
                     determine the starting address of the next link in the chain to jump to - jump
                     LVT[LVTIDX[calling_link]]. This parameter is passed to the
                     rotate_strategy1() procedure to identify the calling link and rotate the IPC's
                     accordingly.
   link_total =      total number of device links present in the IPC (four in this example)
   last_link =       used to identify the last device link that called the procedure          */

void rotate_strategy1(int calling_link)    /* strategy 1 rotate procedure               */
{
    If (calling_link == last_link) {        /* if same link processed consecutively, no need to
                                            rotate device links   */
    return;                                 /* simply return to calling link              */
    }
                                            /* (a) */
    if (lvtidx[0] == 1) {                   /* need to compensate for boundary?          */
        lvtidx[link_total] = 1;             /* return the current high priority link back to its resident
                                            lvtidx[] cell      */
    } else {
        lvtidx[lvtidx[0] - 1] = lvtidx[0];  /* return the current high priority link back to its resident
                                            lvtidx[] cell*/
    }

                                            /* (b) */
    lvtidx[calling_link] = link_total + 1;  /* point the chain's new low priority device link to the
                                            "Safety Net"       */
```

```
                                            /* (c) */
    if (callinglink == link_total) {    /* need to compensate for boundary?              */
        lvtidx[0] = 1;                   /* place newest high priority link at the front of the
                                            chain     */
    } else {
        lvtidx[0] = (calling_link + 1);  /* place newest high priority link at the front of the
                                            chain */
    }

    last_link = calling_link;            /* remember the link that called this procedure last   */
}
```

Figure 7.4.6 Strategy 1 Rotate Procedure - rotate_strategy1()

The first order of business for the rotate procedure is to determine if a rotation is even required. If the same device generates a consecutive request, the device links are already where they need to be and a rotation is not warranted. However, if the device link calling the procedure is not the same as the link that called the procedure last, rotation of the device links is required. The procedure will then update the LVTIDX[] table entries by performing step (a), (b), and (c), update the last_link variable to remember the last device link to call the procedure and return, where the calling link will issue the required Cleanup commands and IRET instruction.

To realize the IPC link rotation method using strategy 1, the **RotateS1.exe** example program in now offered. This program demonstrates the operation of the rotate procedure just described and allows us to observe the dynamic rotation of the device links as requests are being processed. This program and C source code file can be found on the IDPCSD disk in the a:\chpt7 subdirectory. A partial source code listing showing the relevant code segments for RotateS1.exe is given here in Figure 7.4.7.

```
/* rotateS1.c */

define# LINK_TOTAL 4

/* intialize indirect addressing variables */
void interrupt(*lvt[LINK_TOTAL + 2])(void);
char lvtidx[LINK_TOTAL+2];

/* define the director, Safety Net and device links as interrupt */
void interrupt(directorLink(void);
void interrupt(SafetyNet)(void);
void interrupt(dev1Link)(void);
void interrupt(dev2Link)(void);
void interrupt(dev3Link)(void);
void interrupt(dev4Link)(void);
```

```
/* assign common structure to each device link (see common.h) */
deviceLink devLink[LINK_TOTAL];

/* add starting addresses to device link structure */
devLink[0].iSR = dev1Link;
devLink[1].iSR = dev2Link;
devLink[2].iSR = dev3Link;
devLink[3].iSR = dev4Link;

/* initialize Local Vector Table lvt[] */
lvt[1] = devLink[0].iSR;        /* set lvt[1] = device 1 link's starting address   */
lvt[2] = devLink[1].iSR;        /* set lvt[2] = device 2 link's starting address   */
lvt[3] = devLink[2].iSR;        /* set lvt[3] = device 3 link's starting address   */
lvt[4] = devLink[3].iSR;        /* set lvt[4] = device 4 link's starting address   */
lvt[5] = SafetyNet;             /* set lvt[5] = Safety Net                          */

/* initialize the IPC processing order  - 1⇨2⇨3⇨4 */
lvtidx[0] = 1;                  /* director calls device 1 link                    */
lvtidx[1] = 2;                  /* device 1 link calls device 2 link               */
lvtidx[2] = 3;                  /* device 2 link calls device 3 link               */
lvtidx[3] = 4;                  /* device 3 link calls device 4 link               */
lvtidx[4] = 5;                  /* device 4 link calls Safety Net                  */

/* install the director link */
setvect(IRQ_8,directorLink);

/* device links */
void interrupt directorLink()
{
lvt[lvtidx[0]](void);           /* lvtidx[0] entry always points to the device link at  */
}                               /* the front of the processing order               */

void interrupt SafetyNet(void)
{
    disable();                  /* disable interrupts                              */
    outportb(0xa0, 0x20);       /* issue Slave PIC Non-Specific EOI                */
    outportb(0x20, 0x20);       /* issue Master PIC Non-Specific EOI               */
}


void interrupt dev1Link()       /* device 1 service routine                        */
{
    if (devLink[0].irPending) { /* is device 1 requesting service?                 */
        devLink[0].counter++;   /* Yes - service device 1                          */
        /* Reset device request */
        rotate_strategy1(1);    /* rotate processing order - device 1 = lowest priority */
        outportb(0xa0, 0x20);   /* issue Slave PIC Non-Specific EOI                */
        outportb(0x20, 0x20);   /* issue Master PIC Non-Specific EOI               */
    } else {
        lvt[lvtidx[0]]();       /* jump to next link in the chain                  */
    }
}

void interrupt dev2Link()       /* device 2 service routine                        */
{
    if (devLink[1].irPending) { /* is device 2 requesting service?                 */
        devLink[1].counter++;   /* Yes - service device 2                          */
```

```
            /* Reset device request */
            rotate_strategy1(2);              /* rotate processing order - device 2 = lowest priority */
            outportb(0xa0, 0x20);            /* issue Slave PIC Non-Specific EOI          */
            outportb(0x20, 0x20);            /* issue Master PIC Non-Specific EOI
            */
    } else {
        lvt[lvtidx[1]]();                    /* jump to next link in the chain           */
    }
}

void interrupt dev3Link()                    /* device 3 service routine                 */
{
    if (devLink[2].irPending) {              /* is device 3 requesting service?          */
        devLink[2].counter++;                /* Yes - service device 3                   */
        /* Reset device request */
        rotate_strategy1(3);                 /* rotate processing order - device 3 = lowest priority */
        outportb(0xa0, 0x20);                /* issue Slave PIC Non-Specific EOI          */
        outportb(0x20, 0x20);                /* issue Master PIC Non-Specific EOI        */
    } else {
        lvt[lvtidx[2]]();                    /* jump to next link in the chain           */
    }
}

void interrupt dev4Link()                    /* device 4 service routine                 */
{
    if (devLink[3].irPending) {              /* is device 4 requesting service?          */
        devLink[3].counter++;                /* Yes - service device 4                   */
        /* Reset device request */
        rotate_strategy1(4);                 /* rotate processing order - device 4 = lowest priority */
        outportb(0xa0, 0x20);                /* issue Slave PIC Non-Specific EOI          */
        outportb(0x20, 0x20);                /* issue Master PIC Non-Specific EOI        */
    } else {
        lvt[lvtidx[3]]();                    /* jump to next link in the chain           */
    }
}
```

Figure 7.4.7 RotateS1.exe - Partial Source Code Listing (C)

The initialization of the Local Vector Table (LVT[]) is simply a matter of equating the device link starting address with the correct LVT[] entry. The device links are not required to hook the IRx level first and then be retrieved. The only link required to hook the IRx level is the *director*, because it is responsible for directing control to the current high priority device link in the chain. Once the LVT[] is initialized, the LVTIDX[] is setup to reflect the initial processing order of 1⇨2⇨3⇨4 defined back in Figure 7.4.3. All the device links are designed around Locked Slave PIC iSR's and include the call to the rotate procedure. To configure the device links as nested, enable interrupts just before the counter increment and disable interrupts in-between the rotate procedure and the Slave PIC Non-Specific EOI.

RotateS1.exe installs the rotatable IPC behind IR8 (Real Time Clock). Installing the rotatable IPC behind the RTC's IR8 provides an unlimited supply of interrupts for our example to process. The RTC also offers a programmable interrupt rate and the ability to observe the dynamic rotation of the device links at frequencies from 2Hz - 8KHz. Details on the programming and general use of the RTC's periodic interrupt is the subject of section 9.5.

The RotateS1.exe's display is shown here in Figure 7.4.8. As you can see, each device link has its own counter and interrupt pending status represented. The RTC's periodic interrupt rate is also displayed. Because the counters and IR pending status continually change their screen positions along with the device links as they rotate, it can be a bit difficult at 8KHz (or 2Hz for that matter) to determine the exact state of a device's IR pending status. For that reason, a static list of all the devices IR pending status is provided on the upper left hand side of the screen.

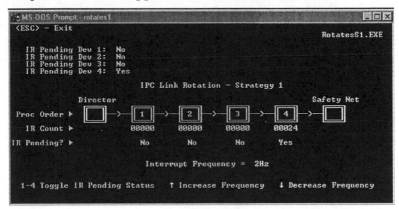

Figure 7.4.8 RotateS1.exe - Output Screen (DOS)

Since the four devices represented by RotateS1.exe do not really exist, the interrupt pending status for each device is simulated by a IR pending status register maintained by the RotateS1.exe program itself. To toggle the interrupt pending status bit ON or OFF for any of the 4 devices, press any one of the following keys:

Press "**1**"   Toggle Device 1's interrupt pending status bit

Press "**2**"   Toggle Device 2's interrupt pending status bit

Press "**3**"   Toggle Device 3's interrupt pending status bit

Press "**4**"   Toggle Device 4's interrupt pending status bit

Because one of the four devices must have asserted its IR signal for the IPC to have been entered, the RotateS1.exe example program ensures that at least one device's interrupt pending status is active at all times. The last remaining active pending status bit can not be toggled inactive.

What you can expect to observe:

When a request arrives, the device currently possessing the highest priority with its active interrupt pending status will see its counter increment. After the counter increments, the device link will call the rotate procedure and the display will reflect the updated processing order showing the companion link of the device just serviced now positioned as the last device link in the IPC. If only one device is pending service, the device link will immediately assume the last device link position in the IPC and stay there while its counter continues to increment.

To observe the true benefit of the IPC link rotation method, set the interrupt rate at 2Hz and enable the interrupt pending status for all four devices. You can now observe the device links rotating around in a circle per the strategy 1 rotate procedure. As each device reaches the front of the processing order, its counter is incremented and it immediately moves to the back of the line.

To slow the interrupt rate down, press the down arrow. To increase it, press the up arrow. Press "Esc" to quit.

Press "↑"   Double the Interrupt Rate (2Hz - 8KHz)

Press "↓"   Half the Interrupt Rate (8KHz - 2Hz)

Press "ESC" Remove IPC, Restore RTC functions and End Program

The RotateS1.exe program will leave no trace of its presence upon exit.

7.4.2 Strategy 2

The second strategy allows interrupt-driven data streams to achieve the maximum throughput any shared IRx level can offer. It requires that the requester follow some specific rules in order for this strategy to work. The principal on which strategy 2 operates is this; an interrupt-driven data stream can achieve a higher throughput rate if the response time to the request is reduced. The link with the lowest response time is the first link in the chain. Therefore to optimize throughput, rotate the device link just processed to the front of the processing order in anticipation of the device's next request. Figure 7.4.8 illustrates this concept.

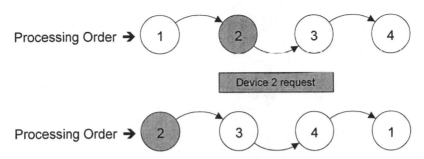

Figure 7.4.7 Strategy 2 - Device Just Serviced Rotates to the Front of the IPC

In this example, device2 has now minimized its response time by assuming the highest priority position in the IPC and can therefore achieve higher throughput rates. A problem arises, however, if device2 has a long stream of data to transfer and other devices are currently pending service. In this instance, the other devices in the chain will be forced to buffer their data until device2 breaks the transfer. To avoid other devices experiencing buffer overflows, long continuous data transfers should be broken up into blocks. After a device transfers a block of data, the device then follows by pulling its IR signal inactive and pausing long enough (maximum expected latency time) for another request pending service to be acknowledged by the processor before reasserting the IR signal. The device only needs to bring the IR signal inactive for a few micro seconds before reasserting. If no other devices are pending service, the recycled IR signal will be acknowledged and the device will transfer another block of data. If another device is requesting service, the inactive IR signal on the first device will allow the second device's active IR signal to be acknowledged by the processor. When it is, the second device will begin transferring data and move immediately into the high priority position in the IPC. Just as the first device did, the second device will briefly cycle its IR signal inactive to let yet another device pending service take over and realize the maximum throughput rate offered by the high priority position in the IPC. It is an honor system of sorts among the various devices. The result is improved data rates for all devices involved.

To develop the strategy 2 rotate procedure, we will assume the familiar four device model given in 7.1, and initialize the LVT[] and LVTIDX[] tables to reflect the 1⇨2⇨3⇨4 processing order shown in Figure 7.4.4. The steps required to rotate the device links per strategy 2 are determined by observing how the processing order rotates as device requests are received and processed by the IPC. Figure 7.4.10 shows us two such examples.

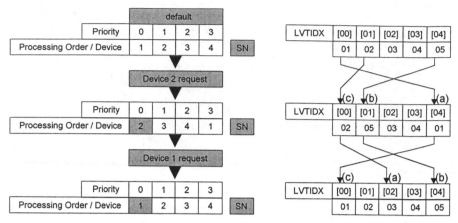

Figure 7.4.10 Strategy 2 - Rotation

After the IPC processes the device2 request, the strategy 2 specification rotates the device 2 link to the front of the IPC. Device2 then continues on with its interrupt-driven data transfer, realizing a minimum response time and increased throughput as a result of its companion links favored position in the chain. The Device1 request is acknowledged and serviced after the Device2 finishes its data transfer. Device 1 is immediately rotated into the high priority position in the IPC. As with strategy 1, we find the same three rules are required to correctly modify the LVTIDX[] table and rotate the device links.

(a) The old high priority device link pointed to by the LVTIDX[00] entry must be returned to LVTIDX[] entry associated with the device that normally calls it.

(b) The newly determined low priority device link must now point to the Safety Net link.

(c) The IPC entry point held in LVTIDX[00] must now point to the new high priority device link's starting address.

Unlike strategy 1 however, the device link that calls the rotate procedure, now assumes the highest priority position in the chain instead of the lowest.

The source code required to perform the (a), (b), and (c) steps illustrated in Figure 7.4.10 and to realize the strategy 2 rotate procedure, is listed here in Figure 7.4.11. The strategy 2 procedure first determines if the IPC needs to be rotated. If the same device generates a consecutive request, the device links are already where they need to be and a rotation is not warranted. If the request is from a different device, the procedure updates the LVTIDX[]

table to reflect the new processing order, updates the last_link variable to remember the last device link to call the procedure and returns to the calling link where the Cleanup commands and IRET instruction are issued.

```
/* calling_link =        device link's local identifier, used to store and access the link's starting address
                         LVT[calling_link] = link's starting address. Also used by the link to
                         determine the starting address of the next link in the chain to jump to - jump
                         LVT[LVTIDX[calling_link]]. This parameter is passed to the
                         rotate_strategy1() procedure to identify the calling link and rotate the IPC's
                         accordingly.
   link_total =          total number of device links present in the IPC (four in this example)
   last_link =           used to identify the last device link that called the procedure           */


   void rotate_strategy2(int calling_link)      /* strategy 2 rotate procedure                      */
   {

        If (calling_link == last_link) {         /* if same link processed consecutively, no need to */
                                                 /* rotate device links                              */
        return;                                  /* simply return to calling link                    */
        }

                                                 /* (a) */
        if (lvtidx[0] == 1) {                    /* need to compensate for boundary?                 */
              lvtidx[link_total] = 1;            /* return the current high priority link back to its */
                                                 /*  resident lvtidx[] cell                          */
        } else {
              lvtidx[lvtidx[0] - 1] = lvtidx[0]; /* return the current high priority link back to its */
                                                 /* resident lvtidx[] cell                           */

        }

                                                 /* (b) */
        if (calling_link == 1) {                 /* need to compensate for boundary?                 */
              lvtidx[link_total] = link_total + 1;  /* point the chain's new low priority device      */
                                                    /* link to the "Safety Net"                      */
        } else {
              lvtidx[calling_link - 1] = link_total + 1;  /* point the chain's new low priority device */
                                                          /* link to the "Safety Net"                */

        }

                                                 /* (c) */
        lvtidx[0] = calling_link;                /* assign the calling link highest priority by placing */
                                                 /*  it at the front of the                          */
                                                 /* chain                                            */

        last_link = calling_link;                /* remember the link that called this procedure last */
   }
```

Figure 7.4.11 Strategy 2 Rotate Procedure - rotate_strategy2()

We will now present the strategy 2 example application program, **RotateS2.exe**. This program demonstrates the operation of the rotate procedure just described and allows us to observe the dynamic rotation of the device links as requests are being processed. This program and C source file can be found on the IDPCSD disk in the a:\chpt7 subdirectory.

source file can be found on the IDPCSD disk in the a:\chpt7 subdirectory. A partial source code listing showing the relevant portions of the RotateS2.exe source is given here in Figure 7.4.12.

```
/* rotateS2.c */

define# LINK_TOTAL 4

/* intialize indirect addressing variables */
void interrupt (*lvt[LINK_TOTAL + 2])(void);
char lvtidx[LINK_TOTAL+2];

/* define the director, Safety Net and device links as interrupt */
void interrupt(directorLink)(void);
void interrupt(SafetyNet)(void);
void interrupt(dev1Link)(void);
void interrupt(dev2Link)(void);
void interrupt(dev3Link)(void);
void interrupt(dev4Link)(void);

/* assign common structure to each device link (see common.h) */
deviceLink devLink[LINK_TOTAL];

/* add starting addresses to device link structure */
devLink[0].iSR = dev1Link;
devLink[1].iSR = dev2Link;
devLink[2].iSR = dev3Link;
devLink[3].iSR = dev4Link;

/* initialize Local Vector Table lvt[] */
lvt[1] = devLink[0].iSR;          /* set lvt[1] = device 1 link's starting address    */
lvt[2] = devLink[1].iSR;          /* set lvt[2] = device 2 link's starting address    */
lvt[3] = devLink[2].iSR;          /* set lvt[3] = device 3 link's starting address    */
lvt[4] = devLink[3].iSR;          /* set lvt[4] = device 4 link's starting address    */
lvt[5] = SafetyNet;               /* set lvt[5] = Safety Net                          */

/* initialize the IPC processing order  - 1⇨2⇨3⇨4 */
lvtidx[0] = 1;                    /* director calls device 1 link                     */
lvtidx[1] = 2;                    /* device 1 link calls device 2 link                */
lvtidx[2] = 3;                    /* device 2 link calls device 3 link                */
lvtidx[3] = 4;                    /* device 3 link calls device 4 link                */
lvtidx[4] = 5;                    /* device 4 link calls Safety Net                   */

/* install the director link */
setvect(IRQ_8,directorLink);

/* device links */
void interrupt directorLink()
{
lvt[lvtidx[0]](void);            /* lvtidx[0] entry always points to the device link at  */
}                                /* the front of the processing order                    */

void interrupt SafetyNet(void)
{
    disable();                   /* disable interrupts                               */
    outportb(0xa0, 0x20);        /* issue Slave PIC Non-Specific EOI                 */
    outportb(0x20, 0x20);        /* issue Master PIC Non-Specific EOI                */
}
```

```
void interrupt dev1Link()              /* device 1 service routine                              */
{
    if (devLink[0].irPending) {        /* is device 1 requesting service?                       */
        devLink[0].counter++;          /* Yes - service device 1                                */
        /* Reset device request */
        rotate_strategy2(1);           /* rotate processing order - device 1 = highest priority */
        outportb(0xa0, 0x20);          /* issue Slave PIC Non-Specific EOI                       */
        outportb(0x20, 0x20);          /* issue Master PIC Non-Specific EOI                      */
    } else {
        lvt[lvtidx[0]]();              /* jump to next link in the chain                         */
    }
}

void interrupt dev2Link()              /* device 2 service routine                              */
{
    if (devLink[1].irPending) {        /* is device 2 requesting service?                       */
        devLink[1].counter++;          /* Yes - service device 2                                */
        /* Reset device request */
        rotate_strategy2(2);           /* rotate processing order - device 2 = highest priority */
        outportb(0xa0, 0x20);          /* issue Slave PIC Non-Specific EOI                       */
        outportb(0x20, 0x20);          /* issue Master PIC Non-Specific EOI                      */
    } else {
        lvt[lvtidx[1]]();              /* jump to next link in the chain                         */
    }
}

void interrupt dev3Link()              /* device 3 service routine                              */
{
    if (devLink[2].irPending) {        /* is device 3 requesting service?                       */
        devLink[2].counter++;          /* Yes - service device 3                                */
        /* Reset device request */
        rotate_strategy2(3);           /* rotate processing order - device 3 = highest priority */
        outportb(0xa0, 0x20);          /* issue Slave PIC Non-Specific EOI                       */
        outportb(0x20, 0x20);          /* issue Master PIC Non-Specific EOI                      */
    } else {
        lvt[lvtidx[2]]();              /* jump to next link in the chain                         */
    }
}

void interrupt dev4Link()              /* device 4 service routine                              */
{
    if (devLink[3].irPending) {        /* is device 4 requesting service?                       */
        devLink[3].counter++;          /* Yes - service device 4                                */
        /* Reset device request */
        rotate_strategy2(4);           /* rotate processing order - device 4 = highest priority */
        outportb(0xa0, 0x20);          /* issue Slave PIC Non-Specific EOI                       */
        outportb(0x20, 0x20);          /* issue Master PIC Non-Specific EOI                      */
    } else {
        lvt[lvtidx[3]]();              /* jump to next link in the chain                         */
    }
}
```

Figure 7.4.12 RotateS2.exe - Partial Source Code Listing (C)

As with strategy 1, the initialization of the Local Vector Table is simply a matter of equating the device link starting address with the correct LVT[] entry. The device links are not required to hook the IRx level first and then be retrieved. Once the LVT[] is initialized, the LVTIDX[] is setup to reflect the initial processing order of 1⇨2⇨3⇨4. The strategy 2 device link design is identical to that shown in Figure 7.4.2 for strategy 1. The only difference being the rotate procedure called. The device links in this example are all designed around Locked Slave PIC iSRs. To conFigure the device links as nested follow the same instructions given for strategy 1 by enabling interrupts just before the counter increment and disabling interrupts in-between the rotate procedure and the Slave PIC Non-Specific EOI.

RotateS2.exe installs the rotatable IPC behind IR8 (Real Time Clock). Installing the rotatable IPC behind the RTC's IR8 provides an unlimited supply of interrupts for our example to process. The RTC also offers a programmable interrupt rate and the ability to observe the dynamic rotation of the device links at frequencies from 2Hz to 8KHz. Details on the programming and general use of the RTC's periodic interrupt is the subject of section 11.6.

Two data transfer modes are provided by the RotateS2.exe. This was done to demonstrate what happens when device's hold their IR signals active indefinitely(continuous mode) and when the device's conform to moving data in blocks and cycling their IR signal inactive after each block is transferred. It becomes apparent when viewing the IPC's operation, that implementing an IPC link rotation method using strategy 2 without the devices conforming to the block transfer and IR signal cycling specification renders the whole strategy 2 concept useless. To toggle between the continuous and block data transfer modes, press the <spacebar>. The data transfer mode currently in operation is displayed in the upper middle portion of the screen.

The RotateS2.exe's display shown here in Figure 7.4.13 is similar to that of RotateS1.exe. The difference is observed in the strategy 2 rotate algorithms operation and the addition of the two data transfer modes.

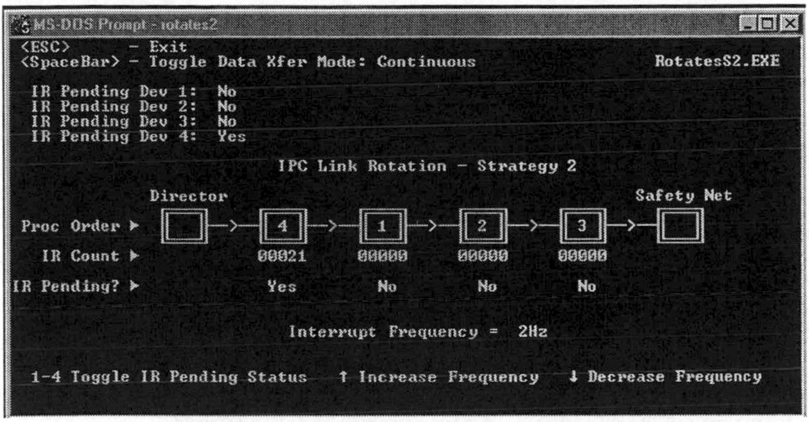

Figure 7.4.13 RotateS2.exe - Output Screen (DOS)

Because we are emulating the devices represented by RotateS2.exe, each device's interrupt pending status is simulated by a virtual device status register maintained by RotateS2.exe program itself. To toggle the interrupt pending status bit ON or OFF for any of the four devices, press one of the following keys:

Press "**1**"   Toggle Device 1's interrupt pending status bit

Press "**2**"   Toggle Device 2's interrupt pending status bit

Press "**3**"   Toggle Device 3's interrupt pending status bit

Press "**4**"   Toggle Device 4's interrupt pending status bit

Since one of the four devices must have asserted its IR signal for the IPC to have been entered, the RotateS2.exe example program ensures that at least one device's interrupt pending status bit is active at all times. The last remaining active pending status bit can not be toggled inactive.

What you can expect to observe:

As a request arrives via the RTC, the device currently possessing the highest priority with an active interrupt pending status will see its counter increment. After the counter increments, the device link will then call the rotate procedure and update the display to reflect the new processing order. The device link just processed is now positioned as the first device link in the IPC. Beyond this point, the operational output diverges as either the continuous or block data transfer mode is selected.

In continuous mode, the device currently holding the high priority position in the IPC with an active IR pending status will see its counter increment indefinitely until such time as the IR pending status for that device is toggled OFF. The next highest priority device currently registering an active IR pending status will then rotate into the IPC's high priority position and begin counting the RTC's incoming requests.

In block mode, the cycling of the device's IR pending status is simulated in software. Each device in block mode will cycle the IR pending status inactive momentarily every 512 counts. After the device records 512 counts, the next highest priority device with its interrupt pending status bit enabled will take over the high priority position in the IPC and register 512 counts before relinquishing the top spot to the next highest priority device requesting service. If no other devices represented in the IPC are requesting service, the highest priority device will maintain its position at the front of the chain and continue to process requests. Two quick notes regarding block mode: First, because the background loop is responsible for noting when the count has reached 512, at higher interrupt rates (256Hz+) the requests can fly past 512 before the background program is able to realize it. What you will see as a result is the counter incrementing beyond the 512 mark before the rotation kicks in. Secondly, an active IR pending status may flicker "NO" briefly as the background program caught the cycling of the IR pending status inactive for a device that had just reached the end of the simulated 512 block transfer. Do not be alarmed, just move quickly and calmly to the nearest emergency exit.

To slow the interrupt rate down, press the down arrow. To increase it, press the up arrow. Press "Esc" to quit.

Press "↑"   Double the Interrupt Rate (2Hz - 8KHz)

Press "↓"   Half the Interrupt Rate (8KHz - 2Hz)

Press "ESC"   Remove IPC, Restore RTC functions and End Program

The RotateS2.exe program will leave no trace of its presence upon exit.

7.5 Designing With Chains

7.5.1 IPC Distribution

A good way to reduce the response time seen by the IPC devices is to break up the IPC and distribute the links over consecutive IRx levels. By distributing over consecutive IRx levels, the priority structure will remain intact while the response time to the devices represented by companion links in the chain will be reduced, resulting in a higher possible throughput. Table 7.5.1 shows an IPC representing five devices installed behind IR9. Whenever device1 requests service, the device 5 - device2 links must check their companion devices for pending status first, before the device1 link is processed. Notice in the example given in Table 7.5.1, that IR10 is available.

8259 PIC IRx Input	Priority Level	Native IRx level	First Implied IRx level	Second Implied IRx level	Third Implied IRx level	Fourth Implied IRx level
IR9	3	device5	device4	device3	device2	device1
IR10	8	available				
IR11	9	JoyStick				

Table 7.5.1 Unbalanced IPC Distribution

By distributing the IPC links over IR9 and the available IR10 similar to the example given in Table 7.5.2, the response time to device1's request is reduced roughly one quarter its original value while the priority structure remains unaffected.

8259 PIC IRx Input	Priority Level	Native IRx level	First Implied IRx level	Second Implied IRx level
IR9	3	device5	device4	device3
IR10	5	device2	device1	
IR11	7	joystick		

Table 7.5.2 Balanced IPC Distribution

This technique can be applied to MCA and EISA devices with vendor supplied drivers. Vendors that provide a full compliment of IRx levels to choose from are preferred when designing with chains for this reason. When deciding a device link's placement within an IPC and the IRx level the IPC will use, simply remember that the assignment of priority within a PC is determined by the transfer rate of each device. The device with the highest transfer rate should be assigned the highest priority (first device link processed by the IPC occupying the highest priority IRx level). The device with the lowest transfer rate should be assigned the lowest priority (last device link processed by the IPC occupying the lowest priority IRx level). Placing PCI devices in the system's interrupt structure is a bit more challenging (refer to Chapter 10 for details)

7.5.2 Equal Priority Methods

PC system designers trying to design complex systems full of modems, network adapter cards or any other interrupt-driven communication devices requiring balanced throughput would benefit from an *equal priority* structure. The throughput imbalance that is associated with the effects of preemption in an implied priority structure (illustrated in Chapter 11.2) simply disappear.

To achieve equal priority among a plurality of devices within a PC requires that all the devices share the same IRx level. This fact is important because the idea of distributing the EPC over two or more IRx levels and expecting to maintain equal priority among all the devices is not possible. As a result, equal priority chain lengths can grow quite long as the number of equal priority devices specified by the design increases. The three EPC methods discussed in section 7.3 process all the links each and every time the EPC is entered as the result of a request. A long EPC therefore imposes significant overhead when considering the response and recovery times seen by a lone EPC device requesting service. The worst case response times need to be considered to verify that the EPC can satisfy the throughput requirements of all its devices. An EPC is most efficient when the EPC length is short (only a couple of devices) and/or when a high percentage of the devices request service simultaneously on a regular basis. Several modems with active sessions would be one such instance.

A more efficient solution to achieving equal priority is to use one of the rotate strategies given in the last section (7.4). Both of the rotate strategies require that the source code for the device links and their processing order be designed into the application program. The IPC link rotation method - strategy 1 works slightly better than an EPC when chain lengths are long and a low percentage of simultaneous requests are encountered. In this case, the rotatable IPC will exit the chain as soon as the device requesting service is found. This potentially reduces the number of links processed each time the chain is entered resulting in a better response time seen by the device. The second rotate strategy (strategy 2) is the most efficient means of achieving equal priority among several devices and affords the highest possible bandwidth possible. The catch - all the devices must inactivate their request signal momentarily when performing long data transfers in order to let other devices pending service reap the benefits of the high priority (minimum response time) spot in the chain. If you are in total control of the software and can establish a mechanism for momentarily cycling the IR signal at the end of the block data transfer, this method is king.

7.5.3 Bullet Proofing the Chain

There were two situations mentioned earlier that could cause the last link (first link to load) in an IPC to jump to the unfamiliar starting address it found and stored when it loaded. A jump to an unfamiliar address in a computer system of any kind is, of course, not a good thing. The first possible cause for such an error would be a misrepresentation by the device of its pending interrupt status. If the device were to inaccurately report to its companion link that no interrupt was pending, then in the instance where no other devices are currently pending service, the last link in the IPC would try to pass control on to the next link by jumping to the unfamiliar address it found in the vector table when it loaded. To eliminate the possibility of a system crash under these circumstances, install a Safety Net at the end of the IPC to absorb any erroneous jumps. It may be desirable to have the IPC Safety Net post a message indicating the error condition just encountered. Note that the installation of a Safety Net link, unless BIOS supplied, is not an option in Plug-and-Play environments such as PCI. This is because the Safety Net link would have no way of loading before the adapter ROMs were scanned and the device links installed at system startup.

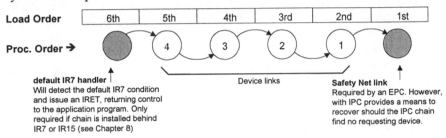

Figure 7.5.1 Most Stable Chain Design - IPC or EPC

As mentioned briefly in section 7.3, the only way to get Safety Nets in place in a Plug-and-Play system such as PCI, is to add a custom adapter ROM to the system that can be recognized by the system prior to all other ROMs and install the Safety Nets.

The second condition that can cause an IPC to fully process with no devices requesting service found, is the 8259's default IR7. Installing a Safety Net link in this instance, will at least stop the last link from jumping into wonderland, but unless an additional link capable of handling the default IR7 is placed at the front of the chain, the PC's interrupt process will come unglued when a default IR7 is encountered. This condition effects both IPCs and EPCs installed behind IR7 or IR15 only. The addition of a default IR7 handler link to a chain installed behind IR7 or IR15 will eliminate the threat to the PC's interrupt process resulting from a default IR7. A default IR7 handler is possible in all PC platforms including Plug-and-Play because the default IR7 handler is installed after all the device links are loaded and do not have to contend with the up-front processing of adapter ROMs. Default IR7 interrupt handler design, both in general and with regards to link design is the subject of Chapter 8.

Figure 7.5.1 illustrates the most stable chain design for both IPCs and EPCs using IR7 or IR15. When using levels other than IR7 and IR15, the front end handling of the default IR7 is not required.

7.5.4 Hybrid Chain - Mixing Link Types

At the beginning of this section, I mentioned a third possible chain type resulting when both IPC and EPC links are combined in a single chain. Although the application for such a chain design is uncommon (usually the result of too few available IRx levels), if you are confronted with such a dilemma, keep the following in mind. It is preferable to place the IPC links at the front of the processing order (install them after the EPC links). The reason is that if the device requesting service is represented by an IPC link, the processing of the chain will end as soon as the IPC device is found and serviced. With the IPC links at the front of the chain, their response time is reduced as the chain does not have to process the EPC links first. To handle the EPC segment, a Safety Net link is required and must reside at the end of the chain. Group all the EPC links together, otherwise the balanced priority they provide their companion devices will not exist.

7.5.5 Looking for Safety Nets using DOS Debug

If you would like to find out if the PC's system BIOS installs Safety Nets (EOI commands followed by an IRET) for available IRx levels, here's one way to go about it. Fire up the DOS debug utility and use the "D" command to dump and record the default addresses installed by the BIOS for the available IRx levels of interest. Table 7.5.3 lists the PC's IRx levels and their associated Vector Table Addresses.

0000:0020	IR0	0000:01C0	IR8
0000:0024	IR1	0000:01C4	IR9 (redirected IR2)
0000:0028	IR2	0000:01C8	IR10
0000:002C	IR3	0000:01CC	IR11
0000:0030	IR4	0000:01D0	IR12
0000:0034	IR5	0000:01D4	IR13
0000:0038	IR6	0000:01D8	IR14
0000:003C	IR7	0000:01DC	IR15

Table 7.5.3 Interrupt Vector Table Physical Addresses

After issuing the debug dump command, here is a sample translation for the four byte address stored in *little endian* format found and displayed by the utility, ex: 43 FF 00 F0 → F000:FF43. Now, using the "U" command, unassemble the code beginning at the address found in the vector table, ex: U F000:FF43. If one (IR[0:7]) or two (IR[8:15]) Non-Specific EOI command(s) followed by an IRET are not immediately noticeable, a call to the BIOS manufacturer may be the only way to determine what the BIOS defaults are regarding unused IRx levels. If you find that Safety Nets are installed by the BIOS, you can incorporate these into your design. Weigh the use of BIOS installed Safety Nets carefully, as the system design will be hardware-platform specific if they are used.

8. The 8259 PIC's default IR7 Feature

8.1 The default IR7 Interrupt Defined

There exists within the 8259 PIC a feature regarded as a nuisance by most, the default IR7. In both edge and level triggered modes, a default IR7 is generated by the 8259 PIC when an IRx input signal transitions from low to high but fails to remain high until it is acknowledged or more specifically until the falling edge of the first INTA# pulse arrives. In this situation, the PIC can't determine which IRx level is responsible for the request, so consequently it provides the interrupt type code associated with its IR7 by default. If the condition for a default IR7 is detected on any of the PIC's eight IRx levels, the result will be a default IR7 interrupt. If default IR7s are not handled properly the system will crash. Figure 8.1.1 illustrates the signal timing condition that causes a default IR7 to be generated when seen by the 8259 PIC IR input.

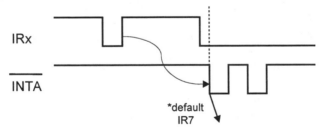

Figure 8.1.1 default IR7 - Signal Timing Requirements

This feature is present on both the Master and Slave 8259 PICs. If the default IR7 condition occurs on a *Master* PIC IRx input, the Master PIC transfers the interrupt type code associated with IR7 during acknowledgment. It follows then that a default IR7 condition detected on the *Slave* PIC should cause the Slave PIC to transfer the interrupt type code associated with its IR7 level, which would appear to the system as an IR15. However, because the Slave PIC cascades to IR2 on the Master PIC, noise or any other condition that might bring about a default IR7 on the Slave PIC, instead causes a default IR7 on the Master PIC as the Master PIC finds no active request on IR2 during the acknowledge cycle.

There is a unique set of conditions though, that if seen on a Slave PIC IRx input, will cause a default IR7 on the Slave PIC which will then appear to the system as a default IR15. For a default IR15 to occur, the Master PIC's IR2 input must be in an *active* high state and the Slave PIC IRx level in an *inactive* state when the falling edge of the first INTA# pulse arrived. A combination of an active IRx input signal, transient noise, the 8259's signal propagation delay, and the untimely arrival of the first INTA# pulse all contribute to the generation of a default IR15. A detailed discussion regarding the generation of default IR15s is presented near the end of the next section.

As a simple matter of probability, nearly all invalid IR input signals (see Figure 8.8.1) that result in a default IR7 or default IR15 will result in a default IR7. At the end of 8.4, a program is given and an experiment suggested that will allow you to generate and observe both default IR7s and default IR15s. To help shorten the terminology, from here on out when referring to both of the independent default IR7s for the Master PIC and Slave PIC within a PC collectively, the term default IR7(IR15) will be used.

The Intel data sheets tell us that the default IR7 is a good way to determine and subsequently reroute an interrupt request inadvertently generated by transient noise. As we will discover in the next section, this is very true. The default IR7 feature is tribute to the 8259's design team. The Intel data sheets recommended that a simple way to handle a default IR7 is to issue an IRET instruction, thereby immediately returning control to the interrupted process. While this may be true in 8259 applications outside the PC environment, when designing an iSR to handle a default IR7(IR15) within a PC environment, a simple IRET instruction will work only when handling a default IR7, never a default IR15. Furthermore, a simple IRET will only handle a default IR7 if the default IR7 is the result of noise (ignorable) and the Master PIC's IR7 is not in use by another iSR (no detection and reroute responsibilities).

Because conditions other than transient noise can generate a default IR7(IR15) as we will see in the next section, and also because IRQs are rarely available in an interrupt-driven design of any complexity, a well thought out approach to handling default IR7(IR15)s is required to arrive at a stable design. The following sections describe common modes found in the PC environment that generate default IR7(IR15)s and then step you through the design of handlers to incorporate into new or current designs, that render default IR7(IR15) requests harmless.

8.2 Noise related default IR7(IR15) interrupts and other false requests

Noise introduced on an 8259 IRx input can cause default IR7 interrupts, default IR15 interrupts, or even what appears to be a valid IRx input request. To fully understand how spurious noise signals can bring about false requests in a PC, the following analysis is offered.

Edge triggered IRx inputs use an edge sense latch to detect a low to high transition on the IRx input. Until the edge sense latch is set, the 8259 IRx input will not recognize an active request which might be pending. Despite its name, the edge sense latch is not actually set by a low to high transition, but rather a low signal level maintained on the IRx input for a minimum of 100nS. Therefore, any noise signal capable of maintaining a low signal level on the edge triggered IRx input for a minimum of 100nS will inadvertently set the IRx input's edge sense latch. Then, with the edge sense latch set and the noise signal strength diminishing, the platform's pull-up resistor returns the IRx input to an active high level and a false request for that 8259's IRx input is generated (not a default IR7).

Level triggered IRx inputs, on the other hand, disable the edge sense latch. In addition, level triggered IRx inputs maintain an inactive high level on the bus to promote interrupt sharing and therefore must invert the bus signal to maintain an inactive low level input signal on the 8259's IRx input. Without the edge sense latch requirement, any valid request or spurious noise is passed directly to the 8259's priority resolver for consideration. Therefore a false request will result anytime the processor samples the INTR line (x 86processors sample the INTR line on instruction boundaries) at the exact moment spurious noise is present and of sufficient strength to pull the IRQx bus line low (INTx# for PCI) and cause an untimely high signal level on the processor's INTR line. Unlike edge triggered IRx inputs, noise on a level triggered IRx input typically results in a default IR7 as the pull-up resistor returns the IRQx bus line to the inactive high level and consequently the 8259's IRx input to an inactive low level before the acknowledge pulses arrive. When the pulses arrive, the 8259 is left with nothing to resolve, resulting in a default IR7.

Further analysis will show that spurious noise is capable of causing false requests as well as default IR7s on both edge and level triggered IRx inputs. To explore all the possible ways noise can wreak havoc on a PC's interrupt process, we begin by reviewing the simplified logic diagram shown in Figure 8.2.1. This diagram is the IRx input portion of the diagram found in the Intel 8259 PIC Datasheet[2]. The two signal lines of the most interest in this analysis are the one entering the negative input and the gate situated just before the interrupt request latch. The interrupt request latch is realized using a transparent D latch. The top input is the control line that determines if the signal appearing on the IRx input is allowed to propagate through the 8259 PIC. If the control line is in a logic 0 state, any signal appearing on the IRx input will appear at the input of the interrupt request latch (transparent D latch) and proceed on into the 8259's interior. If equal to logic 1, the IRx input signal goes unnoticed by the 8259 PIC. By reviewing the logic table in the Figure 8.2.1 call out for the control line, it can be concluded that the only instance in which the IRx signal is kept from propagating through the 8259 PIC, is when the IRx input is edge triggered (LTIM bit set to 0) and the edge sense latch is clear (Q = 0). This makes sense because in edge triggered mode, an edge must be detected first, before the remainder of the IRx input signal is considered.

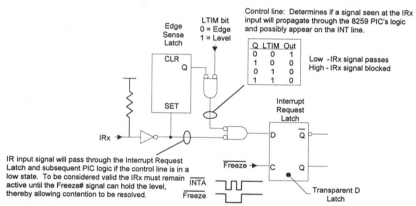

Figure 8.2.1 8259 PIC IR level Front End - Simplified Logic Diagram

From Figure 8.2.1, we see that a low level on the IRx input passes through an inverter (not the IRQx bus line to IRx input inverter) to produce the high level needed to set the edge sense latch. If a noise signal is of sufficient strength and duration to maintain a low signal level on the IRx input for a minimum of 100nS, the inverter shown in Figure 8.2.1 will achieve the positive voltage threshold on the SET pin required to set the edge sense latch. This in turn brings the control line low, which opens the gateway (arms the request latch) and allows the IRx input signal to propagate through the request latch and on to the PIC's priority resolver for consideration. In Figure 8.2.2 we see what happens when a noise signal of sufficient strength appears on an edge triggered IRx input.

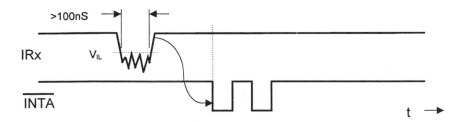

Figure 8.2.2 Noise on Edge Triggered IR Input Generates a False Request

After the noise signal sets the edge sense latch, the pull-up resistor kicks in and pulls the IRx input to an active high level as soon as the noise dissipates. This active request then propagates through the 8259 PIC's interior and appears on the INT line provided the IRx input is not masked. If other requests of higher priority are pending or in service, the false request will remain asserted and quietly wait until the other higher priority requests are processed. Once all higher priority requests are processed, the 8259 will assert the INT line causing the processor to see the active signal on its INTR pin and acknowledge the false request. When the acknowledge pulses arrive, the IRx input that saw the noise signal is found resting in its active high level steady state and the iSR for that IRx level is entered in error. Depending on the device iSR entered, data inconsistencies and other unpredictable system behavior may result. If no iSR was installed behind the IRx level, you could be looking at a system crash. However some PC system BIOS' install EOI and IRET instructions ("Safety Nets") behind the unused IRx inputs at system startup, but don't count on it. This is why unused IRx inputs should always be masked at system startup as a rule.

Edge triggered IRx inputs are also capable of producing default IR7(IR15)s if the right conditions are present. Figure 8.2.3 shows the two conditions under which noise will force default IR7(IR15)s to occur. In Figure 8.2.3(a), the noise arrives at the IRx input after a valid request has been made. The noise is present as the falling edge of the first INTA# pulse arrives, causing a low level to be frozen in the interrupt request latch of the acknowledged IRx level when the Freeze# signal goes active. The result is a default IR7(IR15). In Figure 8.2.3(b), the default IR7(IR15) is produced by two noise signals working together. The first noise signal sets the edge sense latch causing the processor to acknowledge the active high steady state IRx level. The second noise signal causes the IRx input to assume a low logic level as the falling edge of the first INTA# pulse arrives. The result is a default IR7(IR15).

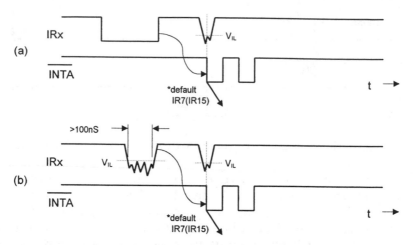

Figure 8.2.3 Noise Conditions on Edge Triggered IRx Inputs that Cause default IR7(IR15)s

When operating in level triggered mode (LTIM bit set to 1), the control line (see Figure 8.2.1) is always in the 0 state, therefore the state of the edge sense latch is of no consequence. The 8259 PIC's front-end circuitry in this case will pass any signal presented to it, whether a valid request or transient noise, on to the PIC's interior where it will appear on the PIC's INT line. Therefore, if no requests of equal or higher priority are pending or in service for a particular IRx level on either the Slave or Master PIC, any valid request or noise signal seen on the IRx input will show up on the processors INTR pin. Figure 8.2.4 shows us what happens next when a level triggered IRx input encounters such a noise signal.

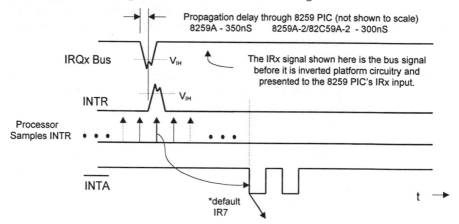

Figure 8.2.4 Noise Condition on Level Triggered IRx Inputs that Generate a default IR7

As covered earlier in section 2.1, level triggered IR lines out on the bus are pumped through an inverter before reaching the actual 8259 IRx inputs. This is done to allow devices to share the IR line using open collectors to ground circuits. The inverter matches up the active low level triggered IRx bus lines with the PIC's active high level requirement. A noise signal seen on the bus will pull the IRx line into a low state. After the platform inverter gets a hold of the noise, we see the inverted signal appear at the IRx input and propagate through to the INTR pin on the processor, as shown in Figure 8.2.4. If the processor samples the INTR line when the noise is present, as in this case, the processor will initiate the acknowledge cycle. When the acknowledge pulses arrive, the level triggered IRx input has returned to its inactive low steady state and a default IR7 results. Even if the noise originated on a Slave PIC IRx input, the chance of a default IR15 being generated is nil. Under the conditions described here, the IR2 line will have returned to an inactive low level long before the falling edge of the first INTA# pulse arrives.

If two noise signals are presented to a level triggered IR input, a possibility exists for the noise to be interpreted as a valid request. This would cause the PC's interrupt process to evoke the device iSR residing behind the IRx input. Again, if no iSR is present you're probably looking at a system crash. If the PC system BIOS had installed Non-Specific EOI and IRET instructions ("Safety Nets") behind the unused IRx inputs at system startup, the system should be able to absorb the false request and remain stable. **Unused IRx inputs should always be masked as a rule.** Figure 8.2.5 demonstrates how noise can create what appears to be a valid request on the level triggered IRx input.

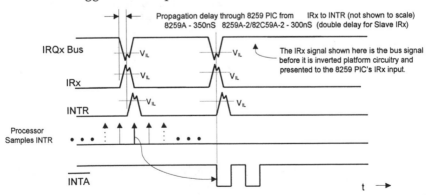

Figure 8.2.5 Noise on Level Triggered IRx Input Generates a False Request

Noise on the IRx input propagates through the 8259 PIC's interior and appears on the INT line (provided the IRx input is not masked, no other requests of equal or higher priority are pending or in service, and interrupts are enabled). The processor then samples the INTR line to find an active request present. A short time later the acknowledge pulses arrive. The second noise signal is present when the falling edge of the first INTA# pulse hits, causing the system to think it has acknowledged a valid request on the IRx level. The second noise signal's presence on the INTR line is of no consequence as the processor stopped recognizing requests at the time it sampled the active high level on the INTR line.

default IR15

After learning the finer points of signal propagation through the 8259 PIC, we can now examine what must take place in order for the rare African albino default IR15 to appear. Provided there exists a clear path through the interrupt processing hardware for our example Slave PIC IRx input, the following sequence of events would cause a default IR15. First, a transient noise signal on either an edge or level triggered IRx input appears and propagates through the Slave and Master PICs. The signal, now present on the INTR line, is sampled by the processor while in the high state, causing the processor to acknowledge the request. Before the falling edge of the first INTA# pulse arrives, a second noise signal occurs. This causes the Master PIC's IR2 input and Slave PIC's IRx input to be at a logical high and logical low level respectively, and a default IR15 is generated. The signal timings that cause a default IR15 on an edge triggered IRx input differ slightly from that of a level triggered IRx input. For that reason, each analysis is discussed here separately.

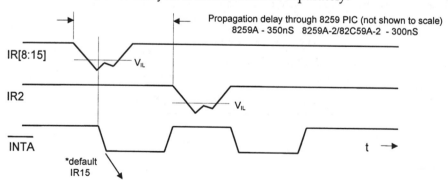

Figure 8.2.6 Noise on Edge Triggered IRx Input that cause a default IR15

The timing diagram given in Figure 8.2.6 describes the condition under which a default IR15 will be produced on an edge triggered Slave PIC IRx input. Just before the falling edge of the first INTA# pulse arrives, a second noise signal appears at the same Slave PIC IRx input. The falling edge of the second noise signal places the Slave PIC IRx input in a low state. As a result of the 8259 PIC's 300nSec propagation delay, the signal does not propagate through the Slave PIC and pull IR2 on the Master PIC low before the falling edge of the first INTA# hits. When the falling edge of the first INTA# pulse arrives, the Freeze# signal shown in Figure 8.2.1 is activated and the IRx inputs on both PICs are frozen in their current states for the remainder of the cycle. IR2 is in the high state and asserts the CAS[0:2] lines. The Slave PIC IRx input responsible for initiating the false request is now in an inactive low state. Next, the Slave PIC recognizes its ID on the CAS[0:2] lines, thereby making it responsible for providing the interrupt vector data to the processor. The Slave PIC then begins to resolve IR[8:15] and finding no pending requests, delivers the vector table data for its IR7 level (IR15) to the processor by default. Voila, a default IR15!

Because the noise signal that causes a default IR15 is inverted before reaching a level triggered IRx input, the analysis is slightly different than for an edge triggered IRx input and proceeds as follows. Referring now to Figure 8.2.7, the second noise signal appears on the Slave PIC IRx input and propagates through the Slave PIC, appearing on the Master PIC's IR2 input just as the falling edge of the first INTA# pulse arrives.

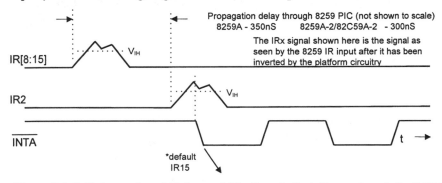

Figure 8.2.7 Noise on Level Triggered IRx Inputs that Generate a default IR15

When the falling edge of the first INTA# pulse arrives, the Freeze# signal described in Figure 8.2.1 is activated and the IRx inputs on both the Slave and Master PICs are frozen in their current states for the remainder of the cycle. IR2 is again in the high state and causes the Master PIC to drive the CAS[0:2] lines with the Slave PIC's ID. The Slave PIC IRx line responsible for initiating the false request is in an inactive low state and as a result of having no pending requests to resolve, drives the data bus with the interrupt vector data for it's IR7 (PC's IR15) by default. The result is a default IR15 generated on a level triggered IRx input.

experiment:

To observe the generation of both default IR7s and default IR15s, the following experiment is offered. Because the PC is open during the experiment and loose wires are involved, it is highly recommended that an expendable or at the very least secondary test PC be used to minimize the impact of any mistakes. **Use caution when performing this experiment and don't electrocute yourself.**

1. Make sure power is *OFF* to your PC and disconnect the power cable.

2. Remove the enclosure cover

3. Attach a *coated* piece of prototyping wire approximately 1 foot long to IRQ11 (refer to appendix A for connector pin-outs). Be sure the wire is connected to IRQ11 only and doesn't come in contact with any other bus pins. To insulate the pin opposite IRQ11 from possible contact, place a piece of paper or some other non conductive material between the pins. Use good judgement.

4. Make sure the free end of the wire is not in contact with any conductive surface.

5. Connect the power cable, turn on the PC and boot up under DOS.

6. Run **default.exe** provided on the IDPCSD diskette in the a:\chpt8 subdirectory.

7. Repeatedly touch the wire to any chassis ground point and observe the counters.

8. Press <ESC> to exit the program.

9. Make sure power is *OFF* before removing the prototyping wire and replacing the enclosure cover.

default.exe maintains counters for all fifteen PC IRQs. Whenever an interrupt request is processed by a particular IRQ, its counter will increment. iSRs installed by default.exe take over IRQ[15, 11, 7, 5] and chain to IRQ([14:12], [10:8], 6, [4:0]). Only IRQ11 and IRQ5 should be used in this experiment and must not conflict with any other devices in the system. The two counters of interest display the number of default IR7 and default IR15 interrupts processed. As the wire attached to IRQ11 is repeatedly touched to ground, the counter for IRQ11 will increment. The erratic signal produced by manually touching the wire to ground will also cause default IR7s and default IR15s to occur. You should observe default IR7s occuring at a rate greater than that of default IR15s for the reasons given in the last section. For a more thorough understanding of default IR7(IR15)s, try attaching the wire to IRQ5. **Do NOT experiment with any IRQs in use by system devices such as IRQ14, IRQ13 or IRQ6.** Without knowing the circuitry on those devices used to generate interrupts, you could permanently damage them. The C source code file **default.c** for **default.exe** is provided on the IDPCSD diskette in the a:\chpt8 subdirectory. iSRs used in **default.exe** to handle the default IR7s and default IR15s are the subject of Section 8.4.

As a final note, the question might come up as to why the designers of the 8259 PIC did not simply capture the rising edge in edge triggered mode and let that stand as the interrupt request? The reason for not doing this is the inevitability of transient noise existing in our physical universe and finding its way to one of the 8259 IRx inputs. If the 8259 PIC let every edge trigger it encountered stand as the request, it would be responsible for firing off interrupt service routines for devices that did not require service. This would throw the entire interrupt-driven system way out of whack and probably wreck something. The default IR7 feature of the 8259 is both necessary and practical for expansion bus applications where IRQx bus lines may be long and un-terminated, making them excellent candidates for hosting transient noise signals.

8.3 Common Conditions That Generate default IR7(IR15) Interrupts

As we just learned in the last section, transient noise appearing on an 8259 PIC's IRx input will result in a default IR7(IR15) if, in the case of an edge triggered IRx input, the noise were to pull the edge triggered IRx input low just as the request was being acknowledged. In the case of level triggered inputs, if the processor samples the INTR line just as the noise seen at the IRx input briefly pulled the INTR line active. Conditions present in an interrupt-driven PC system design and unrelated to noise can result in the generation of default IR7(IR15)s as well. These conditions are related to edge triggered IRx inputs only, like those found on ISA and EISA (if the ELCR is so conFigured) platforms.

The first condition arises as the result of an older interrupt sharing method known as "Shared Pulse". This was an attempt to share interrupts on PC/XT or PC/AT systems using edge triggered IRx inputs. Oddly enough, in some applications this method will work. The problem with it however is twofold. In the rare event two or more mutually exclusive devices have compatible circuitry (usually an open collector to ground) by which they can successfully share an edge triggered IRx input, the request's recognition and subsequent acknowledge cycle is constantly subject to delay. Figure 8.3.1 illustrates this point.

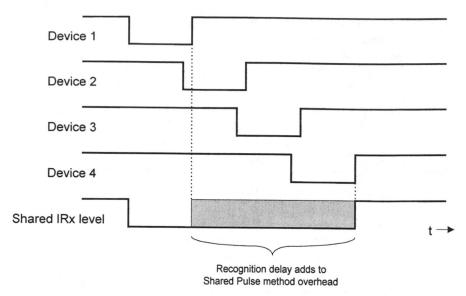

Recognition delay adds to
Shared Pulse method overhead

Figure 8.3.1 Shared Pulse Inherent Request Delay

In this example, device1 sets the edge sense latch and prepares to request service by transitioning low. Before device1 can, and make its active IRx level known to the 8259 PIC, device2 initiates its request by transitioning low. The same scenario repeats for device3 and device4. What we observe on the IRx line is the composite of all the device requests. Where the low to high transition by the device1 IRx line driver should have resulted in the processor recognizing the request, we see the request delayed by devices 2, 3, and 4 instead. Then only after device4 transitions do we see the request being presented to the 8259 PIC. This delay is constantly present and is limiting to any application where speed is an issue. Additionally, only the iSR for device4 in this example will execute when all the other devices clearly requested service. This forces all devices to either have one common iSR capable of polling each device to figure out who needs service and who doesn't or to implement an interrupt chain as discussed in the previous chapter.

The other reason the "Shared Interrupt" method was abandoned, except for the most moderate applications, is that it constantly threatens to produce default IR7(IR15)s. The reason is that interrupt-driven devices request service in an asynchronous manner. The situation like that depicted in Figure 8.3.2 will occur often, producing default IR7(IR15)s.

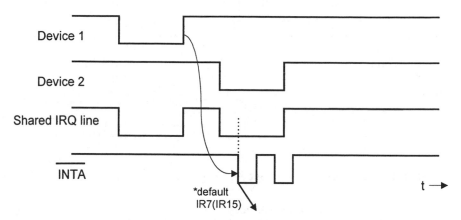

Figure 8.3.2 Shared Pulse Method Generates default IR7(IR15)

In this example, device1 generates a valid request. Before the acknowledge cycle begins, device2 initiates a request by again pulling the IRQ line low. This causes a default IR7(IR15) when the falling edge of the first INTA# pulse arrives only to find no active IRx level present. If the techniques required to handle default IR7(IR15)s are not in place, the Shared Pulse method will cause a constant barrage of misguided IR7(IR15) requests. Additionally, the devices whose requests are involed in a Shared Pulse generated default IR7(IR15) (as device1 and device2 in Figure 8.3.2 are) will go unnoticed by the system during that volley and are forced to reassert their IR signals. Not too many adapter cards I'm aware of come equipted with interrupt request retry circuitry. One way around this would be to program one giant interrupt service routine for all the devices in the system and install it behind IR7 and IR15 to handle the defaults. If that last comment brought a smile to your face, or you're outright laughing, your getting it. These inefficiencies and the outright awkward behavior of the Shared Pulse method is why it is rarely, if ever, used.

There is a much more common situation when designing for edge triggered IRx inputs, other than Shared Pulse, that can generate default IR7(IR15)s. It can occur in any interrupt-driven design using an ISA expansion bus or EISA expansion bus with IRx inputs programmed in edge triggered mode. The default IR7(IR15) in this scenario results when the frequency of the interrupts presented to an IRx input are of such magnitude that the INTA# pulses arrive to acknowledge the request as yet another request is made. Figure 8.3.3 shows how this can happen.

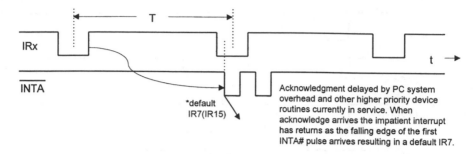

Figure 8.3.3 Interrupt Rate Set Too High Results In default IR7(IR15)

Counter timers and other devices that receive no feedback from their interrupt service routines are the general source for this type of default IR7(IR15). These devices must be forced by design to be sensitive to the overhead imposed by the PC and all devices of higher priority, and should be controlled based on the optimum frequency calculations. The analysis for calculating the optimum frequency to operate a periodic interrupt is given in section 2.3 "Periodic Interrupt-driven Polling".

8.4 Designing iSRs to Detect and Handle default IR7(IR15)s

The only IRx levels that require iSRs capable of handling the default condition are IR7 and IR15. Programming an iSR to detect and handle a default IR7(IR15) takes on many forms. First, if IR7 is unused by any device within the system design, you can program the available IR7 iSR to issue a simple IRET instruction only and be done with it. Likewise, if IR15 is an unused IR level, you can program the iSR to issue an EOI command to the Master PIC followed by an IRET instruction. If however, you intend to use the IR7 and/or IR15 levels in your system design, the simple method just described to handle default IR7(IR15)s won't work. In this case, the following information will be helpful in designing the proper handler. Both the flow chart and source code listings are given for each of the possible iSR designs and source code files in C for each are provided on the IDPCSD diskette in the a:\chpt8 subdirectory.

Before studying how to incorporate a default IR7(IR15) handler into all the possible service routine types described in Chapter 6 and 7, it would probably be a good idea to find out how to discern between a default IR7(IR15) and a valid request when entering the IR7 or IR15 iSR. The 8259 PIC makes this a relatively easy task. When a default IR7(IR15) occurs, the

In-Service bit in the ISR is *not* set when the interrupt is acknowledged. Consequently, if a default IR7 occurs on the Master PIC, bit 7 in the Master PIC's ISR will equal 0. If a default IR7(IR15) occurs on the Slave PIC, bit 7 in the Slave PIC's ISR will equal 0. Any valid request processed by either PIC on the other hand, results in the In-Service bit being set. By reading the PIC's ISR and testing bit 7 at the beginning of the IR7 or IR15's service routine, a determination can be made by the iSR as to whether the request is valid or a default. Testing the ISR's bit 7 works well for *Locked* IR7 and IR15 iSR types, where the iSR maintains the IF switch in the open position (interrupts disabled), thereby preventing any further transient noise from being acknowledge while the Locked IR7 or IR15 iSR is in service.

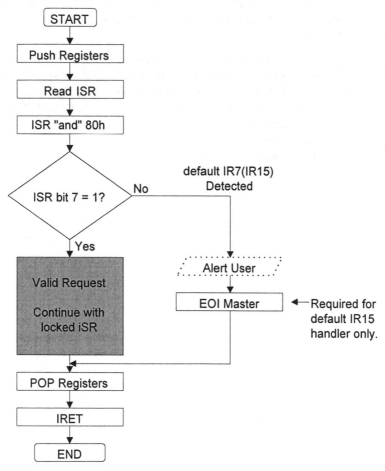

Figure 8.4.1 Generic default IR7(IR15) handler frame for locked iSRs

Figure 8.4.1 shows the flowchart for a generic Locked iSR defaultIR7(IR15) handler frame. The handler first pushes the required registers and reads the ISR of the 8259 PIC responsible for the default IR7(IR15). Next, the handler isolates bit d7 of the ISR by applying a bitwise AND with 80h. If bit 7 in the ISR = 0, a default IR7(IR15) has occurred and the designer may opt to post an "user alert" message to report the anomaly.

If the default IR7 occurred on the slave PIC (default IR15), the default IR15 handler must issue a Non-Specific EOI to the Master PIC before returning to the interrupted process to clear the Master PIC's ISR bit associated with IR2. If this bit was not reset, only IR0 and IR1 would continue to process interrupts. This would mean at the very least, no hard disk or floppy disk access.

In Figures 8.4.2(a) and 8.4.3(a), the generic format of the default IR7(IR15) handler frame for Locked iSRs has been wrapped around standard Master and Slave PIC Locked iSRs to produce the required IR7 iSR and IR15 iSR needed to detect and handle defaultIR7(IR15)s. Regarding Figure 8.4.2, note the Non-Specific EOI command for the Master PIC required to successfully manage the default IR15. All default IR15 handlers require this command to clear the IR2 ISR bit d4.

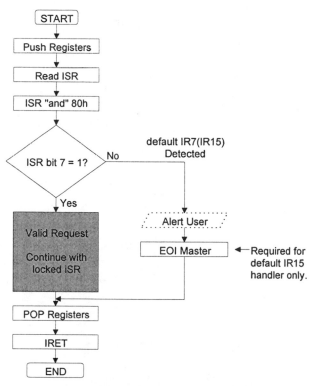

Figure 8.4.2(a) Master PIC locked iSR with default IR7 handler - Flow Chart

```
/* def_Imp.c */

void interrupt LockedMPICiSR(void);

void interrupt LockedMPICiSR()
{
    char mPIC_ISR;

    outportb(0xa0, 0x0b);           /* point to Master PIC ISR                        */
    mPIC_ISR = inportb(0xa0);       /* read Master PIC ISR                            */

    if (mPIC_ISR & 0x80) {          /* IR7 In-Service bit set?                        */

        /* Service Routine Body */
        /* Reset device request if level triggered */

        outportb(0x20, 0x20);       /* No - issue Non-Specific EOI to Master PIC      */

    }
}
```

**Figure 8.4.2(b) Master PIC locked iSR
with default IR7 handler - Source Code**

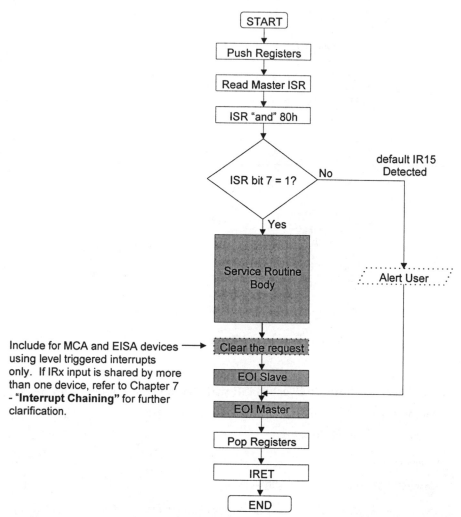

Figure 8.4.3(a) Slave PIC locked iSR with default IR15 handler - Flow Chart

```
/* def_lsp.c */

void interrupt LockedSPICiSR(void);

void interrupt LockedSPICiSR()
{
    char sPIC_ISR;

    outportb(0xa0, 0x0b);              /* point to Slave PIC ISR            */
    sPIC_ISR = inportb(0xa0);          /* read Slave PIC ISR                */

    if (sPIC_ISR & 0x80) {             /* IR15 In-Service bit set?          */

        /* Service Routine Body */
        /* Reset device request if level triggered */

        outportb(0xa0, 0x20);          /* issue Slave PIC Non-Specific EOI  */

    } else {

        outportb(0x20, 0x20);          /* No - issue Non-Specific EOI to Master PIC  */

    }
}
```

Figure 8.4.3(b) Slave PIC locked iSR
with default IR15 handler - Source Code

For *Nested* iSRs using IR7 or IR15, simply testing the In Service bit is not enough to handle a default IR7(IR15). When a nested iSR enables interrupts (closes the IF switch), higher priority IRx levels IR[6:0] or IR[14:8] may encounter an interrupt request signal of insufficient duration or transient noise causing a default IR7(IR15) to occur. A default IR7(IR15) in this instance will cause the Nested iSR for IR7 or IR15 already in service, to be entered twice. If a Nested IR7 or IR15 iSR is entered twice, the second interrupt is necessarily the result of a default IR7(IR15). This condition then needs to be detected before the default IR7(IR15) can be properly handled. Because the ISR bit d7 was set by the valid Nested IR7 or IR15 iSR in service, testing it as we did with the Locked iSRs would now quite incorrectly indicate that the interrupt was valid. So in order to determine when the IR7 or IR15 iSR has been entered a second time, a flag is required within the Nested iSR to indicate when the iSR is in service. Then we can check the flag at the front end of the iSR to determine if the iSR is already in service. If so, the interrupt is a default IR7(IR15) and can be handled accordingly. Figure 8.4.4 gives the generic flowchart for the *Nested* iSR format capable of handling a default IR7(IR15).

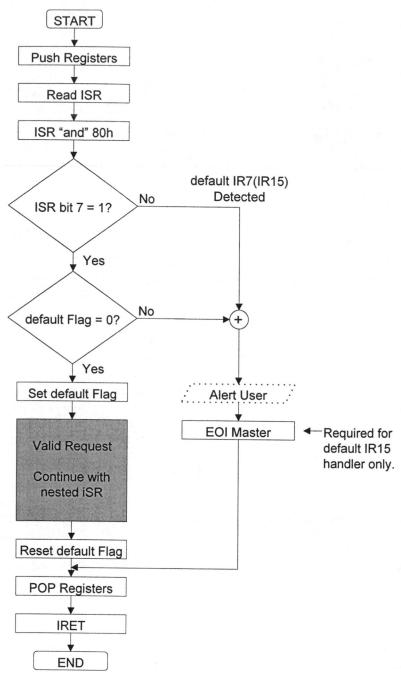

Figure 8.4.4 Generic default IR7(IR15) handler frame for nested iSRs

The ISR bit d7 test is performed first to detect a default IR7(IR15) in the event the IR7 or IR15 iSR was not already in progress. Next, the handler tests to see if the default flag was set by the Nested iSR already in progress. If so, this would indicate that a default IR7(IR15) had caused the iSR to be entered a second time. Both tests are required to detect the default IR7(IR15) for both conditions, and together provide the necessary information needed to determine if the request is valid or if the iSR is being entered as a result of a default IR7(IR15). If both tests indicate that the IR is valid, then the default flag is set, indicating the Nested iSR is currently in progress and the Nested service routine proceeds. After interrupts are disabled for the purpose of issuing the Non-Specific EOI commands and before registers are POP'd, the default flag must be reset. If the default flag is not reset, testing the flag at the front end of the iSR will indicate a default IR7(IR15) every time the iSR is entered, regardless of whether the request is valid or not. The default flag reset is shown correctly located near the end of Figure 8.4.4.

Wrapping the default IR7(IR15)s handler frame for Nested iSRs shown in Figure 8.4.4 around the three basic Nested iSR types is quite different for each. We begin here with the Master PIC Nested iSR format flowcharted in Figure 8.4.5

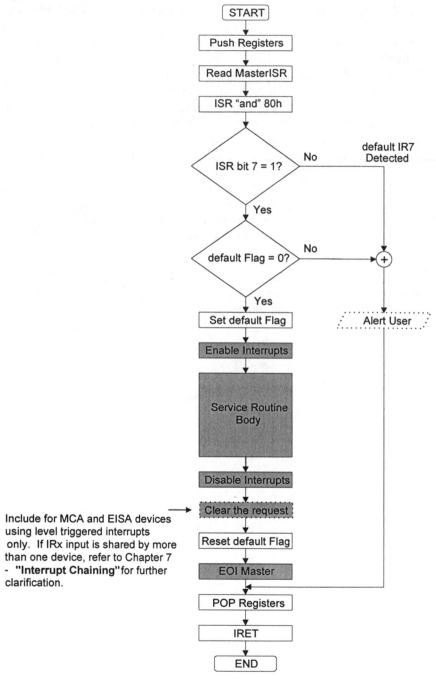

Figure 8.4.5(a) Master PIC Nested iSR with default IR7 handler - Flow Chart

```
/* def_nmp.c */

void interrupt NestedMPICiSR(void);

void interrupt NestedMPICiSR()
{
    static int inService = 0;
    char mPIC_ISR;

    if (mPIC_ISR & 0x80) {          /* IR7 In-Service bit set?     (0=default IR7)    */

        outportb(0x20, 0x0b);       /* point to Master PIC ISR                        */
        mPIC_ISR = inportb(0x20);   /* read Master PIC ISR                            */

        if (inService) {            /* Is iSR already In Service?  (1=default IR7)     */

            /* Post default IR7 message */

        } else {

            inService = 1;          /* set In Service flag                            */

            enable();               /* enable interrupts                              */

            /* Service Routine Body */

            disable();              /* disable interrupts                             */

            /* Reset device request if level triggered */

            inService = 0;          /* reset In-Service flag                          */

            outportb(0x20, 0x20);   /* issue Non-Specific EOI to Master PIC           */
        }

    } else {

        /* Post default IR7 message */
    }
}
```

**Figure 8.4.5(b) Master PIC Nested iSR
with default IR7 handler - Source Code**

The Master PIC Nested iSR fits easily into the generic default IR7 handler frame for Nested iSRs. Before interrupts are enabled, the iSR sets the default flag. Then, after the Service Routine Body completes, interrupts are disabled and the default flag is reset before cleanup commands are issued.

If you remember, the Slave PIC nested ISR lacking the Special Fully Nested Mode SFNM emulation (refer to Chapter 6.4) was an oddball iSR that appears to all IRx levels of higher priority on the Slave PIC as a locked iSR and appears to both IR0 and IR1 on the Master PIC as a nested iSR able to be interrupted. This nested iSR type as it relates to the generation of a default IR15 is considered locked. The reason is, if an IR signal of insufficient duration or noise were to occur on a higher priority Slave PIC IRx level (IR14 - IR8) during the normal execution of the IR15 iSR, the noise would never make it past IR2's open PR switch on the Master PIC. The PR switch remains open because this nested iSR does not include the pseudo SFNM code required to close it. Therefore, this type of nested iSR residing behind IR15 will never be entered a second time. For that reason no tracking by an internal default flag is required. A simple test of the Slave PIC's ISR bit 7 is all that is required with a Slave PIC Nested iSR without SFNM to ensure default IR15s are properly handled. Figure 8.4.6 demonstrates this.

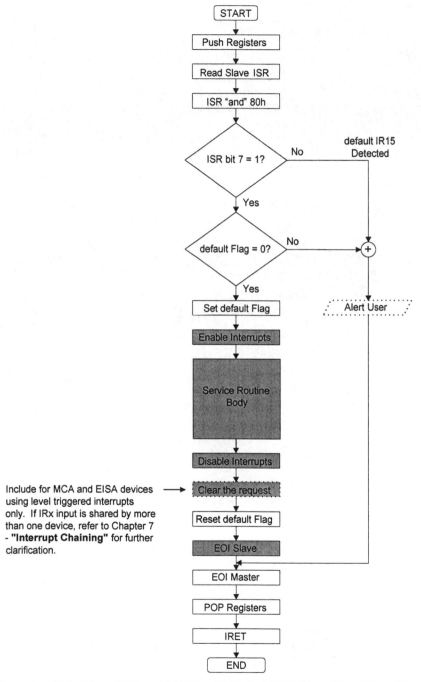

Figure 8.4.6(a) Slave PIC nested iSR with default IR15 handler - Flow Chart

```
/* def_nsp.c */

void interrupt NestedSPICiSR(void);

void interrupt NestedSPICiSR()
{
    static int inService = 0;
    char sPIC_ISR;

    if (sPIC_ISR & 0x80) {              /* IR7 In-Service bit set?      (0=default IR7)      */

        outportb(0xa0, 0x0b);          /* point to Slave PIC ISR                            */
        sPIC_ISR = inportb(0xa0);      /* read Slave PIC ISR                                */

        if (inService) {               /* Is iSR already In Service?   (1=default IR7)      */

            /* Post default IR7 message */
            outportb(0x20, 0x20);      /* issue Non-Specific EOI to Master PIC              */

        } else {

            inService = 1;             /* set In Service flag                               */

            enable();                  /* enable interrupts                                 */

            /* Service Routine Body */

            disable();                 /* disable interrupts                                */

            /* Reset device request if level triggered */

            inService = 0;             /* reset In-Service flag                             */

            outportb(0xa0, 0x20);      /* issue Non-Specific EOI to Slave PIC               */
        }

    } else {

        /* Post default IR7 message */
        outportb(0x20, 0x20);          /* issue Non-Specific EOI to Master PIC              */

    }
}
```

**Figure 8.4.6(b) Slave PIC nested iSR
with default IR15 handler - Source Code**

The Slave PIC nested iSR with SFNM emulation as described in Chapter 6.5 is a Nested iSR type that in addition to the higher priority IR0 and IR1 on the Master PIC, also allows higher priority IRx levels on the Slave PIC to interrupt it. As a result, if a default IR15 were to occur while a valid Slave PIC Nested iSR with SFNM was in service, the valid iSR would be entered a second time. Implementation of the default flag is therefore required, together with the testing of the Slave PIC's ISR bit 7, to make sure the default IR15 is properly handled. Figure 8.4.7 shows how this is accomplished.

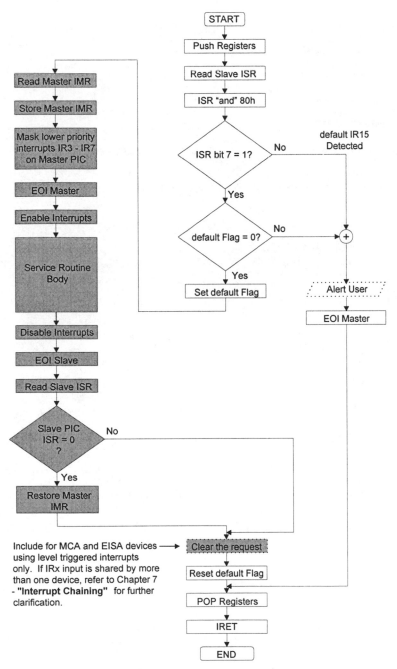

**Figure 8.4.7(a) Slave PIC nested iSR / SFNM
with default IR15 handler Flow Chart**

```
/* def_nsps.c */

void interrupt NestedSPICiSR_sfnm(void);

void interrupt NestedSPICiSR_sfnm()
{
    static int inService = 0;
    char sPIC_ISR;
    int oldMPIC_IMR;

    if (sPIC_ISR & 0x80) {              /* IR7 In-Service bit set?      (0=default IR7)    */

        outportb(0xa0, 0x0b);          /* point to Slave PIC ISR                          */
        sPIC_ISR = inportb(0xa0);      /* read Slave PIC ISR
            */

        if (inService) {               /* Is iSR already In Service?    (1=default IR7)    */

        /* Post default IR7 message */
            outportb(0x20, 0x20);                 /* issue Non-Specific EOI to Master PIC   */

        } else {

            inService = 1;             /* set In Service flag                             */

            oldMPIC_IMR = inportb(0x21);          /* store Master PIC IMR                  */
            outportb(0x21, oldMPIC_IMR | 0xf8);   /* mask IR[3:7]                         */
            outportb(0x20, 0x20);                 /* issue Non-Specific EOI to Master PIC  */

            enable();                  /* enable Interrupts                               */

        /* Service Routine Body */

            disable();                 /* disable Interrupts                              */
            outportb(0xa0, 0x20);      /* issue Non-Specific EOI to Slave PIC             */

            outportb(0xa0, 0x0b);                 /* point to Slave PIC In-Service Register */
            if (inportb(0xa0) == 0) {  /* any lower priority Slave PIC requests still in service? */
                outportb(0x21, oldMPIC_IMR);      /* No - restore Master PIC IMR           */
            }

        /* Reset device request if level trigger */
            inService = 0;             /* enable interrupts                               */

        }

    } else {

        /* Post default IR7 message */
        outportb(0x20, 0x20);                     /* issue Non-Specific EOI to Master PIC  */
    }
}
```

Figure 8.4.7(b) Slave PIC nested iSR / SFNM
with default IR15 handler Source Code

Having demonstrated how all possible iSR types for IR7 and IR15 can be modified to handle default IR7(IR15)s, would it be possible to design a prepackaged TSR that could be chained to either IR7 or IR15 and act as a shield against default IR7(IR15)s? The answer is yes, but only if the IR7 level is available or if in use, all iSRs chained to it are *Locked* iSRs. If a Nested iSR is using the IRx level, the opportunity for a default IR7(IR15) to cause the iSR to be entered twice is present. A Nested iSR that is entered twice can not be handled by a separate default IR7(IR15) handler chained to the IR level. Referring to Figure 8.4.4, the reason is that while the default IR7(IR15) handler could set a default flag for the purpose of detecting a second interrupt, there is no way to reset it as any Nested iSR that hooked the IRx level before the handler would have no knowledge of the default flag. Therefore, from within a stand alone default IR7(IR15) handler, only a test of the ISR bit 7 is possible. If IR7 or IR15 are not in use or if the iSR currently installed behind IR7 or IR15 is Locked, then a stand alone default IR7(IR15) handler installed as a TSR would act as a shield and successfully detect and handle default IR7(IR15)s. On the IDPCSD diskette in the a:\chpt8 subdirectory you will find two such TSRs, one for IR7 (**def_ir7.exe**) and one for IR15 (**def_ir15.exe**). Running either of these executables will install the default IR7 or default IR15 handler link, and under the conditions just mentioned, will eliminate the threat of default IR7(IR15)s crashing the system. Refer to Figure 8.4.8 for the flowchart (a) and partial C source code listing (b) for the default IR7 handler link design. Refer to Figure 8.4.9 for the flowchart (a) and partial C source code listing (b) for the default IR15 handler link design.

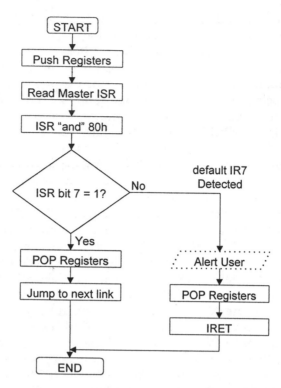

Figure 8.4.8(a) Master PIC default IR7 handler - installable link

```
/* def_ir7.c */

void interrupt newIr7(void);
void interrupt (*oldIr7)(void);

oldIr7 = getvect(0x0f);
setvect(0x0f, newIr7);

void interrupt newIr7()
{
   char mPIC_ISR;

   outportb(0x20, 0x0b);              /* point to Master PIC ISR          */
   mPIC_ISR = inportb(0x20);          /* read Master PIC ISR              */

   if (mPIC_ISR & 0x80) {             /* IR7 In-Service bit set?          */

      oldIr7();                       /* Yes - Far jump to valid IR7 iSR  */

   }
}
```

Figure 8.4.8(b) Master PIC default IR7 handler - installable link

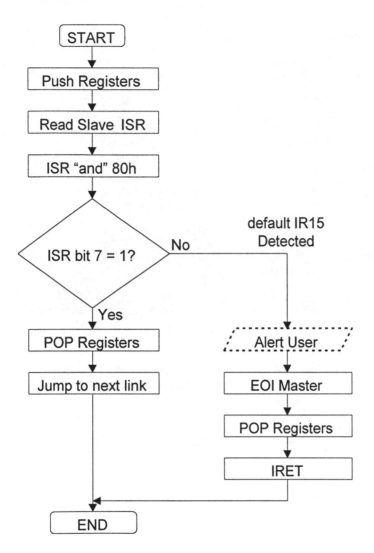

**Figure 8.4.9(a) Slave PIC default IR15 handler
for locked iSRs only - installable link**

```
/* def_ir15.c */

void interrupt newIr15(void);
void interrupt (*oldIr15)(void);

oldIr15 = getvect(0x77);
setvect(0x77, newIr15);

void interrupt newIr15()
{
    char sPIC_ISR;

    outportb(0xa0, 0x0b);          /* point to Slave PIC ISR                      */
    sPIC_ISR = inportb(0xa0);      /* read Slave PIC ISR                          */

    if (sPIC_ISR & 0x80) {         /* IR15 In-Service bit set?                    */

        oldIr15();                 /* Yes - Far jump to valid IR15 iSR            */

    } else {

        outportb(0x20, 0x20);      /* No - issue Non-Specific EOI to Master PIC   */

    }
}
```

**Figure 8.4.9(b) Slave PIC default IR15 handler
for locked iSRs only - installable link**

---

[2] Programmable Interrupt Controller Data Sheet, 8259A-2, Intel Corportation, Order Number 231468-003, Intel Literature Sales - 800-548-4726.

9. PCI Interrupt Processing Hardware

9.1 PCI Interrupt Processing Hardware Overview

PCI supports four sharable interrupt lines known as INTA#, INTB#, INTC#, and INTD#. These lines are routed to level triggered IRQs on the system's interrupt controller. The manner in which the INTx# lines are routed to the IRQs on the systems interrupt controller is up to the system vendor as stated in Section 2.2.6 of the PCI specification revision 2.1.

"The system vendor is free to combine the various INTx# signals from PCI connector(s) in any way to connect them to the interrupt controller. They may be wire-ORed or electronically switched under program control, or any combination thereof. The system designer must insure that *all* INTx# signals from each connector are connected to an input on the interrupt controller."

With this in mind, the INTx# lines may be hard-wired to IRQs on the system's interrupt controller or connected to IRQs through the use of a programmable routing device. The use of a programmable routing device or *"interrupt router"* is preferred because of the flexibility it gives the PCI system's Configuration Manager with regards to IRQ resource assignment.

PC's typically use an interrupt router. The interrupt router is located in the PCI-ISA/EISA/MCA bridge. An illustration of this configuration is shown in Figure 9.1.1. PCI-ISA/EISA/MCA bridge chip data sheets commonly refer to the interrupt router portion of the chip as the *interrupt steering logic*. Along with the interrupt steering logic, the 8259 cores are found in the PCI-ISA/EISA/MCA bridge as well.

195

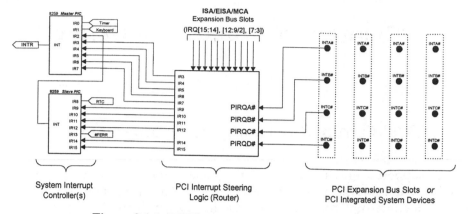

Figure 9.1.1 PCI Interrupt Processing Hardware

The four INTx# system traces arriving from the PCI expansion bus slots are each connected to their respective inputs on the router. These router inputs are referred to as PIRQA#, PIRQB#, PIRQC#, and PIRQD# in both this example and throughout the remainder of this chapter. The number of available IRQs on the system's interrupt controllers for use by any of the four PIRQx# inputs varies from chip set to chip set. Figure 9.1.1 illustrates the 11 IRQs available on Intel's PIIXx series of chipsets.

Each PIRQx# input has an associated PIRQx# route control register on the bridge that allows it to be independently routed to any one of the available IRQs on the system's interrupt controller. More than one PIRQx# input can be routed to the same IRQ. PIRQx# route control registers can also be programmed to disable the PIRQx# input, thereby leaving the PIRQx# input with no IRQ connection. When the PIRQx# route control register is programmed, some chip sets automatically mask the IRQ specified as the target. This fact will become important as we discuss changing the IRQ routes on-the-fly in Chapter 10.

Once a PIRQx# input has been routed to an IRQ, that IRQ must be set to level triggered mode via the Edge/Level Control Registers (See Section 2.6 for details on programming the ELCRs). Additionally, that IRQ is no longer available for use by ISA devices or any other device not designed to share interrupts. Although ISA systems do not require any level triggered IRQs and consequently provide no method of programming them as such, the PCI-ISA bridge does include ELCRs to accommodate PCI's INTx# lines.

* For specific information regarding the programming and general routing options offered by the various PCI-ISA/EISA/MCA bridges, refer to their respective data sheets.

9.2 Single/Multiple Function PCI Device INTx# Pin Binding

9.2.1 Single Function PCI Devices

Single Function PCI devices that require an interrupt must bind the function to the INTA# pin on the edge connector of the add-in board.

9.2.2 Multiple Function PCI Devices

Multi-function PCI devices are defined as any PCI device that incorporates anywhere from of two to eight functions. This definition applies to both PCI add-in cards and integrated PCI devices on the system board. The number of interrupts required by a multi-function device can vary between 0 and 4 (0 indicating no interrupt required). More than one device function is allowed to share an INTx# pin on the PCI device. Interrupt binding on a multi-function PCI device must adhere to the following rules per the PCI Specification ver. 2.1.

1. The number of functions supported by a PCI device (8 max.) and the number of interrupts required to support those functions (4 max.) is at the sole discretion of the designer.

2. Each device function can only bind to one INTx# pin. Therefore, the number of functions a device supports must be equal to (each function connected to a unique INTx# pin) or greater than (group of device functions share the same INTx# pin) the number of interrupts required by that device.

3. If a PCI device requires only one interrupt, all device functions must use INTA#.

4. If a PCI device requires two interrupts, INTA# and INTB# must be used.

5. If a PCI device requires three interrupts, INTA#, INTB#, and INTC# must be used.

6. At least one device function must be bound to each of the INTx# pins used.

The designer is free to bind any PCI device function to any INTx# pin used in any arrangement possible under these general rules. Below are some example configurations to help visualize how the rules above apply.

INTA# ●	INTA# ●●●●●●●●	INTA# ●●●	INTA# ●●●●
INTB#	INTB#	INTB# ●●●	INTB# ●●
INTC#	INTC#	INTC#	INTC# ●
INTD#	INTD#	INTD#	INTD# ●
(single function device)			
INTA# ●●	INTA# ●●	INTA# ●	INTA# ●●
INTB# ●	INTB# ●●	INTB# ●	INTB# ●
INTC# ●●	INTC# ●●	INTC# ●	INTC# ●●
INTD#	INTD# ●●	INTD# ●●●●●	INTD# ●●●
INTA# ●	INTA# ●●	INTA# ●●●●	INTA# ●●●
INTB# ●	INTB# ●	INTB# ●●●●	INTB# ●
INTC# ●	INTC# ●	INTC#	INTC# ●●●●
INTD# ●	INTD# ●●	INTD#	INTD#

● Represents PCI device function   and so on...
bound to INTx# pin

Figure 9.2.1 PCI Device INTx# Pin Binding Examples

Each device function on a PCI device has an associated Interrupt Pin register in its Configuration Space Header Region. The value hard coded in the function's Interrupt Pin register tells the system what INTx# pin on the PCI device that function is bound to. Table 9.2.1 describes the Interrupt Pin values and the INTx# binding they represent. These values allow the system to correctly assign an IRQ resource to the function. For information regarding the PCI IRQ resource assignment process, refer to Section 9.5.

Interrupt Pin register value	Device function is bound to:
00h	No Interrupt Requested
01h	INTA#
02h	INTB#
03h	INTC#
04h	INTD#
05h-FFh	reserved

Table 9.2.1 Interrupt Pin Values

With regards to INTx# binding schemes for multi-function PCI devices where the INTx# pins rely on the router to connect them to IRQ's on the system's interrupt controller (add-in cards), binding to a particular INTx# pin will not guarantee any specific priority assignment when the PCI device is installed in the PC. The system priority assigned to a particular INTx# pin is arbitrary for two reasons. First, the System's Configuration Manager routes the INTx# pins to IRQs on the system's interrupt controller with no guarantees as to what IRQ level and therefore system priority will be assigned a particular INTx# pin. Secondly, INTx# line balancing rotates the INTx# pin assignments between PCI expansion slots and the interrupt router, so depending on what PCI slot you install the device in, the device's INTA# pin may wind up connected to any one of the PIRQB#, PIRQC#, or PIRQD# pins on the router (more on INTx# line balancing in the next section). Device functions that have similar priority should simply be grouped together to use a common INTx# pin. Device drivers associated with these device functions will then hook the same IRQ making all the associated interrupt service routines part of the same interrupt chain. From within the interrupt chain, assigning relative priority among the competing functions is possible (see Chapter 7 for details on interrupt chaining).

9.3 INTx# Line Balancing

As discovered in the last section, the PCI Specification 2.1 requires that all single function PCI devices requiring an interrupt use INTA#. In addition, multi-function PCI devices must assign interrupt usage starting with INTA#. Because of this, on platforms where all the INTx# bus lines are wired pin for pin as illustrated in Figure 9.3.1(a), a *majority* of the system's PCI device function's will necessarily use the INTA# pin and consequently the same IRQ. The interrupt chain resulting when a majority of PCI device drivers hook the same IRQ will be excessive relative to other interrupt chains associated with IRQ's assigned to INTB#, INTC#, and INTD#. To illustrate, refer to the example given in Figure 9.3.2(a) where each INT[D:A]# pin on the bus is connected through the interrupt router to a unique IRQ on the systems interrupt controller. The interrupt latency imposed by this model (a) for device funtion's using INTA# and represented by companion links at or near the end of the resulting interrupt chain on IRQ9 is both unnecessary and unacceptable. Remember, the shorter the chains, the shorter the interrupt latency seen by devices represented by links in those chains. (See Chapter 7 for details).

To correct this imbalance, it is recommended in section 2.2.6 of the PCI specification 2.1 that each of the four INTx# pins for all PCI devices, be connected via system board traces to the PIRQx# inputs on the interrupt router in such a way as to distribute the interrupts evenly over those PIRQx# inputs on the interrupt router. This is referred to as INTx# Line Balancing and an example of this technique is shown in Figure 9.3.1(b).

Using the same system example given in Figure 9.3.2(a) but this time with devices 1 - 4 integrated into the balanced PCI bus slots given in Figure 9.3.1(b), we see in Figure 9.3.2(b) that the interrupt chains are now balanced as well over all four IRQs on the systems interrupt controller.

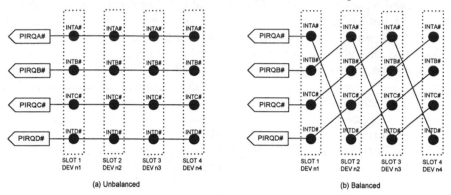

Figure 9.3.1 INTx# Line Balancing Example

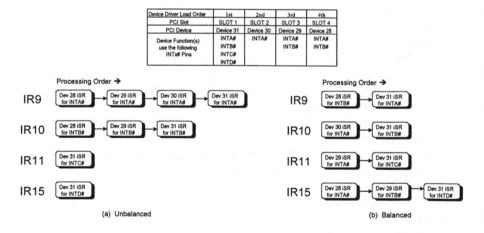

Figure 9.3.2 INTx# Line Balancing's effect on Interrupt Chains

Industry standards regarding INTx# Line Balancing have been developed to ensure consistency over all compliant system boards. Because the placement of a PCI device in a particular slot results in that device being mapped to a particular IRx level on the system's interrupt controller, the relative priority that device will carry in the system's interrupt structure is also determined by the slot the device occupies. If no standard existed, a proven system ported slot for slot onto a different system board

200

could now yield an errant system due to the dramatic change in the interrupt structure. The PCI Industrial Computer Manufacturers Group (PICMG) has defined a widely accepted standard for both active and passive PCI systems. The PICMG PCI-ISA 2.0 specification comliant information with respect to INTx# Line Balancing is presented in Appendix 12.3. *Compact* PCI which uses a Eurocard formfactor similar to VME has a defined PICMG standard as well. For *Compact* PCI INTx# Line Balancing information refer to the PICMG standard developed for *Compact* PCI (www.picmg.com). PCI systems using the PC/104 modular form factor have adopted a standard developed by the PC/104 Consortium known as PC104-*Plus*. PC104-*Plus* Version 1.0 compliant information regarding INTx# Line Balancing requirements are given in Appendix 12.4.

9.4 Routing Tables

As a result of INTx# Line Balancing, if the INTx# pin used by a device function and specified in the device function's Interrupt Pin register is physically wired to a different PIRQx# pin on the interrupt router than the PIRQx# pin the system believes the INTx# pin is connected to, how does the PCI Configuration Manager assign the correct IRQ to the device function? This question would apply to any PCI devices using slots 2, 3, or 4 in Figure 9.3.1(b). The answer is found in the PCI's IRQ *Routing Tables* which provide the information required by the *System Resource Manager* to translate between the INTx# pin the device function is using and the PIRQx# pin that INTx# pin is connected to on the router. This allows the PCI Configuration Manager to correctly identify the IRQ resource assigned to the device function and program the PCI device accordingly.

An interrupt routing table is required for every integrated PCI device and PCI expansion slot in a PCI system.

The routing tables are stored in non-volatile memory on the PC system board. Table 9.4.1 illustrates the layout of an IRQ routing table. Each table is 16 bytes in length and contains the following information:

PCI Bus Number
• PCI bus the integrated PCI device or PCI slot resides on.

PCI Device Number
• The device number encoded in the upper 5 bits of this field.
  (ex: field value = F8h, 11111000b → actual device number = 1Fh or 31d

Link Values for INTA#, INTB#, INTC#, and INTD#
• link value of 00h indicates no interrupt resource is required.

- non-zero link value indicates device function requires an IRQ (link values are covered in detail below)

IRQ bit maps for INTA#, INTB#, INTC#, and INTD#
- Specifies the IRQ routing options for a particular PCI INTx# line.
- Integrated PCI devices may request a specific IRQ not associated with the router (IRQ bit maps are covered in detail below)

Slot Number
- For PCI expansion slots on the system board, this field holds the silk screen or solder mask slot number reference as it appears on the system board. This one-to-one correspondence helps identify the physical slot on the system board that the routing options specified in the table are for. Slot numbering and slot number field values are vendor specific.
- A value of zero indicates the table is assigned to an integrated PCI device.

Offset	Description
0	PCI Bus Number
1	PCI Device Number
2	Link Value - INTA#
3	IRx Bit-Map - INTA#
5	Link Value - INTB#
6	IRx Bit-Map - INTB#
8	Link Value - INTC#
9	IRx Bit-Map - INTC#
11	Link Value - INTD#
12	IRx Bit-Map - INTD#
14	Slot Number
15	Reserved

Table 9.4.1 IRQ Routing Table Layout

9.4.1 Link Values

Link values indicate which INTx# pins located on both integrated PCI devices and PCI expansion slots are wire OR'd together. In addition, link values specify the PIRQx# pin on the interrupt router that all INTx# pins sharing a common link value are connected to. It is the link values found within routing tables that the PCI System Resource Manager uses to translate between INTx# pin and PIRQx# router input pin and correctly program PCI devices with their IRQ routing assignments.

As described in Table 9.4.2, a link value of 00h indicates the INTx# pin on the integrated PCI device or PCI expansion slot in not connected to either a PIRQx# pin on the router or directly to an IRQ on the system's interrupt controller.

Link Value	Description
00h	PCI Device function requires no interrupt resource
01h	PIRQA# interrupt router input
02h	PIRQB# interrupt router input
03h	PIRQC# interrupt router input
04h	PIRQD# interrupt router input
05h-FFh	PCI Device function uses a non-PCI interrupt resource

Table 9.4.2 Link Value Descriptions

As we saw in Figure 9.3.1(b), interrupt line balancing alters the one-to-one correspondence between PCI bus connector's INTx# pin and the PIRQx# input on the router that particular IRQx# line is connected to. The link value given in the PCI bus slot's routing table for a particular INTx# pin indicates which PIRQx# pin on the router the INTx# pin is physically connected to. To demonstrate how routing tables are constructed, an example is given in Figure 9.4.1 showing the routing tables with the appropriate link value entries for four PCI slots using line balancing.

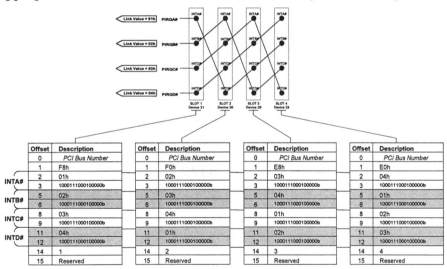

Figure 9.4.1 Routing Table Example

The four link values assigned to the four PIRQx# pins on the router are found primarily in IRQ routing tables associated with PCI expansion slots, not integrated PCI devices. This is because integrated PCI devices generally do not use the interrupt router for IRQ assignment but rather, use IRQs on the system's interrupt controller not made available to PCI. All non-zero link values are arbitrary and vary among chipset manufacturers.

Non-zero link values other than those representing the router's PIRQx# pins, indicate a request for a specific IRQ resource by a PCI device function other than those set aside for use by the router. Typically these link values are used by integrated PCI devices hard-wired to a specific IRQ. For example, the routing table described in Table 9.4.3 for the on-board PCI hard drive controller shows how an integrated PCI device uses a link value and it's corresponding IRQ bit map to request a specific IRQ resource. In this example, the link value FEh indicates that the PCI hard drive controller is requesting a specific IRQ not assigned to the router, and the IRQ bit map associated with link value FEh, indicates the device function is specifically requesting IRQ14. The PCI Configuration Manager in this instance would always program the device function's Interrupt Line register with the value for IRQ14 (see Table 9.5.2 for Interrupt Line register values and their corresponding IRQs).

Offset	Description
0	*PCI Bus Number*
1	*Device Number*
2	FEh
3	0100000000000000b
5	00h
6	0000000000000000b
8	00h
9	0000000000000000b
11	00h
12	0000000000000000b
14	00h
15	Reserved

Table 9.4.3 Integrated PCI Device IRQ Routing Table Example

Other interpretations of the link values being reviewed by PnP Operating System vendors are possible as well. For example, the link value might point to the location in the device's configuration header indicating the correct link value. Additionally, the link value could point to an I/O location holding the correct link value and so on...

9.4.2 IRQ Bit Map

For every non-zero link value in a PCI system there is one unique IRQ bit map associated with that link value. All link values specified in the routing tables that are equal must all share the same IRQ bit map value.

IR15   IR0

IRQ bit map → 1 0 0 0 1 1 1 0 0 0 1 0 0 0 0 0

0 - No routing to this IRQ possible

1 - Routing to this IRQ is possible

IRQ bit maps that specify more than one available IRQ (more than one bit = 1) indicate that some programmable routing device exists between the INTx# pin on the integrated PCI device or the PCI expansion slot and the system's interrupt controller. To illustrate, in a PC you will typically find that the IRQ bit maps associated with each of the four link values representing PIRQA#, PIRQB#, PIRQC#, and PIRQD# on the router are first of all equal, but more importantly provide a number of possible IRQs for the router to use. Hopefully enough IRQs are made available to route each of the four PIRQx# inputs to its own IRQ. A common PC IRQ bit map value is 1000111000100000b, representing IRQ[15, 11:9, 5].

All other non-zero IRQ bit maps are found in routing tables associated with integrated PCI device functions that use a specific IRQ not generally associated with any programmable routing device.

9.5 PnP Device Interrupt Line Configuration

The PCI Device Configuration Manager is responsible for assigning an IRQ resouce on the system interrupt controllers to any PCI device requesting an interrupt. The two PCI device registers involved in this process are located at offset 3Bh and 3Ch respectively in the device's Configuration Space Header Region shown in Figure 9.5.1. The *Interrupt Pin* register is hard coded to reflect the INTx# pin the device function is physically connected to. The *Interrupt Line* register is programmed by the PCI Configuration Manager to let any interested parties, such as the device driver, know what IRQ on the system's interrupt controller the device function is mapped to. This allows the device driver to hook the correct IRQ. The configuration process begins as follows:

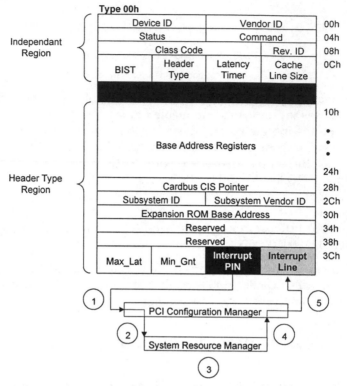

Figure 9.5.1 Device Configuration Space Header Region

1. PCI Configuration Manager reads the Interrupt Pin register located in the device's Configuration Space Header Region. If a 00h is returned, the PCI device function does not use an interrupt line. If however, a value between 01h and 04h is returned, the device function does use an interrupt and the specific INTx# pin hard-wired to the function is described as follows:

Interrupt Pin register value	Device function is bound to:
00h	No Interrupt Requested
01h	INTA#
02h	INTB#
03h	INTC#
04h	INTD#
05h-FFh	reserved

Table 9.5.1 Interrupt Pin Values

2. Once the PCI Configuration Manager has obtained the value of the Interrupt Pin register, it calls the System Resource Manager to assign the actual 8259 IRQ to the device function. In addition to the Interrupt Pin register contents, the Bus, Device, and Function numbers are passed to the System Resource Manager as well.

3. The PCI Interrupt Steering Logic (Router) is programmed by the System Resource Manager during the assignment phase of the Interrupt Line. The algorithm responsible for assigning each of the PCI's four INTx# lines to IRQ on the interrupt controller is very much platform specific. Some aspects of this algorithm however are common across all platforms. At the very least, the IRQ link value and bit map found in the routing tables, along with any user defined CMOS setup parameters regarding IRQ availability must be considered before IRQ assignments are defined.

4. The System Resource Manager returns a value to the PCI Configuration Manager indicating which one of the interrupt controller's IRQs has been assigned to the device function. If no interrupt was requested by the device, the System Resource Manager returns FFh, indicating the device's interrupt line is not connected to the system's interrupt controller. The IRQ represented by returned value is given in Table 9.5.2.

Return Value	IRQ Mapped To:	Return Value	IRQ Mapped To:
00h	IR0	08h	IR8
01h	IR1	09h	IR9
02h	IR2	0Ah	IR10
03h	IR3	0Bh	IR11
04h	IR4	0Ch	IR12
05h	IR5	0Dh	IR13
06h	IR6	0Eh	IR14
07h	IR7	0Fh	IR15
		FFh	No Route

Table 9.5.2 IRQ Route Return Values

5. The IRQ is then written to the Interrupt Line register in the device's Configuration Space Header Region by the PCI Configuration Manager, completing the assignment phase for this device function.

9.6 PCI Device Drivers

There are two distinct differences between ISA/EISA/MCA based device drivers and PCI device drivers. First, the PCI device driver must use the system resources assigned to its companion PCI device by the System BIOS (non-PnP) or the Operating System's Device Class Configuration Manager

(PnP). The PCI device driver obtains the resource assignments by reading the device's Configuration Space Header Region when loading, then uses those resources assigned by the system to access and service its companion device. In comparison, Legacy devices required the system integrator to assign system resources such as Memory base address, I/O base address, DMA, and IRQ usage through on-board jumpers. This effectively hard-wires the resources at the device. Legacy device drivers then typically use command line switches or a configuration utility as a means of porting the resource assignments to the Legacy device driver. The system integrator was then responsible for matching up the device's on board jumper settings with the device driver's software switches. By using resources assigned by the system, PCI device drivers remove the system integrator and any chance of error from the resource assignment phase of system integration.

Next, PCI device drivers must be designed to share interrupts as discussed in detail in Chapter 7 (Interrupt Chaining - Link Design). Since the system decides on IRQ assignments for all PCI devices in the system, it is entirely possible that the system will assign the same IRQ to more than one PCI device. In fact, on some PC platforms, available IRQs for use by PCI devices can be defined through CMOS setup. If the system integrator decides to make only one IRQ available to PCI, all PCI devices requiring an interrupt will share the same IRQ.

Flushing the Posted Write Buffers

Per the revision 2.1 specification, all posted-write buffers between the PCI device and host processor must be flushed to memory before interrupts are delivered to the host processor. If not, data inconsistency could result. Posted write buffers are flushed by one of the following three methods:

1. The system hardware.
2. The device requesting service, if the device has bus master capability.
3. The device's interrupt service routine.

Posted write buffers are flushed by a device with bus master capability when the device reads from the last memory address it wrote to just prior to requesting service. The device's interrupt service routine flushes posted write buffers by reading from any location on the requesting device. All bridges between the requesting device and the host processor will flush their posted write buffers as a result of either action.

It is the responsibility of the device's interrupt service routine to flush the posted write buffers when it is not known if the system hardware or the device itself performs this function. However, interrupt service routines designed to share interrupts must read an interrupt request pending status bit on the device before executing the service routine body to first determine if its companion device was responsible for the request. PCI device drivers by design, therefore, effectively handle the responsibility of flushing posted write buffers.

10. PCI Interrupt Handling

Optimizing Performance

10.1 Performance Objectives

The PCI system's Configuration Manager is responsible for assigning system resources to all PCI devices in a system. Unfortunately, the assignment of interrupt resources does not take into account the relative priority a particular device function carries within that system. The system designer is the only one who can determine that. As a result, high priority device functions are assigned low priority IRQs on the system's interrupt controller and low priority device functions are assigned to high priority IRQs. This is undesirable for two important reasons. First, overall performance is degraded by the increased latency times seen by devices with higher throughput demands being preempted by devices with lower throughput demands. Secondly, critical system events such as error conditions, that require the immediate intervention of the user or the embedded control system, could further aggravate the situation if response to these events is delayed. By putting a little thought into add-in card placement and device driver load order, together with a one time static router modification at system startup, interrupt latencies can be reduced, resulting in a higher performance PCI system.

The primary goal of this chapter is to discuss the techniques that can minimize the effects of latency by organizing the devices across the PC's priority structure such that the highest priority device uses the highest priority IRQ and the lowest priority device uses the lowest priority IRQ. For a discussion on determining a device's relative system priority, refer to section 11.2 "Device Priority Assignment". The PC's priority structure for the 15 system IRQs is given in Figure 10.1.1.

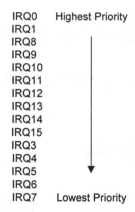

IRQ0	Highest Priority
IRQ1	
IRQ8	
IRQ9	
IRQ10	
IRQ11	
IRQ12	
IRQ13	
IRQ14	
IRQ15	
IRQ3	
IRQ4	
IRQ5	
IRQ6	
IRQ7	Lowest Priority

Figure 10.1.1 PC's IRQ Priority Structure

If a particular IRQ is being shared by several devices, the highest priority device should have its device driver load last and the lowest priority device should load its device driver first to maintain the correct priority order within the interrupt chain. Refer to Chapter 7 for detailed information on interrupt chaining.

If several devices all share similar or identical throughput demands, then the service imbalance imposed by the preemption of devices using lower priority IRQs by devices using higher priority IRQs diminishes real-time system performance. Software techniques that equalize priority among a plurality of devices like those discussed in 7.3 ("Equal Priority Chains") and 7.4 ("IPC Link Rotation") work well when the devices are able to share the same IRQ. If, however, all PCI device functions requiring balanced priority are unable to share the same IRQ, or so many functions assigned to the same IRQ result in long interrupt chains, producing unacceptable latencies, the technique of rotating IRQ assignments via the PCI interrupt router as described in Section 11.4 will prove valuable.

10.2 Organizing PCI Devices in the PCI Interrupt Structure

Before any decisions regarding the organization of PCI devices in the PCI system's interrupt structure can be made, two questions must be answered. First, how are the INTx# pins for each PCI bus connector and integrated PCI device routed via system board traces to either the PIRQx# inputs on an interrupt router or directly to the IRQs on the system's interrupt controller? And second, how does the routing algorithm in the system's

Configuration Manager assign the PIRQx# inputs on the router to IRQs on the system's interrupt controller? Once this information is known, PCI devices can be installed such that the relative priority each device is assigned by the designer is preserved when the Configuration Manager programs the interrupt router and assigns the IRQ resources to the device. Gathering the information needed to map the platforms interrupt structure and piece together the routing algorithm's operation is best accomplished through the use of *PCI System BIOS Software Extensions* described next.

PCI System BIOS Software Extensions are a set of routines that give anyone designing with a PCI system access to the PCI hardware. For example, these functions can be used to retrieve all PCI system routing tables, program the interrupt router, or read from or write to the PCI device configuration space. A complete list of the PCI BIOS software functions is given in Table 10.2.1. Functions highlighted in Figure 10.2.1 are relevant to this text and complete descriptions for them can be found in Appendix 12.5. For a complete description of all PCI BIOS functions listed in Table 10.2.1, including 32 bit calling conventions, refer to "PCI Hardware and Software Architecture and Design" by Solari/Willse. To determine if a system BIOS supports PCI BIOS functions, use the *Get PCI BIOS Present Status* function. This function returns status indicating whether the services exist or not.

PCI Function	AH = B1h
	AL
Get PCI BIOS Present Status	01h
Find a PCI Device	02h
Find a PCI Class Code	03h
Generate A PCI Special Cycle	06h
Read a PCI Configuration Byte	08h
Read a PCI Configuration Word	09h
Read a PCI Configuration DWord	0Ah
Write a PCI Configuration Byte	0Bh
Write a PCI Configuration Word	0Ch
Write a PCI Configuration DWord	0Dh
Get PCI Interrupt Routing Options	0Eh
Set PCI Hardware Interrupt	0Fh

See Appendix 12.5 for details on highlighted functions

Table 10.2.1 PCI System BIOS Software Extensions

The *Get PCI Interrupt Routing Options* function is useful in determining how the INTx# system board traces are routed to PIRQx# inputs on the router for all PCI bus slots as a complete set of PCI system IRQ routing tables is returned by the function. With a complete set of the system's routing tables in hand, it is possible to integrate add-in PCI devices into the system such that device functions with like priority are physically connected to the same PIRQx# input on the interrupt router and thereby use the same IRQ. The *Get PCI Interrupt Routing Options* function is not required to determine the platform's interrupt structure if the system is PICMG or PC/104-*Plus* compliant. Refer to Appendix 12.3 for PICMG PCI-ISA Revision 2.0 compliant INTx# bindings or Appendix 12.4 for the PC/104 *Plus* revision 1.0 compliant INTx# bindings. For *Compact*PCI bindings please refer to the PICMG *Compact*PCI standard (www.picmg.com).

Discovering how the System Resource Manager's interrupt routing algorithm assigns IRQs to the PIRQx# inputs on the router during startup is a two step process. First, the Interrupt Line register for a known PCI device function is read to determine the IRQ assigned to the device function by the System Resource Manager. To read a PCI device function's Interrupt Line register using the *Read a PCI Configuration Register Byte* function described in Appendix 12.5 requires knowledge of the PCI device's Bus Number and Device Number. Knowing the PCI bus slot the device occupies, you can look up the PCI device's Bus/Device Number in the IRQ routing table.

Knowing the INTx# pin the PCI device function is using (which can be read from the device function's Interrupt Pin register), along with the Link Value associated with that INTx# pin (given in the IRQ routing table for the PCI slot the device occupies), and the IRQ assigned to the device function, you can quickly determine the System Resource Manager assigns IRQs to each of the four Link Values (PIRQx# inputs) at startup. Another way to ascertain the interrupt router assignments would be to read each of the four PIRQx# route control registers directly from within the interrupt router itself. However, this requires platform specific knowledge on how to access the Legacy bridge registers.

Having the knowledge of which IRQs the System Resource Manager assigns to each of the four PIRQx# inputs on the interrupt router, and the Link Values (given in the IRQ routing tables) associated with each add-in bus slot, allows us to assign a particular PCI device function a specific priority through the physical placement of the device in a specific PCI bus slot. The physical placement of PCI devices alone does not always allow the relative device priorities to be preserved within the PCI's interrupt structure, no matter what combination of add-in card to bus slot is attempted. In this instance, a *static router modification* can be used to force the interrupt structure to more closely resemble the designer's relative priority structure. A static router modification is when, after the Configuration Manager has completed assigning IRQs to all PCI device functions, the interrupt router is programmed with the custom IRQ routes required. A static router modification is part of the example coming up.

Once the system's device placement and subsequent interrupt priority structure is set for a particular design, any addition, subtraction, or change in available IRQs will require the routing algorithm to take this new information into account and change the routing assignments to compensate. Therefore, the knowledge of how the algorithm will assign interrupts and the arrangements made by the system designer to optimize the interrupt structure are only valid if the available IRQs both in number and level remain consistent. If a change is required, the interrupt structure will need to be re-evaluated.

To better understand the methods described so far, the following real world example is presented. Assume there are 6 PCI devices we wish to integrate into a system with 6 PCI bus slots. All devices are single function and require an interrupt. It has been determined based on functionality, what the relative priority of each device should be with respect to each other in the system. This priority order is given in Table 10.2.2. The device numbers shown are chosen arbitrarily, it just happens to be the order in which the devices fell out of the antistatic bubble wrap and onto the carpet.

	Device 1	Device 2	Device 3	Device 4	Device 5	Device 6
INTA#	1	3	1	4	4	2
INTB#	-	-	-	-	-	-
INTC#	-	-	-	-	-	-
INTD#	-	-	-	-	-	-

1 - Highest Priority
4 - Lowest Priority

Table 10.2.2 Relative Priority Assignment (example)

Using the *Get PCI Interrupt Routing Options* function, we ascertain the link values associated with the INTx# pins for all six PCI bus slots. The results can be seen in Figure 10.2.1.

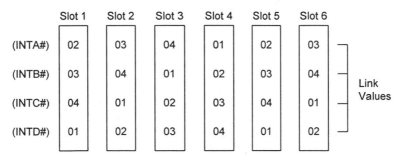

	Slot 1	Slot 2	Slot 3	Slot 4	Slot 5	Slot 6	
(INTA#)	02	03	04	01	02	03	
(INTB#)	03	04	01	02	03	04	Link
(INTC#)	04	01	02	03	04	01	Values
(INTD#)	01	02	03	04	01	02	

Figure 10.2.1 PCI Bus Slot INTx# Routing (example)

Next, to determine how the system's System Resource Manager assigns IRQ's to each of the four PIRQx# inputs, we have installed four of the PCI devices in four successive PCI bus slots such that each of the four PIRQx# inputs are in use by at least one device. After the system has started up, we then read the contents of the Interrupt Line register using the *Read a PCI Configuration Byte* function for each of the four PCI device functions. From the IRQ routes indicated in each of those registers, it is determined that the System Resource Manager assigns IRQs to the PIRQx# inputs as described in Table 10.2.3.

Router Input (Link Value)	IRQ Route (Priority)
PIRQA# (01)	IRQ10 (1)
PIRQB# (02)	IRQ11 (2)
PIRQC# (03)	IRQ15 (3)
PIRQD# (04)	IRQ5 (4)

1 - Highest Priority
4 - Lowest Priority

Table 10.2.3 Router Assignments (example)

Now that the Platform's Interrupt Structure is known, we can begin the process of determining which PCI bus slots each of our 6 PCI devices should occupy. To start we notice in Table 10.2.2 that devices 1 and 3 as well as devices 4 and 5 have the same relative priority assignments, 1 and 4 respectively. If, at all possible, we want to group like priority device functions so that they use the same IRQ. This is done by placing PCI devices in PCI bus slots such that like priority device functions use INTx# pins with the same link value assignments. In our example, where all 6 PCI devices are single function and therefore all use INTA#, grouping like priority devices is accomplished by placing the devices in PCI bus slots that have identical link value assignments for INTA# - INTD#.

As shown in Figure 10.2.1, slots 1 and 5 have the same link value assignments as well as slots 2 and 6. To group devices 1 and 3, we will assign them to slots 1 and 5 respectively as shown in Table 10.2.4 and devices 4 and 5 will be assigned slots 2 and 6. Device 2 is assigned slot 3 and device 6 slot 4.

	Device 1	Device 2	Device 3	Device 4	Device 5	Device 6
INTA#	1	3	1	4	4	2
INTB#	-	-	-	-	-	-
INTC#	-	-	-	-	-	-
INTD#	-	-	-	-	-	-
Slot Assignment	Slot 1	Slot 3	Slot 5	Slot 2	Slot 6	Slot 4

1 - Highest Priority
4 - Lowest Priority

Table 10.2.4 PCI Device Slot Assignments (example)

By reviewing the original decisions regarding the desired order of devices based on relative priority as shown in 10.2.2 and again in 10.2.4, we find the desired order to be device 1, 3, 6, 2, 4, 5. The order of devices based on priority resulting from the slot assignments just made is 6, 1, 3, 4, 5, 2 as described in Table 10.2.5. Immediately it is clear that the current order does not resemble the order we are trying to achieve. However, because we bound (grouped) the device functions of like priority to the same PIRQx# inputs, a simple static router modification is all that's required to realize the desired device order within the system's interrupt structure.

Devices	Router Input (Link Value)	IRQ Route (Relative Priority)
6	PIRQA# (01)	IRQ10 (1)
1, 3	PIRQB# (02)	IRQ11 (2)
4, 5	PIRQC# (03)	IRQ15 (3)
2	PIRQD# (04)	IRQ5 (4)

1 - Highest Priority
4 - Lowest Priority

Table 10.2.5 Interrupt Structure After Slot Assignments (example)

Table 10.2.6 shows how the devices are ordered correctly (1, 3, 6, 2, 4, then 5) after the interrupt router is reprogrammed (static router modification).

Devices	Router Input (Link Value)	IRQ Router (Relative Priority)
1,3	PIRQB# (02)	IRQ10 (1)
6	PIRQA# (01)	IRQ11 (2)
2	PIRQD# (04)	IRQ15 (3)
4,5	PIRQC# (03)	IRQ5 (4)

Table 10.2.6 Interrupt Structure After Static Router Modification (example)

Summary

Correctly ordering the PCI devices by priority in the system's interrupt structure optimizes overall system performance as higher priority devices see reduced latency times relative to the priority each carries. The example just given shows how to order the devices by priority, and the following list summarizes the steps recommended to accomplish this task.

1. Map the system board traces to determine which INTx# pins are wired-ORed together. Routing tables provide this information via Link Values. If the platform is PICMG or PC/104 Plus compliant, refer to Appendix 12.3

and 12.4 respectively for the INTx# binding specification. Knowing this allows the installation of PCI devices such that like priority PCI device functions can be made to share the same PIRQx# input on the interrupt router and consequently the same IRQ.

2. Determine which IRQs the system's Resource Manager assigns to each of the PIRQx# inputs on the router. Start by installing a PCI device in each PCI bus slot, such that each PIRQx# input slated for use in the final design is represented, and boot the system. Then, if you know the layout of the platform's interrupt router, you can read the PIRQx# route control registers directly. Otherwise, read the Interrupt Line register from each device and determine the IRQ assignments using the IRQ routing tables.

3. Install the PCI devices such that device functions of like priority share INTx# pins with the same link value, thereby using the same PIRQx# input on the router. If possible, install the PCI devices such that not only do like priority device functions share the same PIRQx# input, but also the priority order of the devices is preserved within the system's interrupt structure. If there is no way to preserve the priority order of the devices, then assign them to PIRQx# inputs arbitrarily and perform a static router modification to correct.

With only four INTx# lines available to PCI, and the inherent complexities of trying to preserve the relative priority order when adding multi-function PCI devices, sometimes it's best to try various arrangements to see which one works best. A logical approach to this process would be to first group all PCI devices such that all priority 1 device functions use the same PIRQx# pin on the interrupt router. On the next iteration, start by grouping all priority 2 device functions and so on until the most efficient arrangement is found.

In some instances, PCI device functions sharing a common IRQ will unavoidably not have the same or even similar relative priority. To arrange device functions by priority that share the same IRQ resource requires that the load order of the device drivers be specified, as described in Chapter 7. Device drivers that load first carry the lowest priority in an interrupt chain, while device drivers that load last enjoy the highest priority. Software techniques for balancing priority among a plurality of devices are also discussed in Chapter 7 (specifically 7.3 "Equal Priority Chains" and 7.4 "IPC Link Rotation"). In the next section, an adaptation of the rotate technique given in 7.4 is applied to the PCI interrupt router to achieve a balanced priority among a plurality of devices by rotating the router assignments on-the-fly.

10.3 Static Modification of the Interrupt Router

Below is the step-by-step list of events required to complete a successful modification of the PCI interrupt router after the system startup is complete and the system's Configuration Manager has completed all IRQ assignments.

1. Disable Interrupts system wide (see Section 5.5 for details).

2. Program the interrupt router to route the PIRQx# inputs to the desired IRQs and disable and unused PIRQx# inputs. Once a PIRQx# input has been routed to a particular IRQ, that IRQ is no longer available for use by ISA devices or any other device not designed to share interrupts.

3. Program the Edge/Level Control Register (ELCR) to make sure the IRQ routed to is configured as level triggered (see Section 2.6 for details)

4. Update the Interrupt Vector Table IVT(Real Mode) or Interrupt Descriptor Table IDT(Protected Mode) so that the interrupt chains starting address which hooked the original IRQ's IVT/IDT location is copied to the new IRQ's IVT/IDT location. Be sure not to clobber a valid starting address in the process.

5. Update the Interrupt Line register in the PCI Configuration Space for every PCI device function effected by the routing change. This step is only required for hot-swap systems or any system that might load a device driver after the Static Router Modification. Embedded systems generally do not fall into this category and subsequently do not require this step to operate successfully.

6. Note: The *Write a PCI Configuration Register Byte* function is used to complete this step. Details on this function can be found in Appendix 12.5.

7. Immediately after the interrupt router is reprogrammed and the IVT/IDT and Interrupt Line registers are updated, unmask the IRQs routed to, as some chip sets mask the IRQ when the PIRQx# route control registers are programmed to route a PIRQx# input to a specific IRQ.

8. Enable Interrupts system wide.

10.4 Rotating Interrupt Router Assignments OTF

This section is geared toward the embedded system designer and is intended to describe a means by which the interrupt router can be used to achieve equal priority among a plurality of PCI devices. Until the advent of PCI and the broad application of programmable interrupt routers, the only way to balance priority among a plurality of devices was to use one of the interrupt chaining techniques described in Chapter 7 (See Sections 7.3 "Equal Priority Chains" and 7.4 "IPC Link Rotation"). The programmable interrupt router, with its unique ability to route any PIRQx# input to any available IRQ, adds yet another technique of achieving balanced priority. It is the intent of PCI to provide a resource-conflict free environment. As such, it was made very clear that the interrupt router was the domain of the PCI System BIOS and PnP operating systems only. However, if the system is embedded, the constraints of an open system design, under which the specification was written, no longer apply. So there is nothing to preclude the use of an interrupt router to achieve balanced priority by rotating the PIRQx# to IRQ router assignments on-the-fly.

Both of the rotate Strategies discussed in Chapter 7.4 "IPC Link Rotation" can be successfully applied to the rotation of IRQ router assignments. Strategy 1 specifies that a device requesting service will assume the lowest priority "go to the Back of the Line" after the device is serviced. Strategy 2 specifies that the device requesting service will assume the highest priority or "go to the Front of the Line" after it is serviced. With the techniques described in Section 7.4, this meant rotating the device links in the chain. Here however, rotating the priority of the PCI device functions is accomplished by rotating the IRQ router assignments.

To help visualize what the rotate procedures effect on the interrupt router, the following example is offered. In this example, assume four single function PCI devices each occupying a PCI add-in card slot.

Device1's INTA# pin is connected to PIRQA# with a Link Value = 01h.

Device2's INTA# pin is connected to PIRQB# with a Link Value = 02h.

Device3's INTA# pin is connected to PIRQC# with a Link Value = 03h.

Device4's INTA# pin is connected to PIRQD# with a Link Value = 04h.

Therefore all for PIRQx# inputs on the router are used in this example. Further assume that IRQ's [9, 11, 12, 15] are available to PCI.

Figure 10.4.1(a) shows the Strategy 1 rotate procedure's effect on the IRQ routes after successive requests are processed.

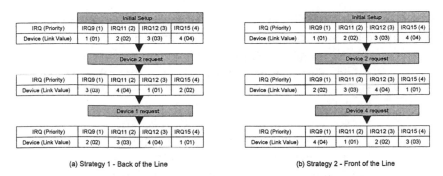

(a) Strategy 1 - Back of the Line   (b) Strategy 2 - Front of the Line

Figure 10.4.1 Rotating the Interrupt Router Assignments On-The-Fly

First, device2 requests service, after which it is assigned the IRQ with the lowest priority, IRQ15 in this example. The remaining devices are rotated accordingly. Next device1 requests service and is moved to the lowest priority IRQ level (IRQ15) after service. Again, all other devices are rotated accordingly after device1 is serviced.

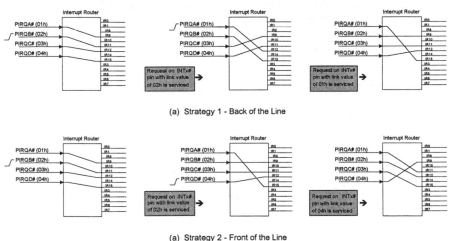

(a) Strategy 1 - Back of the Line

(a) Strategy 2 - Front of the Line

Figure 10.4.2 Graphical Illustration of Rotating Router Assignments

Figure 10.4.2(a) further illustrates this point by describing the interrupt routers new assignments per Strategy 1· for the above example in a graphical form. Figures 10.4.1(b) and 10.4.2(b) illustrate the Strategy 2 rotate procedure's effect on IRQ routes after the processing of successive requests. Conceptually, that's how it works.

In order to facilitate the rotation of the interrupt router assignments on-the-fly, a few rules, steps, and considerations must be observed. To begin

221

presenting the design process for implementing this scheme, **the two rules that apply to the system and must be followed are:**

- All device drivers must load before the first rotate procedure is called. This eliminates the need to update the Interrupt Line registers of all interrupt-driven PCI device functions effected by the new routes each time the rotate procedure is called.

- IRQs involved in the rotation process must be all Master 8259 PIC IRQs (IR[7:0]) or all Slave 8259 PIC IRQs (IR[15:8]). In a PC, the latter is typical since most IRQs available to PCI are on the Slave PIC. Because of the additional Non-Specific EOI command required by Slave PIC iSRs, a mixing of Master and Slave PIC iSR types in the rotate process is not allowed, as it would result in a Slave PIC iSR responding to a request originating on a Master PIC or a Master PIC iSR responding to a request originating on a Slave PIC. This of course, would end system bliss.

The design procedure that leads to the successful development of a system that rotates interrupt router assignments is accomplished by following the step-by-step list given below. Following this list is a detailed discussion of each item.

1. Record the IRQs and PIRQx# inputs involved in the rotation. Any number of PIRQx# (4 max.) inputs and any number of IRQs (4 max.) may be specified for use in the rotate procedure provided the number of PIRQx# inputs specified is equal to or greater that the number of IRQs.

2. Verify that the IRQs picked for the rotate procedure do not conflict with other devices in the system. This includes ISA, EISA or MCA devices, as well as integrated PCI devices. Any device, other than those for which the rotate procedure is intended and which use a PIRQx# input involved in the rotate procedure should be reviewed, to ensure system stability and performance criteria for that device are not jeopardized. Such a device might be heard saying, "It's a twister!" or "I don't think we're in Kansas anymore, Toto!"

3. Organize the PCI devices in the PCI interrupt structure such that device functions involved in the rotation are physically balanced over the PIRQx# inputs involved in the rotation. This minimizes latency as a result of the shortened interrupt chains. Section 10.3 covers this organization process. A static router modification may be required if any or all of the IRQs involved in the rotation are available, but not assigned by the system's Configuration Manager at startup. If the static router modification does not update the Interrupt Line registers for all effected PCI devices, then the respective device drivers must have the IRQ hard coded into them.

4. Design the iSRs. Link Values for device functions are now known. (see description below)

5. Design the rotate procedure. Link Values for device functions are now known. (see description below)

6. Stage the following sequence of events to occur at system startup
   - Disable Interrupts
   - Mask IRQs involved in rotation
   - Initialize the interrupt router. This includes disabling unused PIRQx# inputs.
   - Configure IRQs involved as level triggered.
   - Enable Interrupts
   - Load Device Drivers
   - Unmask IRQs involved in rotation and stand back.

10.4.1 Device Driver related issues

PCI device drivers are responsible for using the system resources assigned by the system's Configuration Manager to access their device. Additionally, PCI device drivers must be designed to share interrupts (refer to 9.6 for discussion on PCI device drivers). PCI device drivers use the IRQ assignment made by the system's Configuration Manager and stored in the Interrupt Line register to install the interrupt service routine behind the correct IRQ vector table entry. Some consideration must be made then for a design that includes a static router modification as part of the staging sequence, as this will cause a discrepancy between the value stored in the Interrupt Line register and the actual IRQ the device function is routed to. If a static router modification is performed before any device drivers load and no effort is made to update the Interrupt Line registers of all effected PCI devices, the interrupt service routines will hook the incorrect IRQ vector table entry. In an embedded system, this is easily overcome by hard-coding the known IRQ assignment that results from the static router modification into the device driver. If the Interrupt Line registers are, on the other hand, updated as part of the staging sequence, devices drivers can rely on the Interrupt Line register values to hook the correct IRQ vector table entry.

10.4.2 Interrupt Service Routines (iSRs)

Interrupt service routines (iSRs) representing PCI devices involved in the rotation may be designed as either Locked or Nested. As stated earlier, all IRQs involved in the rotation must be all Master 8259 PIC IRQs (IR[7:0]) or

223

all Slave 8259 PIC IRQs (IR[15:8]). All iSRs servicing devices involved in the rotation will therefore all be designed as either all Master or all Slave PIC iSRs. This eliminates the faulty interrupt handling that would result from an iSR designed to handle a Slave PIC request being rotated to a Master PIC IRQ and vice versa.

One of the key elements involved in the success of an iSR designed to rotate the IRQ router assignments is knowledge of the Link Value for the INTx# pin used by the PCI device function it represents. This value is required by the rotate procedure to facilitate the correct rotation of the IRQ assignments. An iSR may simply be designed with the Link Value hard coded in it, or the device driver may determine and store the Link Value when loading. The latter requires the device driver to know how either the Configuration Manager's routing algorithm operates or how the static router modification routes the IRQs. Either will allow the device driver to read the Interrupt Line register on the device and "knowing" the routes back to the PIRQx# inputs, obtain the Link Value assigned to that PIRQx# input. It is imperative that the Interrupt Line registers contain the value associated with the IRQ the PCI device function is actually using. Therefore, if a static router modification was performed during the staging sequence, and the Interrupt Line registers were not updated, the Interrupt Line register values will be incorrect and there will be no way for a device driver to determine the Link Value. Subsequently, in this instance all Link Values will have to be hard coded. The easiest way though is to lock down the PCI bus slot the device will be using and hard code the Link Value into the iSR.

A Nested Slave PIC iSR example is presented in Figure 10.4.3 to illustrate the characteristics of an iSR designed to work in an environment described in this section. Figure 10.4.3(b) lists the C source required to realize the iSR as flowcharted in Figure 10.4.3(a). Of particular interest is the way the IMR is handled and the Link Value is passed to the rotate procedure.

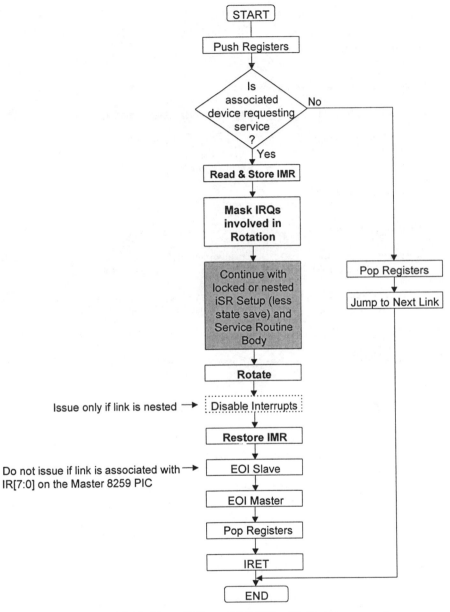

Figure 10.4.3(a) Nested Slave PIC iSR with Rotate example

```
/* ipc_lnkr.c */

void interrupt ipc_lnkr(void);
void interrupt (*Original_iSR)(void);
int ourDevicePending;

void interrupt ipc_lnkr()
{
    if (ourDevicePending) {            /* Is companion device pending service?    */

        oldSPICIMR = inportb(0xa0)     /* store original Slave PIC IMR             */
        outportb(0xa1, oldSPICIMR | 9a /* mask IR[15, 12, 11, 9] involved in rotation */
        enable();                      /* enable interrupts                        */

        /*Service Routine Body*/
        /*Reset device request if level triggered*/

        rotate_strategy1(1);           /* rotate the device links                  */

        disable():                     /* disable interrupts                       */
        outportb(0xa1, oldSPICIMR)     /* restore original Slave PIC IMR           */

        outportb(0xa0, 0x20);          /* issue Slave PIC Non-Specific EOI         */
        outportb(0x20, 0x20);          /* issue Master PIC Non-Specific EOI        */

    } else {

        Original_iSR();                /* Far Jump to next link in the chain       */
    }
}
```

Figure 10.4.3(b) Nested Slave PIC iSR with Rotate example

Following the flowchart given in Fig. 10.4.3(a), the iSR begins by satisfying its interrupt sharing obligation by first checking its companion device function for an active pending request condition. If its device function is requesting service, the iSR services the device and rotates the IRQ assignments. Before the iSR begins processing however, *Nested* iSRs must mask all IRQs involved in the rotation prior to the Nested iSR enabling interrupts. To accomplish this, the contents of the IMR are first read and stored before all IRQs involved in the rotation are masked (see 5.3 for details on masking IRQs). This results in the iSR appearing locked to the IRQs involved in the rotation, but nested to all remaining IRQs in the system. Masking IRQs involved in the rotation before interrupts are enabled prevents lower priority requests currently in service from being rotated to an unmasked higher priority IRQ, where the still active request signal from the first request will cause its iSR to be entered a second time for the same request. This ill fated rotation could either be caused by a higher priority request calling the rotate procedure or by the original

226

request itself calling the rotate procedure with a second request sharing the same PIRQx# input pending service.

With the IRQs involved in the rotation masked, the required Setup procedures and Service Routine Body for the specified iSR type service the PCI device function. Next, the rotate procedure is called. When the iSR calls the rotate procedure, it passes the Link Value associated with the INTx# pin it uses to the rotate procedure. The Link Value passed to the rotate procedure is the key by which the rotate procedure is able to identify the PIRQx# input it needs to assign to the IRQ with either the lowest (Strategy 1) or highest (Strategy 2) priority. Once the first PIRQx# input is assigned the appropriate IRQ, all remaining PIRQx# input assignments follow accordingly. The rotation of the router assignments is accomplished by either issuing a series of *Set PCI Hardware Interrupt* functions (see 10.2 or Appendix 12.5 for details) or programming the interrupt router directly. Direct software access to the interrupt router during the rotation procedure is preferred, as this minimizes the overhead involved in the rotation process. Next, the rotate procedure rotates the stating addresses of the interrupt chains within the Interrupt Vector Table IVT(Real Mode) or Interrupt Descriptor Table IDT(Protected Mode) such that the interrupt chains match up with the new IRQ assignments. Figure 10.4.4 shows a flowchart of the rotate procedure.

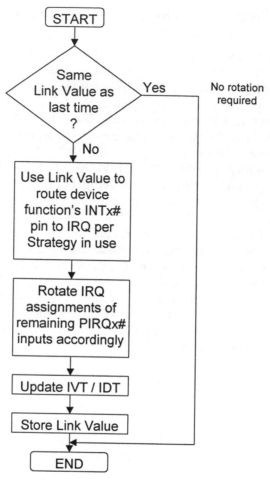

Figure 10.4.4 Rotate Procedure (Flow Chart)

To help reduce overhead, the rotate procedure starts out by determining if the Link Value passed is the same Value passed the last time the procedure was called. If so, there is no need to rotate the IRQ assignments. However, if the Link Value is different, the rotate procedure just described will proceed. As a last step, the rotate procedure stores the new Link Value for future reference before returning to the iSR

After the Service Routine Body and call to the rotate procedure are complete, the IMR is restored, thereby unmasking all IRQs that were masked when the iSR was entered. The IMR (OCW1) should only be restored when interrupts are disabled. The remainder of the iSR marks the clean-up segment.

11. Application Development

11.1 Locked Vs. Nested iSRs

As discussed in Chapter 6.1, Locked iSRs add to the Latency Time seen by higher priority iSRs by keeping interrupts disabled (IF=0) until the iSR completes. For this reason, nested iSRs are always preferred unless a unique situation should arise requiring the use of a locked iSR. Throughout the previous chapters, a number of such situations have been described and the list below summarizes those situations where the use of a Locked iSR is advantageous.

- **High data throughput devices assigned to lower priority IRQs.** Consider the case where a device with a relatively high data throughput rate (*device A*) is assigned a lower priority IRQ than a device with a low data transfer rate (*device B*) out of necessity. If device A's iSR is *Nested*, then *device B* can interrupt *device A's* data transfer. Therefore device A's data throughput rate suffers due to the increased latency times resulting from its low priority IRQ standing. The situation is further aggravated as *device A's* request, once acknowledged and in service, is then subject to interruption by *device B* with secondary throughput needs. In this instance, system performance might benefit from *device A's* ability to fully complete its single or block data transfer without interruption through the use of a *Locked* iSR.

- **IRQ7 iSRs designed to handle default IR7.** As described in Chapter 8, a default IR7 occurs whenever an active interrupt request signal is seen by the processor but is removed before the INTA# pulses arrive. Finding no active requests present, the 8259 PIC responds by driving the data bus with vector data associated with IR7. To detect this situation and handle it properly, the In Service bit for IR7 is tested. If equal to 1 the request is a valid device request, if equal to 0 the request is a default IR7. This test works well provided a valid *Nested* iSR for IRQ7 is not already in progress. When a *Nested* iSR is in service for IRQ7 and a default IR7 condition occurs, the IS bit set when the valid Nested iSR was entered remains set, and the iSR will mistakenly be entered a second time. To eliminate the threat of the iSR being entered a second time and reduce the default IR7 handler to a simple test of the IS bit, design the IRQ7 device iSR as *Locked*. A *Locked* iSR once in service will prevent a default IR7 condition from ever being acknowledged because the transient noise will be rejected by the open IF switch (interrupts disabled). Also, with the test for a default IR7 condition reduced to a simple test of the IS bit for IR7, the possibility for a generic TSR program that chains to IRQ7 and handles the default IR7 condition exists. Chapter 8.4 "Programming an iSR to Detect and Handle a default IR7(IR15)" details the design of iSRs used to detect and handle default IR7 and default IR15s. Also, a TSR program like the one referred above that acts as a shied against default IR7s is provided in the a:\ch8 subdirectory on the IDPCSD diskette in both source and executable form. **def_IR7.exe** chains to the Master PIC's IRQ7 (interrupt 0Fh) and **def_IR15.exe** chains to the Slave PICs IRQ15 (interrupt 78h) to handle any default IR7s that might occur on the Slave PIC

- **Localized data synchronization.** In a time critical data acquisition operation where an unpredictable delay would make it impossible to guarantee data accuracy, a Locked iSR allows the timing mechanism (software timing loop or timer tick monitor) to accurately meter the time before the iSR's next event.

11.2 Device Priority Assignment

The system's interrupt processing hardware which includes the IRQ bus lines, interrupt controller chips, processor, and the memory that holds the interrupt vector table is collectively referred to as the system's *interrupt structure*. The unique priority levels assigned to each of the IRQ resources in a system is commonly referred to as the system's *priority structure*. Figure 11.2.1 shows the priority structure for IRQs in a PC.

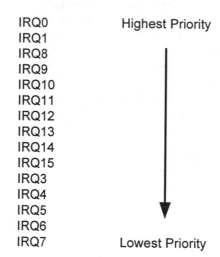

IRQ0   Highest Priority
IRQ1
IRQ8
IRQ9
IRQ10
IRQ11
IRQ12
IRQ13
IRQ14
IRQ15
IRQ3
IRQ4
IRQ5
IRQ6
IRQ7   Lowest Priority

Figure 11.2.1 PC's Priority Structure

The fact that each IRQ resource has a higher or lower priority relative to all other IRQs allows the system designer to adjust a device's access to processor bandwidth relative to all other interrupt-driven devices by simply assigning a particular IRQ to that device. Devices assigned to high priority IRQs enjoy faster response times and once in service, are able to complete their service cycles with fewer interruptions than lower priority IRQs. There are two basic classes of interrupt-driven devices found in a system.

- Critical System Functions requiring fast response times with generally low data throughput.

- Communication, Data Acquisition, and Control devices with varied data throughput demands.

System functions such as the familiar system timer (IRQ0) and keyboard (IRQ1) are examples of devices with low interrupt rates that require immediate response. Because these functions are critical to the system operation at least in the consumer market place, these functions are assigned the highest priority IRQs in the system so as never to be missed. Other examples of critical system functions include a "nuclear reactor nearing meltdown" interrupt or the even more critical "Kick off in 5 minutes" interrupt.

After the critical system functions are assigned the highest priority IRQs, all remaining IRQs are assigned to the data acquisition and control devices. As mentioned above, the ability to access processor bandwidth is directly related to the relative priority of the IRQ assigned. The higher the priority, the more processor bandwidth is available to the device. Therefore when deciding relative priority among several devices, the device demanding the highest data throughput should be assigned the highest priority IRQ on down to the device with the lowest data throughput demand being assigned the lowest priority IRQ.

If several devices have equal data throughput demands, a difficulty arises when trying to provide balanced access to processor bandwidth because of the PC's rigid priority structure. Devices assigned higher priority IRQs can interrupt or *preempt* devices using lower priority IRQs and as a result are able to obtain service more often with less interruptions than their lower priority counterparts. To illustrate this point, consider the following example. Assume four interrupt-driven devices, device1 - device4 each with assigned priorities 1 - 4 respectively, 1 being the highest. Furthermore, each device carries with it an identical data throughput demand and uses the same data transfer method to move an equal amount of data with each interrupt processed. Starting at a low enough interrupt rate, such that all four devices are able to transfer data comfortably with plenty of processor bandwidth to spare, we begin to increase the interrupt rate and subsequent demand on processor bandwidth simultaneously to the point where the processor runs out of enough bandwidth to effectively handle all four devices. If the overall throughput of each device were graphed over increasing interrupt rates, the results would resemble the chart shown below in Figure 11.2.2.

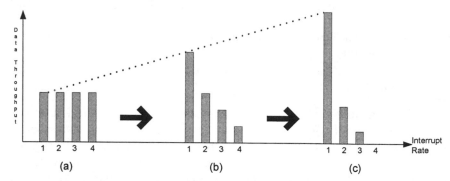

Figure 11.2.2 Effects of Preemption at Increasing Interrupt Rates

Figure 11.2.2(a) illustrates the service distribution for the four devices as the interrupt rate reaches the point where exactly 100% of processor bandwidth is utilized and the throughput demands of all four devices are still met, but with remaining headroom. As the interrupt rate increases further and the data transfer of all four devices combined begins to exceed all available processor bandwidth, the preemption of lower priority devices by higher priority devices results in the unbalanced servicing described in 11.2.2(b). This skew in the distribution of service is the direct result of lower priority devices losing their ability to effectively initiate and sustain their data transfers uninterrupted. This is due to preemption by higher piority interrupt requests, which first hinder lower priority requests from being acknowledged and then continue to interrupt the lower priority device iSRs once in service. Eventually, still greater increases in the interrupt rate will cause the effects of preemption to become so severe as to completely block the service of lower priority devices altogether, as shown in 11.2.2(c). A rigid priority structure and *preemption* are desirable when critical system functions require a more immediate processor response and when the processing order of devices with varying data throughput demands needs to be established.

There are several software techniques discussed throughout this book that describe how to establish equal priority among several devices. These techniques achieve balanced distribution for the devices involved. The benefit to balancing priority is that service to the devices and consequently the end users of those devices is balanced. To demonstrate how preemption has no effect on a balanced priority scheme, assume the same

four devices, data transfer methods and interrupt rates given in the example illustrated in Figure 11.2.2. If one of the techniques used to balance priority is applied, the resulting service distributions will remain balanced even as the interrupt rate is increased beyond what the processors can handle. This fact is illustrated in Figure 11.2.3.

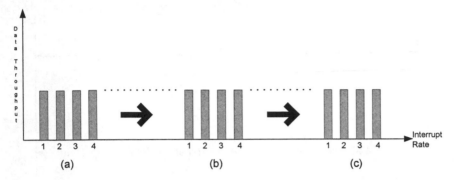

Figure 11.2.3 Balanced Priority Methods not subject to Preemptive Effects

For information on techniques that establish equal priority among a plurality of devices, refer to the following sections:

*   Chapter 2   - Section 2.3 "Periodic Interrupt-driven Polling"
*   Chapter 7   - Section 7.3 "The Equal Priority Chain (EPC)"
*   Chapter 7   - Section 7.4 "IPC Link Rotation"
*   Chapter 10 - Section 10.4 "Rotating Interrupt Router Assignments On-the-Fly"

11.3 Maximum Interrupt Rates

Knowing the maximum possible interrupt rate for a given IRQ is important for two reasons. First, it allows you to establish a guaranteed minimum service time. This is particularly important to Periodic Interrupt-driven Polling, where the timer rate is dependent on the device that requires attention most frequently. In this instance, knowing the minimum service time achievable lets you know immediately whether the system has enough available bandwidth for the Periodic Interrupt-driven Polling operation. Secondly, the maximum interrupt rate allows you to establish the guaranteed maximum data transfer rate for a particular design. Once the maximum interrupt rate is known, an immediate determination as to whether the data transfer method is sufficient can be made.

There are two ways to go about determining the maximum interrupt rate for a given design. The first requires that you calculate it based on the

processor speed, bus speed, data throughput rates, and data transfer methods of all devices using higher priority IRQs. The second and more realistic approach, uses a digital storage oscilloscope to observe the maximum interrupt rate that precipitates out after many trials.

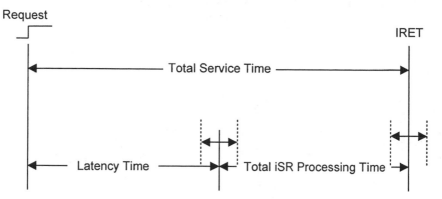

Figure 11.3.1 Total Service Time

The period of time between the assertion of an interrupt request to the time when the iSR issues the IRET instruction is the *Total Service Time* required to service the device once. This *Total Service Time* varies due to fluctuations in both the *Latency Time* and *Total iSR Processing Time*. Latency Time variations are based on the number of higher priority devices already in service when the interrupt request is asserted. Total iSR Processing Time is effected by the number of higher priority devices that interrupt the request while it's in service. Since interrupts are asynchronous events, the moment when a higher priority interrupt request is asserted is purely random (which is why many trials are required to capture the longest observed Total Service Time during a worst case condition). The longest observed Total Service Time then immediately yields the maximum interrupt rate through a simple inversion (1/Total Service Time).

For this method to be successful, all devices that occupy higher priority IRQs and are therefore able to interrupt the test iSR, must be in place and fielding requests as they would under normal operating conditions. To determine the maximum interrupt rate over *several* IRQs requires that you start with the highest priority IRQ and proceed to the lowest priority IRQ, bringing each device operational for each completed IRQ first before continuing. Also, the test iSR used in the process must take the same amount of processing time as the actual device iSR intended for use with the IRQ. For a Periodic Interrupt-driven Polling (PIDP) design, this means that the iSR should execute both the polling *and* service routines for all PIDP associated devices for every request.

11.3.1 Measuring the Maximum Interrupt Rate

The output of a programmable timer will act as the interrupt source. Connect the first probe to the timers output and setup the oscilloscope to trigger off the rising edge of the timer output for edge-triggered IRQs and the falling edge of the timer output for level triggered IRQs. Remember that on level triggered IRQs a software mechanism in the iSR is required to reset the request *before* interrupts are enabled (to avoid a second request from being generated).

The timer output acts as the starting point for measuring the *Total Service Time*. A second signal source is required to mark the elapsed time between the active request signal and the IRET. Because the IRET command produces no signals we can easily probe, the end point can be defined by having the iSR write to an I/O port on a known device and then probe the chip select line on that device shortly before the IRET command is issued. To avoid any inaccuracies, the OUT command used to mark the end point must be issued after the iSR disables interrupts. If the oscilloscope is in storage mode and the number of stored samples is set to its maximum, the resulting display will show the maximum *Total Service Time* resulting from the many samples the scope stores. Over many trials, a reliable maximum *Total Service Time* is observed. To adjust the Total Service Time and account for the processing time between the OUT command and the IRET instruction, simply combine the processing times for each instruction after the OUT command in the test iSR and add it to the observed time. To attain the final maximum interrupt rate, simply invert the combined time.

To properly interface a timer output signal to a level triggered IRQ therefore requires a circuit like the example shown in Figure 11.3.1(a). The circuits timing characteristics are illustrated in Figure 11.3.1(b).

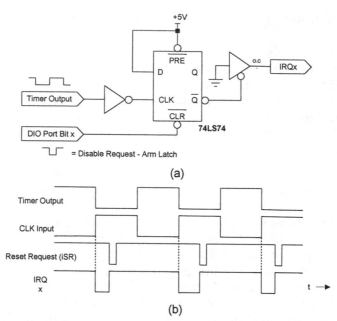

Figure 11.3.2 Timer Output to Level Triggered IRQ Interface Circuit

First, when the timer output transitions low, the D type latch's /Q output goes low. This opens a path to ground through the open collector output of the tri-state buffer connected to the IRQx bus line and an active request is asserted on the level triggered IRQ. After the request is recognized, the iSR is entered and begins by resetting the active request first, before interrupts are enabled. This is accomplished in this example by first writing a 0 and then a 1 to a digital I/O port tied to the D latch's /CLR pin. Cycling the /CLR input signal low deasserts the request by tri-stating the buffer and the second transition back high arms the latch for the next request.

11.4 CPU Exceptions and Vector Table Relocation

Intel processor specification dictates that interrupts 00 - 2F are to be reserved for exception faults. IBM, when designing the original PC, decided to assign the eight IRQs on the 8259 PIC to interrupts 08 - 0F in the interrupt vector table. This was of no immediate threat since the 8088 only used the first four interrupts 00h - 03h for exceptions. However, starting with the x286, a direct conflict between processor exceptions and hardware interrupts IRQ0 - IRQ7 arose. Table 11.4.1 lists the exceptions that conflict with interrupt 08h - 0fh.

Interrupt	Address	Type	Description
8	0:20h	Hardware	IRQ0 - System Timer
		CPU, 286	*Interrupt out of Range*
		CPU, 386+	*Double Exception*
9	0:24h	Hardware	IRQ1 - Keyboard
		CPU, 286+	*Coprocessor Segment Overrun*
A	0:28h	Hardware	IRQ2 - EGA/Slave 8259 Cascade
		CPU, 386+	*Invalid TSS*
B	0:2ch	Hardware	IRQ3 - Serial Port (COM2)
		CPU, 386+	*Segment not Present*
C	0:30h	Hardware	IRQ4 - Serial Port (COM1)
		CPU, 386+	*Stack Exception*
D	0:34h	Hardware	IRQ5 - Fixed Disk/ Parallel Port (LPT2)
		CPU, 286	*Segment Overrun Exception*
		CPU, 386+	*General Protection Fault*
E	0:38h	Hardware	IRQ6 - Floppy Drive
		CPU, 386+	*Page Fault*
F	0:3ch	Hardware	IRQ7 - Parallel Port (LPT1)

Table 11.4.1 Conflicting Exceptions/Faults

CPU exception interrupts are for the most part restricted to V86 or protected mode, with the exception of interrupt 0dh. On all 386 and subsequent processors, interrupt 0dh represents the General Protection fault and can occur in both real and protected mode. In real mode, no attention is given to the exception when it occurs, which results in the IRQ5 iSR processing what it believes to be a valid request. This is easily avoided if the iSR is designed to first validate the In-Service bit before processing the real mode request. In V86 mode, the exception is handled first by the protected mode manager, before control is passed to the IRQ5 iSR. Even if the interrupt is a valid IRQ5 request, the processor still passes control to the protected mode manager first. In V86 mode however, the additional overhead imposed by the exception handler results in lower possible data transfer rates for IRQ5 that other hardware IRQs. For this reason, it is sometimes desirable to redirect interrupt vectors 8h - Fh associated with hardware interrupts IRQ0 - IRQ7 to 50h - 57h when operating in V86 mode.

To relocate interrupts IRQ0 - IRQ7 to 50h - 57h requires the following steps:

1. Disable interrupts

2. Initialize the Master 8259 PIC setting ICW2 = 50h

3. Copy interrupt vectors 8h - Fh to 50h - 57h

4. Enable interrupts

The following C program example **relocate.c** is offered to demonstrate how the relocate procedure is accomplished. Both **relocate.c** and **relocate.exe** are on the IDPCSD disk in the a:\chpt11 subdirectory. Once redirected, any device iSRs that hook the original interrupts 8h - Fh will never be called. Before calling the relocate proceedure, make sure no other programs are currently using interrupts 50h - 57h. This can be done by checking all eight vector table entries for the system BIOS segment - *F000h*. If any of the entries show starting addresses with anything other than the system BIOS segment F000, the IRQ has been hooked by another program. To accomodate the interrupts already in use at 50h - 57h, simply modify the **relocate.c** program to first read and store the original starting addresses for interrupts 50h - 57h before calling the relocate proceedure. After the relocate proceedure, restore any of the original 50h - 57h interrupt's starting addresses that were in use. Avoid overwriting any of the valid vector table entries relocated from interrupts 8h - Fh when restoring from the original 50h - 57h interrupts. If an unresolvable conflict arises, post an error message and exit leaving the vector table unchanged.

```
/* relocate.c /*

void main()
{
    disable();

    /* Initialize Master 8259 PIC with 50h */
    outportb(0x20, 0x11);    /* ICW1 - Edge Triggered Mode, Cascaded PIC, ICW4 required to define µPM    */
    outportb(0x21, 0x08);    /* ICW2 - Set PIC offset to 50h, the PC's Master PIC IVT base Address       */
    outportb(0x21, 0x04);    /* ICW3 - Slave PIC attached to IR2 Input                                   */
    outportb(0x21, 0x01);    /* ICW4 - Set PIC operation to 8086/8088 Mode                               */

    /* relocate Vector Table */
    for (i = 0; I < 8; i++){
        tempVector = getvect(0x08 +i);
        setvect(0x50 + i, tempVector);
    }
    enable();
}
```

Figure 11.4.1 relocate.c - Relocates interrupts 08h - 0Fh to 50h - 57h

Once interrupts are relocated to 50h - 57h, any iSRs that hook the vacant 08h - 0Fh interrupts after the fact will never be called. Therefore all iSRs should be installed before interrupts are relocated. Also because IRQ2 interrupts are "redirected" through IRQ9, the BIOS handler for IRQ9 will no longer jump to a valid starting address once interrupts are relocated. An example of the IRQ9 redirection iSR and a TSR program **ir9_ir2.exe** which provides the required redirection is given in Chapter 4.3. To complement the **relocate.exe**, a modified version of ir9_ir2.exe TSR program, named **ir9_ir2r.exe** is located on the IDPCSD diskette in the a:\chpt11 subdirectory. It installs an IRQ9 iSR that redirects IRQ2 requests to interrupt 52h, IRQ2's new home.

11.5 Using the System Timer's 1Ch Extension

All PC's have at least three onboard counters responsible for supporting internal system operations. The Original PC and PC/XT used an Intel 8253. All other PC platforms use an Intel 8254 Programmable Interval Timer (PIT). As illustrated in Figure 11.5.1, counter 0 is used to provide the timer tick interrupt on IRQ0, critical to both updating the *timer tick count* used to derive the system's time-of-day and generating the motor off delay used to shut the diskette drive motor down after a seek operation. Counter 1 initiates all system memory refresh cycles by prompting the DMA controller's channel 0 to perform a dummy read of the system's DRAM once every 15.12µS. Counter 2 outputs a squarewave used to generate tones on the system's audio speaker.

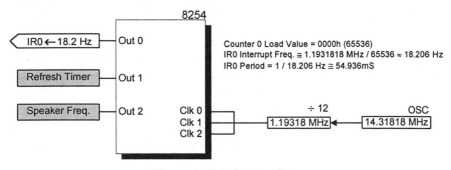

Figure 11.5.1 System Timer

All three counters are fed by a 1.193182MHz input clock derived from the PC's onboard 14.31818MHz oscillator.

Of particular interest to the design of interrupt-driven systems is the operation of counter 0 as it relates to maintaining the system's time-of-day tick count. Counter 0 is set up in Mode 3 (Windows sets up counter 0 in Mode 2) and initialized with a count of 65536. With the counter 0 GATE pin permanently enabled (pulled up to +5V), the resulting *18.206Hz* (1.1931818MHz / 65536) free running periodic signal on counter 0's output pin continuously interrupts the processor on IRQ0 once every *54.936mS*

(1/18.206Hz). Each time the timer tick interrupt occurs, the real mode IRQ0 (interrupt 8h) handler installed by the system BIOS first updates the timer tick count stored in the double word located at 40:6Ch in the BIOS RAM area. The timer tick count represents the total number of timer tick counts (interrupts) since midnight. Every midnight, the timer tick count rolls over to 0 when the count reaches 1800B0h. *1800B0h* is the PC's standard total number of counts in a 24 hour period. When a power on sequence occurs, the timer tick count held in 40:6ch is cleared. The system's Real Time Clock is then probed for the correct time of day and the timer tick count at 40:6ch is updated such that the count will reach 1800B0h at exactly midnight. After the tick count is updated, the IRQ0 handler checks to see if the diskette drive motor needs to be shut off. Following the diskette drive motor check, the IRQ0 handler issues a software INT 1Ch instruction before issuing the clean-up commands and returning from the timer tick interrupt. It is this call to a *user definable* software interrupt handler that is of interest to us.

The 1Ch extension is a free onboard periodic interrupt resource that can be used to drive any periodic interrupt-driven polling routine where a 54.936mS polling period is fast enough to satisfy the polling requirements of the device(s) involved. See 2.3 "Periodic Interrupt-driven Polling" for a discussion on determining the optimum periodic interrupt rate. In addition, the onboard system timer's interrupt 1Ch extension can be used to manage devices and events that occur on the order of seconds, hours, days or even years without the need for any additional hardware. Home automation ("smart home"), building security systems, and the monitoring of slowly changing environmental conditions are all examples of potential applications.

As illustrated in Figure 11.5.2, an iSR designed to handle the 1Ch software interrupt call differs slightly than an iSR designed to handle a standard hardware interrupt.

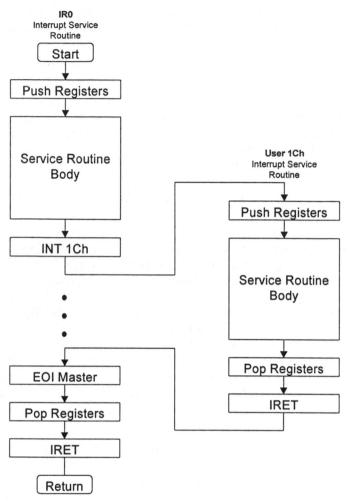

Figure 11.5.2 System timer user interrupt 1Ch - flow chart

First, the 1Ch iSR pushes the registers it intends to use onto the stack. The extent to which the BIOS supplied IRQ0 handler has pushed various registers upon entry is unknown, unless you review the source code. So to be safe, push any registers targeted for use by the 1Ch iSR. There is no need to enable interrupts during the 1Ch iSR's execution since it is servicing the highest priority IRQ in the system. Because interrupt 1Ch is a software interrupt, Non-Specific EOI command(s) are not issued by the 1Ch iSR. This is the responsibility of the calling iSR (interrupt 08h) and will take place when the 1Ch handler returns to the IRQ0 BIOS handler. A simple programming example that hooks the 1Ch extension and displays a counter showing the current timer tick count and the current time-of-day calculated based on the timer tick count at 04:6Ch is included on the IDPCSD diskette. Both the source code file **timer_1c.c** in C and the resulting executable **timer_1c.exe** can be found in the a:\chpt11 subdirectory.

If the system timer tick interrupt rate does not provide adequate resolution or if the rate exceeds what is required by the periodic interrupt-driven polling procedure thereby burdening the CPU with baseless polling cycles, you may want to consider the Real Time Clock's more flexible *Periodic Interrupt* (IRQ8), which is the subject of the next section. Barring that, a counter/timer add-in card with interrupt capability can provide almost any resolution desired. It is possible to load the system timer's counter 0 with a count lower than 65536 to produce periodic interrupt rates higher than 18.206Hz. In this case the handler must chain to IRQ0 (interrupt 08h) and reliably pass control to the original BIOS routine once every 54.936mS, the original rate. This allows the iSR to initiate polling cycles at the desired rate while accounting for the increased interrupt rate and maintaining an accurate timer tick count at BIOS RAM location 40:6Ch. Designing a custom handler to mimic the BIOS IRQ0 handler is another matter altogether, and outside the scope of this book. However, if you are designing one for an *MCA system*, the level triggered request must be reset before enabling interrupts at the end of the iSR. To reset the timer tick interrupt on an MCA system, first read the contents of I/O port 61h, "OR" the value read with 80h and write the new value back to I/O port 61h.

In application development involving time of day calculations, it is often necessary to initialize the application with the correct time of day and in some instances date. Given in Table 11.5.1 below are two common INT 21 functions used to initialize an event scheduling application with the correct Time and Date. The time and date are read from the system's RTC.

INT 21 function 2Ah - *Get System Date*
entry: AH = 2Ah
return: CX =   year (1980 - 2099)
         DH =   month
         DL =   day
         AL =   day of week (00h = Sunday)

INT 21 function 2Ch - *Get System Time*
entry: AH = 2Ch
return: CH =   hour
         CL =   minute
         DH =   second
         DL =   hundredths of a second in .055 increments
                  (On some systems DL will always return 0)

Table 11.5.1 DOS Date and Time INT21h Function Calls

To demonstrate the calculation required to derive the current time in Hrs:Min:Sec from the timer tick count realized in the **timer_1c.exe** programming example, consider the following: A read of the BIOS RAM location 04:6Ch yields a value of 0c3f00h. The standardized total number of timer ticks for a 24 hour period is 1800b0h (1573040d). Dividing 1800b0h by the total number of seconds in a day yields the number of tick counts per second as shown below.

$$1573040 / 60sec/60min/24hr = \textbf{18.2064815} \text{ tick counts/sec}$$

This PC system constant is the basis on which all accurate calculations of time of day are made.

example:

$[04:6Ch] = 0c3f00h = 802,560d$

raw seconds	= 802,560/18.2064815	= 44081.00489
raw minutes	= raw seconds / 60	= 734.6834148
raw hours	= raw minutes / 60	= 12.24472358

Hrs	= integer(raw hours) = 12	
Min	= integer(raw minutes) - Hrs*60 = 14	
Sec	= integer(raw seconds) - Hrs*3600 - Min*60	= 41

12:14:41pm (lunch time!)

11.6 Using the RTC's Periodic Interrupt on IRQ8

Beginning with AT systems, all PC's come equipped with a Motorola MC146818 Real Time Clock chip or compatible that is responsible for storing the systems setup parameters in its CMOS RAM component and maintaining the correct time and date when the system is powered down. The RTC is also capable of producing a *Periodic Interrupt* in the form of a square wave, perfect for *Periodic Interrupt-driven Polling* applications. In a PC, the periodic interrupt uses IRQ8. Periodic interrupt rates are programmable on the RTC and range anywhere from 2Hz to 8KHz. At system startup, the PC's system BIOS sets up the RTC's *Periodic Interrupt* to operate at a frequency of 1KHz. This 1KHz periodic interrupt rate is meant for use by a couple of rather obscure BIOS interrupt INT 15 functions, namely Function 83h - *Set or Clear Wait Time Interval* and Function 86h - *Wait Until Time Interval has Elapsed*. These functions are not required by any of the standard PC system operations. Therefore, unless required by another program, the RTC's periodic interrupt is up for grabs. In fact, all of the sample programs offered in Chapter 7 use the RTC's periodic interrupt to power the examples.

To setup and utilize the RTC's periodic interrupt requires three of the RTC's four status registers - Status Register A, Status Register B and Status Register C. To access these registers via the RTC's indirect addressing scheme, first write the register value to I/O port address 70h, then read from or write to the specified register using I/O port address 71h. Status Register A is used to establish the periodic interrupt rate by programming the RATE select bits shown in Figure 11.6.1(a) with a value between 3 and F. The resulting periodic interrupt rate is then produced by the RTC based on the following formula:

$$\text{Periodic Interrupt Rate} = 65535 / 2^{RATE}$$

0Ah - Status Register A

d7	d6	d5	d4	d3	d2	d1	d0
UIP	0	1	0	x	x	x	x

Shaded information not relevant to Periodic Interrupt applications

RATE - Interrupt rate = 65535 / 2 ^{RATE} (see Table 11.6.1 for valid values)

BASE - Defines RTC's Time Base (standard value is 010 = 32Kz)

Update In Progress
0 - RTC Date/Time accessible
1 - RTC Date/Time updating

0Bh - Status Register B

d7	d6	d5	d4	d3	d2	d1	d0
SET	PI	AI	UI	SQU	DM	24h	DLS

Shaded information not relevant to Periodic Interrupt applications

Daylight Savings
0 - Disabled   1 - Enabled

Time Mode
0 - 12 Hr Clk   1 - 24 Hr Clk

Data Mode
0 - Binary   1 - BCD Date/Time

Square-Wave Signal
0 - Disabled   1 - Enabled

Update Interrupt
0 - Disabled   1 - Enabled

Alarm Interrupt
0 - Disabled   1 - Enabled

Periodic Interrupt
0 - Disabled   1 - Enabled

Set Update Cycle
0 - Disabled   1 - Enabled

Figure 11.6.1 RTC Status Register Definitions (A, B, and C only)

0Ch - Status Register C

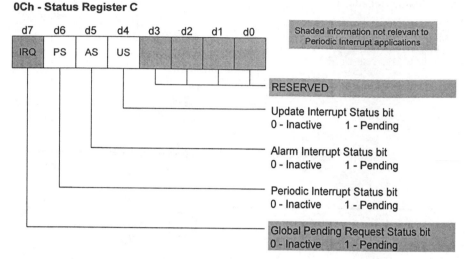

Figure 11.6.1 RTC Status Register Definitions (A, B, and C only) continued

Table 11.6.1 shows a complete list of all available periodic interrupt rates/periods and the Status Register A programming values required to achieve them.

RATE	Status Register A Value	Interrupt Rate (Hz)	Period
3	23h	8K	125 µS
4	24h	4K	250 µS
5	25h	2K	500 µS
6	26h	1K	1 mS
7	27h	512	1.95 mS
8	28h	256	3.91 mS
9	29h	128	7.81 mS
A	2Ah	64	15.625 mS
B	2Bh	32	31.25 mS
C	2Ch	16	62.5 mS
D	2Dh	8	125 mS
E	2Eh	4	250 mS
F	2Fh	2	500 mS

Table 11.6.1 RTC Periodic Interrupt Reference

Along with the *Periodic Interrupt*, two additional functions within the RTC can produce interrupts on IRQ8. The first is the *Update Interrupt*, which if enabled generates an interrupt after each complete update of the time and date in CMOS RAM. The second is the *Alarm Interrupt*. After every update the RTC checks to see if the updated time matches the alarm time. If so, and the Alarm Interrupt is enabled, an interrupt request on IRQ8 is asserted. All three RTC interrupt types share the same output pin tied to the PC's IRQ8. The *PI*, *UI*, and *AI* bits in Status Register B correspond to each of the three RTC interrupt types, and are used to either enable or disable each type respectively. Because an interrupt request asserted by the RTC can result from a Periodic, Update, or Alarm interrupt, an iSR designed to handle the *Periodic Interrupt* only must distinguish between the three interrupt types. To accomplish this, the iSR first reads the RTC's Status Register C, described in Figure 11.6.1, which includes status bits *PS*, *US*, and *AS*. These status bits indicate whether a particular RTC interrupt type is pending service or not. When Status Register C is read, all bits are cleared and the Periodic, Update, and Alarm interrupts on the RTC are all reset and re-enabled. Therefore, any iSR designed to handle RTC interrupts is required to read Status Register C.

Any iSR designed to handle an RTC interrupt type is required to read Status Register C to reset and re-enable interrupts.

Because all three interrupt types are reset and re-enabled by reading Status Register C, chaining individual iSRs behind IRQ8 to handle each of the three interrupt types is not an option. If all three RTC interrupt types need to be handled, it will have to be done in one iSR.

To demonstrate an iSR designed to handle the Periodic Interrupt, refer to Figure 11.6.2.

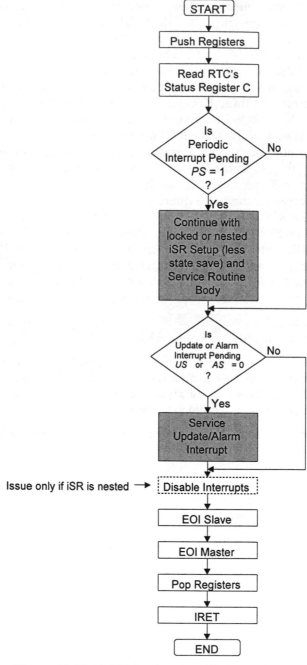

**Figure 11.6.2(a) iSR Designed to Handle RTC's
Periodic Interrupt (flow chart)**

```
/* rtc_ISR.c */

void interrupt( rtcPI_ISR)(viod);
 void interrupt(*Original_ISR)(void);

Original_ISR = getvect(70);                   /* remember previously loaded iSRs starting address   */
setvect(70, rtcPI_ISR);                       /* install PI link starting address behind IR8        */

void interrupt rtcPI_isr()

       unsigned char
       status_reg_c;

    outportb(0x70, 0x0c);                     /* point to RTC's Status Register C                   */
    status_reg_c = inportb(0x71);             /* read RTC's Status Register C                       */

    if (stat_reg_c | 0x40) {                  /* is Periodic Interrupt pending service?            */

       enable();                              /* enable interrupts if iSR is nested                */

          /* Service Routine Body                      */
          /* Reset device request if Level Triggered   */

    }

    if (status_reg_c | 0x30); {               /* Update or Alarm interrupts pending?               */

       /* Yes - service Update or Alarm Interrupt   */

    }

    disable();                                /* disable interrupts if iSR is nested               */
    outportb(0xa0, 0x20);                     /* issue Slave PIC Non-Specific EOI                  */
    outportb(0x20, 0x20);                     /* issue Master PIC Non-Specific EOI                 */

}
```

**Figure 11.6.2(b) iSR Designed to Handle RTC's
Periodic Interrupt (source code)**

From the flowchart given in 11.6.2(a), the first order of business after the iSR has pushed the required registers is to determine whether a Periodic Interrupt caused the request. This is accomplished by reading the *PS* bit d6 in Status Register C. If the return value is 0, the Periodic Interrupt was not responsible for the request and the iSR then checks the US and AS bits, looking for an active Update or Alarm request. If the PS return value is 1 however, the Periodic Interrupt is serviced, after which the US and AS bits are checked. If an Update or Alarm interrupt is pending, their respective Service Routine Bodies execute as well. The iSR then falls through to the cleanup commands and the RTC interrupt processing cycle completes.

rtc.exe, a coded example demonstrating Periodic Interrupt handling and its C source file **rtc.c** are provided on the IDPCSD diskette in the a:\chpt11 subdirectory. To give the example some meaning, **rtc.exe** first initializes the RTC to generate a 1KHz interrupt signal, then displays three counters, one for each of the three RTC's interrupt types. The Periodic Interrupt counter is incremented with each periodic interrupt processed. Counters for the Update and Alarm interrupts are incremented any time the *US* or *AS* indicate a pending request in Status Register C. The periodic interrupt rate for the RTC is selectable using the *up arrow* and *down arrow* keys and produces interrupt rates from 2Hz to 8KHz.

11.7 Synchronized Timer Interrupt

When a computer system is required to perform control operations, many times the application will call for specific timing requirements. Industrial controls and the synchronizing of user input/output devices are areas where time dependent applications are common. As mentioned in Chapter 2, trying to manage data synchronization though the use of software timing/polling loops is costly in terms of both software complexity (development costs) and throughput. Interrupts, on the other hand, offer a tremendous boost in our ability to get much more out of the systems we design. Even with interrupts though, sometimes an application's timing requirements are such that specific timing delays need to be executed before the next action is taken. In this instance, the interrupt, while useful in marking the beginning of the service cycle, still requires a software timing loop to achieve the appropriate delay and complete the cycle. Specific timing delays in a complex system design are highly impractical and downright difficult to achieve in software. This is where the *Synchronized Timer Interrupt* method can help.

The Synchronized Timer Interrupt method uses counters to mark off the required timing delays and produce interrupts at the precise moment they are needed. There are two methods of timing generation within the Synchronized Timer Interrupt structure known as *Dependent Timing* and *Independent Timing*. Dependent timing is when one timing event acts as the reference that other timing events are based upon. An example of Dependent Timing would be where the output of one counter is tied to the GATE of another and acts as a trigger, causing the second counter to count down and assert an interrupt request upon reaching terminal count. *Dependent Timing* always involves the OUT pin of one counter being tied to the GATE pin of another. *Independent Timing* results from timing events that occur independent of other timing events in the system. A counter with its GATE pin permanently enabled (tied to +5V), and therefore free from influence by another counter, is an example of Independent Timing. The Periodic Interrupt-driven Polling method, described in Section 2.3, uses Independent Timing to produce the free running periodic interrupt signal.

To demonstrate the application of synchronized timer interrupts, consider the following example: Every 5 minutes the system triggers a physical event, after which three distinct service routines are required to obtain the resultant data. Additionally, the three service routines are time dependent, meaning the first service routine (a) must acquire its data precisely 10 seconds after the event trigger, the second (b) 45 seconds afterwards and the third (c) a full 2 minutes following the trigger. As a final requirement, both the first (a) and second (b) service routines must trigger a fourth service routine (d) precisely 5 seconds after each executes. Available hardware consists of two 8253 programmable counter/timer chips supported on an ISA add-in card and an AT system with an ISA bus operating at 8.00MHz. Any of the counter outputs can be tied to any of the IRQs available on the ISA bus. The BCLK signal line is used to supply the counter/timer add-in card with an 8.00MHz clock source.

The design begins by selecting one counter to act as a *prescaler* to create a system wide time base that will be act as the CLK source for all remaining counters in the design. In this example, counter 0 on the first 8253 is chosen to fill this role of *Application Time Base*, as shown in Figure 11.7.1.

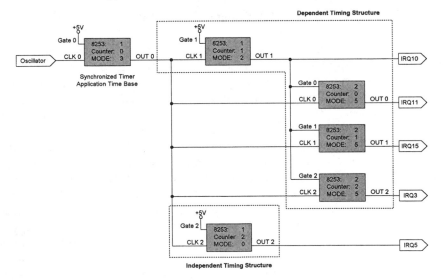

Figure 11.7.1 Dependent and Independent Timing Application example

By initializing the Application Time Base with a count of 40,000d, the 8MHz input frequency (125nS period) is divided down to 2KHz, producing a universal CLK source with a period of 5mS. This is slow enough to allow another 16 bit counter to achieve the maximum period of 5 minutes required by our example application and all points in between.

The counter acting as the Application Time Base is configured to operate in Mode 3 (Square Wave). While Mode 2 also produces a periodic signal, the negative going pulse in Mode 2 is only one clock period in duration. At sufficiently high frequency, the negative going pulse produced in Mode 2 is too short to meet the 8253 CLK input's 150nS low signal minimum for stable operation (1/8.00MHz = 125nS), hence Mode 3. For a listing of all counters involved in the design and their configurations relative to this application example, refer to Table 11.7.1.

8253	Counter	Mode	Timing	GATE	CLK	Count	OUT (period)
1	0	3	Independent	+5V	8.00 MHz	40,000d (9C40h)	Synchronized Timer - Application Time Base (5 mS)
1	1	2	Independent	+5V	200Hz	60,000d (EA60h)	Dependant Timing Trigger IRQ10 (5 min)
2	2	5	Dependent	1/1 OUT	200Hz	1999d (07CFh)	IRQ11 (10 sec after Trigger)
2	0	5	Dependent	1/1 OUT	200Hz	8999d (2327h)	IRQ15 (45 sec after Trigger)
2	1	5	Dependent	1/1 OUT	200Hz	23,999d (5DBFh)	IRQ3 (2 min after Trigger)
1	2	0	Independent	+5V	200Hz	10,000d (2710h)	IRQ5 (50 sec after IRQ11 iSR counter load)

Table 11.7.1 Counter Configurations

Once the Application Time Base is in place, the dependent timing portion of the application needs to be established. In this example, one counter must be chosen to interrupt the processor every 5 minutes and provide the trigger source for three additional counters to mark off times of 10 sec, 45 sec and 2 min before interrupting the processor. From Figure 11.7.1 we see that counter 1 on the first 8253 was chosen in this example as the *dependent timing trigger source*. It receives a 200Hz input signal on the CLK pin from the Application Time Base and asserts a periodic interrupt once every 5 minutes by loading an initial count of 60000 ((5mS * 60000) / 60 = 5 min). Additionally, the counter is operated in Mode 2 (Rate Generator). Because Mode 2 produces a free running periodic signal, it is perfect for both generating the periodic interrupt request needed to trigger the "physical event" and synchronize the three data acquisition counters in our example. With a CLK input frequency of 200Hz, Mode two's negative output pulse will remain low for 5mS, well above the minimum 100nS required by the 8259's IR inputs and the 100nS required by the 8253's GATE input. Mode 2 has the following operational characteristics. After the initial count N is loaded, the count begins to decrement on the very next CLK pulse. When it reaches a count of 1, the output goes low for one CLK period, after which the initial count N is automatically reloaded and the cycle repeats.

Each of the three counters on the *second* 8253 are used in this example to mark off specific timing delays and interrupt the processor when those delays are achieved. All three are operated in Mode 5 (Hardware Triggered Strobe). When operated in Mode 5, a counter will do nothing until it sees a trigger (rising edge) on its GATE pin. After which, the counter will reload the initial count and begin counting down. When the count reaches 0, a negative going pulse 1 clock period in duration (5mS) is produced and the counter returns to an idle state until the next trigger. Because the negative going pulse occurs after $N + 1$ counts in Mode 5, the initial count value loaded should be $N - 1$ to correctly achieve a specific time period. To realize the 10 second delay required by the first iSR (a) in this example, a count of $N=2000$ is required (5mS * 2000 = 10 seconds). For the second iSR (b), a delay of 45 seconds requires $N=9000$ (5mS * 9000 = 45 seconds) and for the third iSR (c) requiring a 2 minute delay, $N=24000$ ((5mS * 24000) / 60 = 2 minutes). Initial count values for all counters in this example are given in Table 11.7.1.

With the dependent timing requirements achieved, we move on to the one independent timing operation required by our example application to satisfy the requirements of the first (a) and second (b) iSRs. Following the interrupts asserted by the counters responsible for the 10 and 45 second delays, it was specified that a fourth service routine (d) be executed precisely 5 seconds after both the (a) and (b) service routines executed. To meet this requirement, the remaining counter, counter 2 on the first 8253, is set up in Mode 0 (Interrupt on Terminal Count). Each of the two iSR's can then invoke the required service routine precisely 5 seconds after they execute by simply writing to the Mode 0 counter and loading it with an initial count of 1000 (5mS * 1000 = 5 Sec.). In Mode 0, counting begins only after the initial count is loaded. Then while counting down, the output remains low. When the terminal count is reached, the output goes high and remains high until the count is reloaded. An independent counter configured to operate in Mode 0 becomes a hired gun. If you want something specific to happen at any given time, simply load the counter with the initial count that defines the delay you want and design the iSR accordingly.

With all specifications met and counters in place, all that remains is to initialize the Synchronized Timer application example. The steps shown below outline the process.

1. Disable interrupts.

2. Install the iSRs.

3. Set Modes and load initial counts on all counters.

4. Enable interrupts.

As a final note, for very low resolution applications where a periodic interrupt on the order of minutes, hours, days, or even *years!* is required, just a few counters cascaded together can produce surprisingly long interrupt periods. For instance, using just one of the 8253's given in this example, if all three counters were cascaded as shown in Figure 11.7.2, configured as Mode 2, initialized with maximum counts (65536) and the CLK pin on counter 0 fed an 8MHz input signal, the PC would see a request from the OUT pin of counter 2 once every 1.12 Years!

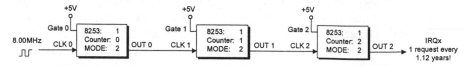

Figure 11.7.2 Cascaded Counters

* For a complete description of the 8253's various operating Modes, including the four Modes (0, 2, 3, and 5) used in this example and details on programming, refer to the Intel data sheets.

11.8 Non-Maskable Interrupt (NMI)

As its name implies, the PC's *Non-Maskable Interrupt* or *NMI* uses the NMI pin present on all x86 processors to provide a hardware interrupt resource that cannot be masked (disabled). Unlike the INTR pin, which supports the processor's maskable interrupt resource, the NMI pin is *not* influenced by the IF bit 9 in the Flags register or the CLI and STI instructions that control it. The NMI has priority over all other hardware interrupts in the PC and has therefore been reserved for handling only those events which jeopardize system integrity. Such events include memory parity errors, I/O channel errors, Failsafe (Watchdog) Timer time-outs, and power failure detection. When a low to high transition is detected on the NMI pin, the processor responds on the next instruction boundary by issuing an INT 02h instruction invoking the handler installed behind Interrupt 02h. The handler then determines the source of the NMI by polling status bits located in system owned I/O ports and handles the error. To prevent the NMI from being re-entered, the processor disables the NMI until the IRET instruction is executed by the NMI handler.

Because of its non-maskable nature, the NMI is vulnerable during the initialization sequence of the PC, when potential NMI sources are still in an undefined state and the system BIOS has not quite gotten around to hooking Interrupt 02h with the NMI handler. If the NMI were to see an active request pending during this time, a jump to an erroneous location in memory would result. For this reason, all PCs starting with the Original PC are equipped with an I/O Port bit that acts as a software controlled "on/off switch", allowing the NMI to be disabled during the initialization sequence. More recent applications involving high resolution event timing often use this feature to disable the NMI while measuring the event time to ensure accuracy. In addition to the NMI itself, potential NMI sources, such as RAM parity and I/O channel check have I/O port bits defined that can be used to enable or disable each via software. The platform also provides each NMI source with a status bit that is used by the NMI handler to determine the source of the request. Not surprisingly, I/O port and bit definitions relevant to the NMI structure along with the potential NMI sources have not remained consistent throughout the PCs evolution. We'll start at the beginning.

Figure 11.8.1(a) illustrates the NMI structure for the Original PC and PC-XT. I/O port bits responsible for controlling both the NMI and NMI sources are shown next to the "switches" they represent.

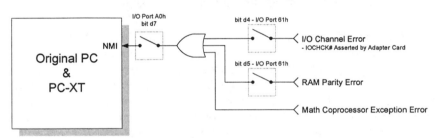

**Figure 11.8.1(a) Non-Maskable Interrupt Structure
for Original PC and PC-XT Systems**

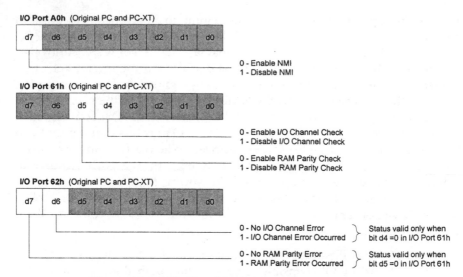

**Figure 11.8.1(b) Non-Maskable Interrupt Structure
for Original PC and PC-XT Systems**

The Original PC, the PC-XT and in fact all PC-AT ISA, MCA and EISA platforms have two primary sources of NMI requests, the system's memory parity logic and the IOCHCK# bus signal used to indicate an I/O channel error (CHCK# for MCA). During a memory write, the memory parity logic calculates the parity for the byte being written and stores it along with the byte in the 9th bit position (even = 0, odd = 1). When the byte is read from memory, the parity is again calculated and compared to the parity bit stored during the write phase. If the parity bits are not equal, an NMI is generated to indicate the RAM error.

The IOCHCK# bus signal (CHCK# for MCA) is a shared signal line used to indicate an I/O channel error and may be driven active low by any expansion bus resource. That is, an expansion bus resource such as an adapter card, able to sense an on-board parity error, general bus failure, overflow condition, or any other conceivable error that jeopardizes system integrity can assert the IOCHCK# and cause an NMI.

If IOCHCK# is asserted while a DMA or Refresh cycle is in progress (i.e. the platform CPU is not the bus owner), the request must wait until the platform CPU regains control of the bus before it can be recognized and handled.

Definitions of each I/O port bit relevant to the Original PC and PC-XT's NMI structure are illustrated in Figure 11.8.1(b). Bit d7 of I/O port A0h allows the NMI to be disabled system wide. NMI sources, RAM parity check and I/O channel check, are controlled through bits d5 and d4 respectively in I/O port 61h. The NMI handler is able to determine which source was responsible for the NMI by reviewing status bits d7 for the RAM parity error and d6 for the I/O channel error in I/O Port 62h.

PC-XT systems have a third unique NMI source. Because of a limited number of IRQ resources on the PC-XT, the Math Coprocessor's Exception interrupt was tied to the NMI. The Exception interrupt can be masked via bit d7 ("M" bit) in the 8087's Control Word. Pending status regarding the Math Coprocessor Exception interrupt is held in bit d7 ("IR" bit) of the 8087's Status Word.

Because the I/O ports used to control the NMI structure are shared with other resources, always read the I/O Port first, modify only the bit or bits required, then write the data back. (Section 5.3 covers setting and resetting select bits)

Figure 11.8.2(a) illustrates the NMI structure for PC-AT ISA, MCA, and EISA expansion bus platforms. For *all* PC-AT systems, bit d7 in I/O port 70h controls the NMI. This would appear to conflict with the Real Time Clock's indirect address register. However, the RTC only decodes the 6 low order bits d[5:0] at I/O port 70h. Some platforms with extended CMOS capabilities will decode the 7 low order bits d[6:0]. Either way, bit d7 in I/O port 70h remains available and acts as the NMI control bit.

Caution: The RTC's I/O port 70h on many PC-AT platforms is unreadable and will yield a bogus value such as FFh or 00h when read, regardless of the actual value held there. For this reason, be sensitive to the state of bit d7 when programming the RTC to avoid inadvertently enabling or disabling the NMI.

On PC-AT ISA, MCA, and EISA platforms, both RAM parity check and I/O channel check control and status bits are found in I/O port 61h. I/O port bit definitions relevant to the NMI structure for all PC-AT systems are defined in Figure 11.8.2(b).

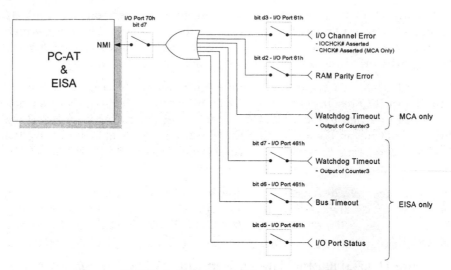

**Figure. 11.8.2(a) Non-Maskable Interrupt Structure
for PC-AT ISA, MCA, and EISA Systems**

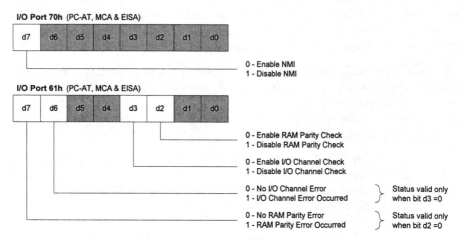

**Figure. 11.8.2(b) Non-Maskable Interrupt Structure
for PC-AT ISA, MCA, and EISA Systems**

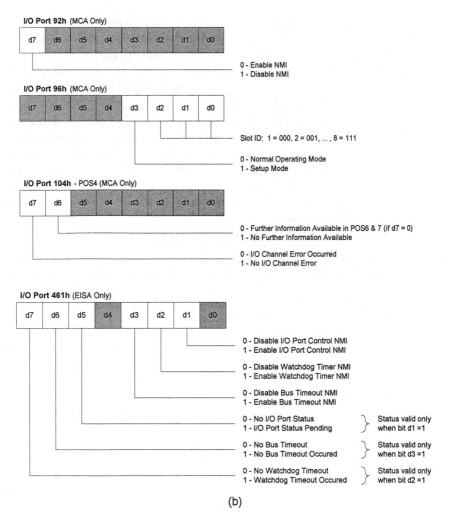

(b)

**Figure. 11.8.2(b) cont. Non-Maskable Interrupt Structure
for PC-AT ISA, MCA, and EISA Systems**

MCA and EISA systems both implement a second 8253/8254 PIT to
provide a *Failsafe Timer* also referred to a *Watchdog Timer (WDT)* which
causes an NMI on terminal count to prevent errant code from permanently
hanging the system. Some PC-AT ISA systems are also equipped with a
second 8253/8254 PIT and provide the WDT feature. Unfortunately, no
standard I/O port bits are defined for the control of a Watchdog Timer on
PC-AT ISA platforms, and as such it is best to refer to the manufacturer's
technical reference for details.

On MCA systems, bit d4 in I/O port 92h is used by the NMI handler to determine if a WDT time-out occurred. Also unique to MCA systems is the ability to pin point which adapter card was responsible for an I/O channel error. Referring now to Figure 11.8.2(b), bit d7 in I/O port 104h (Programmable Option Select 4) for each adapter provides the I/O channel error status. Furthermore, if bit d6 in the same I/O port 104h = 0, additional information regarding the error may be obtained from the adapters POS6 and POS7 registers. To activate the POSx register set for a specific adapter, place the adapter in setup mode by setting bit d3 = 1 and specifying the adapter's slot (Slot 1 = 000, Slot 2 = 001, ... , Slot 8 = 111) using bits d[2:0] in I/O port 96h. For example, to look at the POSx register set for an adapter residing in Slot 5, write 0000 1100b to I/O port 96h, then read the desired POSx register.

Each of the three EISA specific NMI sources, Watchdog Timer, Bus Time-out, and I/O Port Status shown in Figure 11.8.2(a) is represented by a separate control and status bit in I/O Port 461h, as detailed in Figure 11.8.2(b).

While the NMI is not regarded as a hardware interrupt resource open to the system designer, chaining a device iSR to Interrupt 02h and using the IOCHCK# as a level triggered IRQ resource is possible if the platform is willing. Specifically, this technique requires that the platform provide a mechanism through which the I/O channel error status bit can be reset via software. While this may sound trivial, a good many platforms do not provide this capability. Furthermore, the iSR designed to chain to Interrupt 02h and service the device must be able to determine whether or not the device was responsible for the request in order to avoid mistaking a "legitimate" I/O channel error for a device request. This means the device must possess a pending status bit that can be interrogated by the iSR. If the pending status bit is active, process the request, reset the pending status bit on the device, reset the I/O channel error status bit, and IRET. If the pending status bit is not active, immediately pass control to the original NMI handler. The only hazard of using this technique is when a legitimate I/O channel error occurs at the same time the device is pending service. Once the device iSR finds the device's pending status bit active, it services the device and *clears the I/O Channel check status bit*. At that moment, the legitimate I/O channel error loses its registration with the system. In most instances however, the source of the legitimate I/O channel error will continue to drive the IOCHCK# active until reset. This will cause another NMI to occur on the very next instruction boundary so that the legitimate I/O channel error will then be handled. It should be noted that I/O channel errors are extremely rare.

The following are guidelines for using the NMI on a PC-AT platform that does provide a software means of resetting the I/O channel error's pending status bit. Because IOCHCK# is a shared bus resource, the IOCHCK# must be asserted using an open collector to ground approach like that described for level triggered interrupts in Section 3.2. Provided the I/O channel check NMI source is enabled (bit d3 in I/O port 61h = 0), the asserted IOCHCK# will be latched by the I/O port, thereby setting bit d6 = 1 in I/O port 61h. Next, if the NMI itself is enabled (I/O Port 70h bit d7 = 0) on the next instruction boundary, the processor will finish its current task and enter the device handler chained to Interrupt 02h. Upon completion of the device handler's service routine, the handler must then reset the pending status bit on the device first, then reset the I/O channel error's status bit, in that order before issuing the IRET. The order of resetting the pending status bits is important as it prevents a second bogus request from being latched between reset procedures. Some platforms allow you to clear the I/O channel error pending status bit (I/O Port 61h bit d6) on a PC-AT by cycling the I/O channel check control bit (bit d3 in I/O port 61h) high (disabled) then low (re-enable). The following example code segment in C shows how this is done:

```
outportb(0x61, inportb(0x61) | 0x08);  /* disable I/O channel check   */
outportb(0x61, inportb(0x61) & 0xf7);  /* re-enable I/O channel check */
```

Finally, the iSR may be designed to do one of two things. First the iSR can take the time to evaluate the pending status of all other NMI sources on the platform to determine if it should pass control to the original NMI handler, or it can simply bypass the evaluation of other NMI sources and issue the IRET knowing that any pending NMI sources will be recognized and handled on the very next instruction boundary. Skipping the evaluation of other NMI sources on the platform shortens the processing time of the device iSR and consequently the latency time of all other IRQ resources in the system.

12. Appendices

12.1 XT/ISA/EISA, MCA, & PCI Connector Diagrams with Interrupt Pin Call Outs

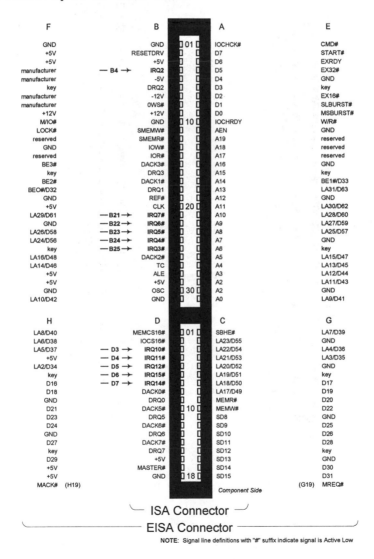

F		B		A	E
GND		GND	01	IOCHCK#	CMD#
+5V		RESETDRV		D7	START#
+5V		+5V		D6	EXRDY
manufacturer	← B4 →	IRQ2		D5	EX32#
manufacturer		-5V		D4	GND
key		DRQ2		D3	key
manufacturer		-12V		D2	EX16#
manufacturer		0WS#		D1	SLBURST#
+12V		+12V		D0	MSBURST#
M/IO#		GND	10	IOCHRDY	W/R#
LOCK#		SMEMW#		AEN	GND
reserved		SMEMR#		A19	reserved
GND		IOW#		A18	reserved
reserved		IOR#		A17	reserved
BE3#		DACK3#		A16	GND
key		DRQ3		A15	key
BE2#		DACK1#		A14	BE1#/D33
BE0#/D32		DRQ1		A13	LA31/D63
GND		REF#		A12	GND
+5V		CLK	20	A11	LA30/D62
LA29/D61	← B21 →	IRQ7#		A10	LA28/D60
GND	← B22 →	IRQ6#		A9	LA27/D59
LA26/D58	← B23 →	IRQ5#		A8	LA25/D57
LA24/D56	← B24 →	IRQ4#		A7	GND
key	← B25 →	IRQ3#		A6	key
LA16/D48		DACK2#		A5	LA15/D47
LA14/D46		TC		A4	LA13/D45
+5V		ALE		A3	LA12/D44
+5V		+5V		A2	LA11/D43
GND		OSC	30	A2	GND
LA10/D42		GND		A0	LA9/D41

H		D		C	G
LA8/D40		MEMCS16#	01	SBHE#	LA7/D39
LA6/D38		IOCS16#		LA23/D55	GND
LA5/D37	← D3 →	IRQ10#		LA22/D54	LA4/D36
+5V	← D4 →	IRQ11#		LA21/D53	LA3/D35
LA2/D34	← D5 →	IRQ12#		LA20/D52	GND
key	← D6 →	IRQ15#		LA19/D51	key
D16	← D7 →	IRQ14#		LA18/D50	D17
D18		DACK0#		LA17/D49	D19
GND		DRQ0		MEMR#	D20
D21		DACK5#	10	MEMW#	D22
D23		DRQ5		SD8	GND
D24		DACK6#		SD9	D25
GND		DRQ6		SD10	D26
D27		DACK7#		SD11	D28
key		DRQ7		SD12	key
D29		+5V		SD13	GND
+5V		MASTER#		SD14	D30
+5V		GND	18	SD15	D31
MACK#	(H19)				(G19) MREQ#

Component Side

⌐ ISA Connector ⌐

⌐─────────────── EISA Connector ───────────────⌐

NOTE: Signal line definitions with "#" suffix indicate signal is Active Low

263

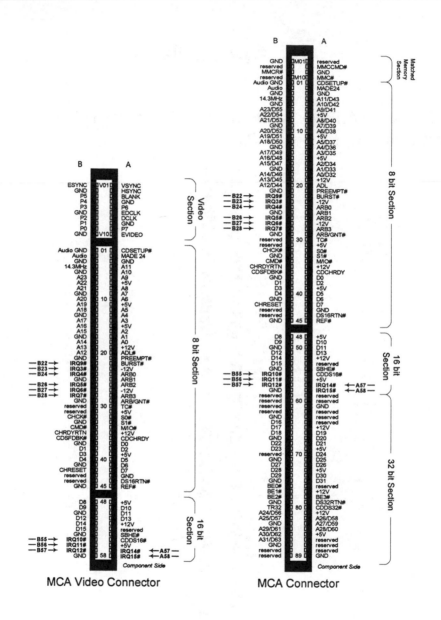

MCA Video Connector

MCA Connector

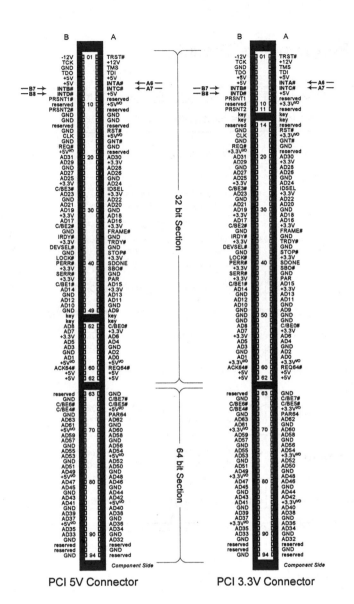

PCI 5V Connector   PCI 3.3V Connector

12.2 Programmers Toolkit

	Funcion	Borland C	MicroSoft C	iAPX
M A S T E R 8 2 5 9	Read the IMR	IMR = inportb(0x21)	IMR = _inp(0x21)	in al, 21h
	Write to the IMR	outportb(0x21,0xdd)	_outb(0x21,0xdd)	mov al, mask out 21h, al
	Read the IRR	outportb(0x20, 0x0a); IRR = inportb(0x20);	_outb(0x20, 0x0a); IRR = _inp(0x20);	mov al, ah out 20h, al in al, 20h
	Read the ISR	outportb(0x20, 0x0b); ISR = inportb(0x20);	_outb(0x20, 0x0b); ISR = _inp(0x20);	mov al, 0bh out 20h, al in al, 020h
	Non-Specific EOI	outportb(0x20, 0x20);	_outb(0x20, 0x20);	mov al, 20h out 20h, al
S L A V E 8 2 5 9	Read the IMR	IMR = inportb(0xa)	IMR = _inp(0x21)	in al, a1h
	Write to the IMR	outportb(0x21,0xdd)	_outb(0x21,0xdd)	mov al, mask out a1h, al
	Read the IRR	outportb(0xa0, 0x0a); IRR = inportb(0xa0);	_outb(0xa0, 0x0a); IRR = _inp(0xa0);	mov al, 0ah out a0h, al in al, a0h
	Read the ISR	outportb(0xa0, 0x0b); ISR = inportb(0xa0);	_outb(0xa0, 0x0b); ISR = _inp(0xa0);	mov al, 0bh out a0h, al in al, a0h
	Non-Specific EOI	outportb(0xa0, 0x20);	_outb(0xa0, 0x20);	mov al, 20h out a0h, al
	Disable Interrupts	disable();	_disable();	CLI
	Enable Interrupts	enable();	_enable();	STI

266

12.3 PICMG 2.0 Interrupt Binding Specification

	Device Number	Slot Number	IDSEL#	Interrupt Binding				To Router ← Inputs
				PIRQA#	**PIRQB#**	**PIRQC#**	**PIRQD#**	
	31	1(*n*)	AD31	INTB#	INTC#	INTD#	INTA#	
PCI-PCI Bridge *n*	30	2(*n*)	AD30	INTC#	INTD#	INTA#	INTB#	
	29	3(*n*)	AD29	INTD#	INTA#	INTB#	INTC#	
	28	4(*n*)	AD28	INTA#	INTB#	INTC#	INTD#	

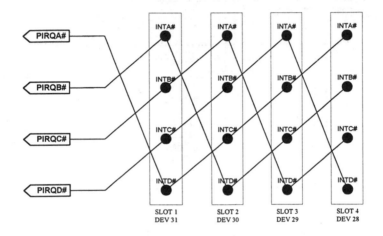

12.4 PC/104+ Interrupt Binding Specification

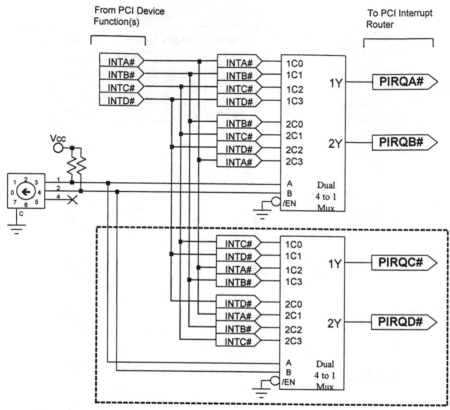

Second Mux only required on a PC/104+ multifunction
PCI device requiring more than two INTx# lines.

Switch Position	Module Slot	IDSEL#	IDSEL Binding	Interrupt Binding				To Router ← Inputs
				PIRQA#	PIRQB#	PIRQC#	PIRQD#	
0 (4)	1	IDSEL0	AD20	INTB#	INTC#	INTD#	INTA#	
1 (5)	2	IDSEL1	AD21	INTC#	INTD#	INTA#	INTB#	
2 (6)	3	IDSEL2	AD22	INTD#	INTA#	INTB#	INTC#	
3 (7)	4	IDSEL3	AD23	INTA#	INTB#	INTC#	INTD#	

12.5 PCI BIOS Extensions

The 16 bit PCI BIOS Extensions are additions to the ISA compatible INT 1Ah software interrupt. The new function identifier that indicates the request of a PCI BIOS service is B1h. B1h is passed during the call in the AH register. The specific function being requested is passed in the AL register. To request a PCI BIOS service in real mode, an iAPX INT 1Ah instruction is issued. In protected mode, the INT 1Ah instruction must be simulated. To simulate the INT 1Ah instruction in protected mode, perform the following:

1. Push the Flags register onto the stack using the iAPX PUSHF instruction.

2. Make a far CALL to the INT 1Ah interrupt service routine at physical address FFE6:Eh.

    • The code segment descriptor must have a base address of F000:0h and a limit of 64K.

    • The INT 1Ah interrupt service routine uses the caller's stack.

    • The INT 1Ah interrupt service routine will issue an iAPX IRET instruction which will restore the IP, CS, and Flags registers in that order.

PCI BIOS functions described in this appendix are listed in Table 12.5.1. A complete list of the PCI BIOS function completion codes, which are returned to the caller in the AH register to indicate the completion status of the requested function, are listed in Table 12.5.2.

PCI BIOS Function	AH	AL
Get PCI Interrupt Routing Options	B1h	0Eh
Set PCI Hardware Interrupt	B1h	0Fh
Read a PCI Configuration Byte	B1h	08h
Write a PCI Configuration Byte	B1h	0Bh
Get PCI BIOS Present Status	B1h	01h

Table 12.5.1 PCI System BIOS Software Extensions

Completion Code	AH
Successful	00h
Function_Not_Supported	81h
Bad_Vendor_ID	83h
Device_Not_Found	86h
Bad_Register_Number	87h
Set_Failed	88h
Buffer_Too_Small	89h

Table A.E.2 PCI BIOS Function Completion Codes

Get PCI Interrupt Routing Options

Purpose:
This function returns the routing tables for each integrated PCI device and PCI bus connector on the platform. The routing tables provide the link values that indicate how the INTx# pins on integrated PCI devices and PCI bus connectors are routed to either PIRQx# inputs on the interrupt router or directly to IRQs on the system's interrupt controller. Furthermore, the routing tables provide the Bus Number and Device Number (in upper 5 bits) needed to call the *Read a PCI Configuration Register Byte* function and determine how the routing algorithm programmed the interrupt router (see section 11.2).

Additionally, an IRQ bit-map reflecting the IRQ assignments exclusive to PCI devices is returned.

Entry:
[AH]   B1h
[AL]   0Eh
[BX]   0000h

16 Bit Real Mode
[DS]   Segment for BIOS data. The base address value in [DS] must resolve to F0000h.
        The limit value for [DS] must equal 64k.
[ES]   Segment to caller's data structure.
[DI]   16 bit offset address to caller's data structure

16 Bit Protected Mode
[DS]   Selector for BIOS data. The base address value in [DS] must resolve to F0000h.
        The limit value for [DS] must equal 64k.
[ES]   Selector to caller's data structure.
[DI]   16 bit offset address to caller's data structure

Exit:

[AH]   Return Code
        00h   Successful
        81h   Function not supported
        89h   Buffer too small

[BX]   IRQ bit-map. Indicates which IRQs are exclusively used by PCI devices.
        0 = IRQ not exclusive to PCI   1 = IRQ exclusive to PCI
[ES]   16 bit offset address to caller's data structure
[DI]   Segment (Real Mode) or Selector (Protected Mode) to caller's data
structure.
[CF]   Completion Status
        0 = Successful
        1 = Error

NOTES:

ES:DI contains a far pointer to the caller's data structure. The caller's data structure is used to pass the size and location of the data buffer the function will use to transfer the IRQ routing tables back to the caller.

Buffer Size - Offset 00h

- This 2 byte field contains the size in bytes of the caller's data buffer when the call is first made. If the buffer size specified here is greater than the actual size of all IRQ routing tables combined, this field will be updated to reflect the smaller accurate size.

- A zero returned in this field indicates that no integrated PCI devices or PCI bus connectors exist on the platform.

- If the buffer size specified by the caller is too small, the system BIOS will update this field with the buffer size required. No IRQ routing tables will be returned.

Data Buffer - Offset 02h

- This 2 byte field contains the far pointer to the caller's data buffer. When this function completes successfully, the callers data buffer will contain IRQ routing tables for every integrated PCI device and PCI bus connector. Refer to Section 10.5 for the definition and layout of routing tables.

Set PCI Hardware Interrupt

Purpose:
This function will route a particular INTx# pin on a PCI device to a specific IRQ on the system's interrupt controller provided the IRQ is available. In a PC environment, this function allows the caller to reprogram the interrupt router.

Entry:
[AH]	B1h
[AL]	0Fh

[BH]	PCI Bus Number where device resides
[BL]	PCI Device Number and Function Number in the following format:

Bits	Definition
[7:3]	Device Number (0 - 31)
[2:0]	Function Number (0 - 7)

[CL]	INTx# pin on PCI Device to route to:
	0Ah INTA#
	0Bh INTB#
	0Ch INTC#
	0Dh INTD#

[CH]	IRQ to route the device's INTx# pin to:
	00h IRQ0
	.
	.
	0Fh IRQ15

16 Bit Real Mode
[DS]   Segment for BIOS data. The base address value in [DS] must resolve to F0000h.

The limit value for [DS] must equal 64k.

16 Bit Protected Mode
[DS]   Selector for BIOS data. The base address value in [DS] must resolve to F0000h.

The limit value for [DS] must equal 64k.

Exit:
[AH]	Return Code
	00h Successful
	81h Function not supported
	88h Operation failed

[CF]	Completion Status
	0 = Successful
	1 = Error

NOTES:

- Caller is responsible for ensuring no conflict with other system devices such as ISA devices will result from the call. Check IRQ bit map associated with PIRQx# input's link value and CMOS setup for valid IRQs available to PCI.

- Caller is responsible for configuring the IRQ to operate in level triggered mode. (refer to Section 2.6 for details)

- Caller is responsible for updating the Interrupt Line register in the configuration space for all effected device functions. Each device function using an INTx# pin that is wire-ORed (shares a common link value) with the one specified in the call will be effected. Before updating any Interrupt Line registers, verify the successful completion of the function.

- A return code of 88h indicates the requested IRQ was unavailable.

Read a PCI Configuration Register Byte

Purpose:
This function returns a byte of data from the configuration space of a PCI device. Reading the Interrupt Line register (offset 3Ch) of a PCI device after POST executes defines how the Configuration Manager programs the interrupt router (see Section 11.2 for details).

Entry:
[AH]   B1h
[AL]   09h

[BH]   PCI Bus Number where device resides. (Found in Routing Table offset 0)
[BL]   PCI Device Number and Function Number in the following format:

Bits	Definition
[7:3]	Device Number (0 - 31) - Found in Routing Table offset 1 (upper 5 bits)
[2:0]	Function Number (0 - 7)

[DI]   Configuration Space register to read. (3Ch - Interrupt Line register)

Exit:
[AH]   Return Code
        00h   Successful

[CL]   Byte Value read
[CF]   Completion Status
        0 = Successful
        1 = Error

NOTES:
Bits 0 and 1 in [DI] must equal 0.
Return values of 87h in the AH register and 1 in the CF register will result if this condition is not met.

Write a PCI Configuration Register Byte

Purpose:
This function writes a byte of data to the configuration space of a PCI device. Writing to the Interrupt Line register (offset 3Ch) of a PCI device after POST facilitates the assignment of a new IRQ resource (see Section 11.3 for details).

Entry:
[AH]	B1h
[AL]	0Bh
[BH]	PCI Bus Number where device resides. (Found in Routing Table offset 0)
[BL]	PCI Device Number and Function Number in the following format:

Bits	Definition
[7:3]	Device Number (0 - 31) - Found in Routing Table offset 1 (upper 5 bits)
[2:0]	Function Number (0 - 7)

[CL]	Byte Value to write
[DI]	Configuration Space register to Write. (3Ch - Interrupt Line register)

Exit:
[AH]	Return Code
	00h Successful
[CF]	Completion Status
	0 = Successful
	1 = Error

Get PCI BIOS Present Status

Purpose:
This function verifies the existence of PCI BIOS services. Other information returned includes the PCI BIOS interface level, the Number of the last PCI bus in the system, the hardware mechanism used to access PCI configuration space, and special cycle support status.

Entry:
[AH]   B1h
[AL]   01h

Exit:
[AH]   Return Code
        00h   PCI BIOS services exist if the contents of [EDX] equal = "PCI "

Bit(s)	Value	Definition
0	0	Configuration Mechanism #1 not supported
	1	Configuration Mechanism #1 supported
1	0	Configuration Mechanism #2 not supported
	1	Configuration Mechanism #2 supported
3:2	0	Return value is always 0
4	0	Special Cycle not supported through Mechanism #1
	1	Special Cycle supported through Mechanism #1
5	0	Special Cycle not supported through Mechanism #2
	1	Special Cycle supported through Mechanism #2
7:6	0	Return value is always 0

[BH]   PCI BIOS Interface revision Major Version Number in BCD
[BL]   PCI BIOS Interface revision Minor Version Number in BCD
        ex: Version 2.1   BH = 02   BL = 01

[CL]   Number of the last PCI bus in the system
[EDX]   PCI signature ASCII string

Bits	Value	ASCII Character
[7:0]	50h	'P'
[15:8]	43h	'C'
[23:16]	49h	'I'
[31:24]	20h	' '

[CF]   PCI BIOS services status
        0 = PCI BIOS services are present if the contents of [EDX] equal "PCI "
        1 = PCI BIOS services are not present

12.6 Software Cross Reference

	Figure	Source	Executable
Chapter 3 - a:\chpt3			
3.5 8259 PIC BIOS Initialization PC/XT	Figure 3.5.1	xt_init.c	xt_init.exe
3.5 Master/Slave 8259 PIC BIOS Initialization AT-ISA	Figure 3.5.2	isa_init.c	isa_init.exe
3.5 Master/Slave 8259 PIC BIOS Initialization PS/2-MCA	Figure 3.5.3	mca_init.c	mca_init.exe
3.5 Master/Slave 8259 PIC BIOS Initialization AT-EISA	Figure 3.5.4	eisainit.c	eisainit.exe
Chapter 4 - a:\chpt4			
4.3 IRQ9 Reroute to IRQ2 Routine	Figure 4.3.1	ir9_ir2.c	IR9_IR2.exe
Chapter 6 - a:\chpt6			
6.2 Locked Master PIC iSR	Figure 6.2.1(b)	lmp_isr.c	
6.3 Locked Slave PIC iSR	Figure 6.3.1(b)	lsp_isr.c	
6.4 Nested Master PIC iSR	Figure 6.4.1(b)	nmp_isr.c	
6.5 Nested Slave PIC iSR	Figure 6.5.1(b)	nsp_isr.c	
6.6 Nested Slave PIC iSR / SFNM	Figure 6.6.1(b)	nsp_sfnm.c	
Chapter 7 - a:\chpt7			
7.2 The Implied Priority Chain	Figure 7.2.3(b)	ipc_link.c	
7.2 The Implied Priority Chain	Figure 7.2.4	ipc.c	ipc.exe
7.3 The Equal Priority Chain - Method 1	Figure 7.3.3(b)	epc1_lnk.c	
7.3 Safety Net	Figure 7.3.4(b)	snet_lnk.c	
7.3 The Equal Priority Chain - Method 1	Figure 7.3.7	epc1.c	epc1.exe
7.3 The Equal Priority Chain - Method 2	Figure 7.3.5(b)	epc2_lnk.c	
7.3 The Equal Priority Chain - Method 2	Figure 7.3.8	epc2.c	epc2.exe
7.3 The Equal Priority Chain - Method 3	Figure 7.3.6(b)	epc3_lnk.c	
7.3 The Equal Priority Chain - Method 3	Figure 7.3.9	epc3.c	epc3.exe
7.4 IPC Link with Rotate	Figure 7.4.2(b)	ipc_lnkr.c	
7.4 IPC Link with Rotate	Figure 7.4.7	RotateS1.C	RotateS1.exe
7.4 IPC Link with Rotate	Figure 7.4.12	RotateS2.C	RotateS2.exe
Chapter 8 - a:\chpt8			
8.4 Locked Master PIC iSR with default IR7 Handling	Figure 8.4.2(b)	def_lmp.c	
8.4 Locked Slave PIC iSR with default IR15 Handling	Figure 8.4.3(b)	def_lsp.c	
8.4 Nested Master PIC iSR with default IR7 Handling	Figure 8.4.5(b)	def_nmp.c	
8.4 Nested Slave PIC iSR with default IR15 Handling	Figure 8.4.6(b)	def_nsp.c	
8.4 Nested Slave PIC iSR/SFNM with default IR15 Handling	Figure 8.4.7(b)	def_nsps.c	
8.4 Prog. an iSR to Detect and Handle a default IR7(IR15)		default.C	default.exe
8.4 Prog. an iSR to Detect and Handle a default IR7(IR15)	Figure 8.4.8(b)	def_IR7.C	def_IR7.exe
8.4 Prog. an iSR to Detect and Handle a default IR7(IR15)	Figure 8.4.9(b)	def_IR15.C	def_IR15.exe
Chapter 11 - a:\chpt11			
11.4 CPU Exceptions and Vector Table Relocation	Figure 11.4.1	relocate.c	relocate.exe
11.4 CPU Exceptions and Vector Table Relocation		ir9_ir2r.c	ir9_ir2r.exe
11.5 Using the System Timer's 1Ch Extension		timer_1c.c	timer_1c.exe
11.6 Using the RTC's Periodic Interrupt on IRQ8		rtc.c	rtc.exe
11.6 iSR Designed to Handle RTC's Periodic Interrupt	Figure 11.6.3(b)	rtc_iSR.c	

12.7 References and Other Interesting Reading

Publications

S. Savitzky, 1985, Real-Time Microprocessor Systems, Van Nostrand Reinhold Company, Inc., New York, NY.

S. G. Shiva, 1988, Introduction to Logic Design, Scott, Foresman and Company, Glenview, IL.

G. A. Gibson and Y. Liu, 1980, Microcomputers for Engineers and Scientists, PTR, Prentice-Hall, Inc., Englewood Cliffs, NJ

H. W. Johnson and M. Braham, 1993, High Speed Digital Design - A Handbook of Black Magic, PTR Prentice-Hall, Englewood Cliffs, NJ.

E. Solari and G. Willse, 1996, PCI Hardware and Software, 3rd Ed., Annabooks, San Diego, CA.

E. Solari, 1992, ISA & EISA Theory & Operation, Annabooks, San Diego, CA.

T. Shanley and D. Anderson, 1995, PCI System Architecture, 3rd Ed., MindShare Inc., Richardson TX.

L.C. Eggebrecht, Interfacing to the IBM Personal Computer, 2nd Edition., 1990, Howard W. Sams & Co., Indianapolis, IN.

M. Sargent and R. L. Shoemaker, 1995, The Personal Computer from the Inside Out, 3rd Ed., Addison Wesley Publishing Co., Reading, MA.

F. Van Guilluwe, 1994, The Undocumented PC, Addison-Wesley Publishing Co., Reading, MA.

R. Brown and J. Kyle, 1994, PC Interrupts, A Programmer's Reference to BIOS, DOS, and Third-Party Calls, 2nd Ed., Addison-Wesley Publishing Co., Reading, MA.

R. Lai, 1992, Writing MS-DOS Device Drivers, 2nd Ed., Addison-Wesley Publishing Co., Reading, MA.

H. P. Messmer, 1995, The Indispensable PC Hardware Book, 2nd Ed., Addison-Wesley Publishing Co., Reading, MA.

W. L. Rosch, 1994, The Winn L. Rosch Hardware Bible, 3rd. Ed., Brady Publishing, Indianapolis, IN.

Manuals / Data Sheets / Application Notes

Intel Architecture Software Developer's Manual, Volume 1: Basic Architecture, Order number 243190, Intel Literature Sales - (800) 548-4726.

Intel Architecture Software Developer's Manual, Volume 2: Instruction Set Reference Manual, Order number 243190, Intel Literature Sales - (800) 548-4726.

Intel Architecture Software Developer's Manual, Volume 3: System Programming Guide, Order number 243190, Intel Literature Sales - (800) 548-4726.

PowerPC Microprocessor Family: The Programming Environments for 32-bit Microprocessors, Motorola Inc., Document number MPCFPE32B/AD r1

PowerPC Microprocessor Family: The Programming Environments for 64-bit Microprocessors, Motorola Inc., Document number MPCFPE/AD r1

PowerPC Microprocessor Family: The Programmer's Reference Guide, Motorola Inc., Document number MPCPRG/D

Peripheral Components, 1993 Order number 296467-004. Intel Literature Sales - (800) 548-4726

82371FB (PIIX) and 82371SB (PIIX3) PCI ISA IDE Xcelerator Order number 290550-001. Intel Literature Sales - (800) 548-4726

82420/82430 - PCIset ISA and EISA Bridges Order number 290481-001. Intel Literature Sales - (800) 548-4726

8259A-2 Programmable Interrupt Controller Order number 231468-003. Intel Literature Sales - (800) 548-4726

8253/8253-5 Programmable Interval Timer Order number 231306-001. Intel Literature Sales - (800) 548-4726

8254 Programmable Interval Timer Order number 231164-004. Intel Literature Sales - (800) 548-4726

R. Jigour, 1979, AP-59 - Using the 8259 Programmable Interrupt Controller, Intel Corporation, Order number 121500-001

PowerPC 603 Hardware Interrupt Latency in Embedded Applications, Motorola Corporation, Document number AN1267/D

D. Long - Microsoft Developer Technology Group, 1993, Article - "Exploring the Mystery and Manifestrations of Interrupt Processing in Microsoft Windows version 3.1".

Specifications:

PCI-ISA Rev. 2.0 Card Edge Connector for Single Board, PICMG, Wakefield, MA.

PPBB Rev. 1.02 PCI-PCI Bridge Board Connector for Single Board Computers, PICMG, Wakefield, MA.

CPCI Rev. 2.1 CompactPCI, PICMG, Wakefield, MA.

PCI Specification Rev. 2.2, PCI Special Interest Group, Hillsboro, OR

PCI BIOS Specification Rev. 2.1, PCI Special Interest Group, Hillsboro, OR

PCI to PCI Bridge Specification Rev. 1.0, PCI Special Interest Group, Hillsboro, OR

Index

Notes

Other Annabooks Titles

Designing with Flash Memory
Dipert & Levy, 0-929392-17-5, $34.95

Developing USB PC Peripherals
Tan, 0-929392-38-8, $29.95

Fuzzy Logic for Real World Design
Heske & Heske, 0-929392-24-8, $49.95

ISA & EISA Theory and Operation
Solari, 0-929392-15-9, $89.95

NCP: Programmer's Guide to the NetWare Core Protocol
Conner & Conner, 0-929392-31-0, $34.95

PCI Hardware and Software, Architecture & Design, 4th Edition
Solari & Willse, 0-929392-59-0, $97.95

PCI Hot-Plug Application and Design
Goodrum, 0-929392-60-4, $39.95

The PC Handbook, 6th Edition
Choisser & Foster, 0-929392-36-1, $9.95

The PCI Handbook
Dipert, 0-929392-25-6, $14.95

The USB Handbook
Jaff, 0-929392-39-6, $24.95

USB Hardware and Software, Architecture & Design
Garney, Solari, Callahan, Jaff, & Hosler, 0-929392-37-X, $94.95

USB Peripheral Design
Koon, 0-929392-46-9, $49.95

A full catalog of Annabooks titles, along with the titles we distribute, can be found on our website at www.annabooks.com. Orders may also be placed by mail, phone, or fax.

Annabooks
11838 Bernardo Plaza Court, Ste. 102A
San Diego, CA 92128
619-673-0870, fax 619-673-1432
info@annabooks.com